A Passion for History

Habent sua fata libelli

Early Modern Studies Series

General Editor
Michael Wolfe
St. John's University

NATALIE ZEMON DAVIS

Edited by Michael Wolfe
Translated by Natalie Zemon Davis
and Michael Wolfe

Early Modern Studies 4
Truman State University Press

tsup.truman.edu

Translated from *L'Histoire tout feu tout flamme: Entretiens avec Denis Crouzet* © Editions Albin Michel S.A. - Paris 2004.

Cover art: Conseil general de la Haute-Garonne/Archives départementales, Toulouse/ 1 B 3432. This is the opening of the final decision in the Martin Guerre case, in which the judges of the Parlement of Toulouse upheld the conviction of Arnaud du Tilh for imposture and adultery by a lower court and condemned him to death. The passage fully visible on the cover reads as follows:

> Jeudi douziesme jour du moys de septembre an 1560 en la chambre criminel. Presens Messieurs de Mansencal, Daffis, Latomy, et Du Faur presidens, Reynier, Cognard, Papus, P. Robert, Bonald, Lafitau, Sabatier, Carriere, de Ferrieres, et de Coras.
>
> Veu le proces faict par le Juge de Rieux a Arnaud du Tilh dict Pancette, soy disant Martin Guerre, prisonnier en la Conciergerie, appellant dudit Juge. L'inquisition d'office faicte par ordonnance de la court aiant dire droit sur l'appel dudict du Tilh. Les auditions et responses de Bertrande de Rolz, femme de Martin Guerre, et de Pierre Guerre, oncle dudict Martin, jadiz prisonniers pour raison de la matiere. Recollemens et confrontations et exhibition de tesmoings. Ensemble les conclusions et recommandations du procureur general du Roy sur ce baillees par escript et aultres procedures faictes en la matiere. Et icelluy du Tilh prisonnier ouy en sa cause d'appel.
>
> Il sera dict que la cour a mis et mect l'appellation dudit du Tilh, et cela dont a este appelle, au neant...

English translation:

> Thursday, the twelfth day of September, 1560, in the Criminal Chamber. Present: Messieurs de Mansencal, Daffis, Latomy and Du Faur, presiding; Reynier, Cognard, Papus, P. Robert, Bonald, Lafitau, Sabatier, Carrière, de Ferrièrres, and de Coras.
>
> Having seen [the records of] the trial conducted by the Judge of Rieux of Arnaud du Tilh alias Pancette, calling himself Martin Guerre, prisoner in the Conciergerie, appealing [the decision of] the judge... [And having seen] the hearings and responses of Bertrande de Rolz, wife of Martin Guerre, and of Pierre Guerre, uncle of Martin Guerre, formerly prisoners in connection with this case. [And having seen] the challenges and confrontations [between Arnaud du Tilh and the witnesses] and the evidence presented by the witnesses, together with the conclusions and recommendations of the king's attorney... And having heard the prisoner du Tilh make his appeal.
>
> It is announced that the court has rejected and rejects the appeal of the said du Tilh...

The decision goes on to condemn Arnaud du Tilh for "imposture, false supposition of name and person, and adultery" and sentences him to demand pardon publicly in the village of Artigat, and to be hanged in front of the house of Martin Guerre and his body then burned.

Cover design: Teresa Wheeler
Type: Legacy Sans ITC and Legacy Serif ITC © URW Software; CaslonAntiqua © Phil's Fonts
Printed by: Thomson-Shore, Dexter, Michigan USA

Library of Congress Cataloging-in-Publication Data
Davis, Natalie Zemon, 1928-
[Histoire tout feu tout flamme. English]
A passion for history / Natalie Zemon Davis ; conversations with Denis Crouzet.
p. cm. – (Early modern studies series ; 4)
Includes bibliographical references and index.
ISBN 978-1-931112-97-0 (pbk. : alk. paper)
1. Historiography. 2. Historians–France–Interviews. 3. Davis, Natalie Zemon, 1928–Interviews. 4. Crouzet, Denis, 1953–Interviews. I. Crouzet, Denis, 1953- II. Title.
D13.2.D3813 2010
907.2'02–dc22

2010003974

The paper in this publication meets or exceeds the minimum requirements of the American National Standard for Information Sciences–Permanence of Paper for Printed Library Materials, ANSI Z39.48-1992.

Contents

Acknowledgments	vii
Foreword by Orest Ranum	ix
1 Wonderments	1
2 Encounters	30
3 Fashionings	63
4 Memories	93
5 Women	109
6 Commitments	130
7 Hopes	158
Epilogue	180
Works by Natalie Zemon Davis	184
Works by Denis Crouzet	203
Index	211

Acknowledgments

I often tell my students that "making history" really means entering into a conversation about the past that began long ago and, thankfully, will never end so long as people remain willful and unpredictable. How lucky we are to be able to listen in on this conversation between Natalie Zemon Davis and Denis Crouzet, two historians who make history so masterfully. I am sure that students and scholars alike will learn or be reminded that the pursuit of history is a matter for both the heart and the mind. The idea for an American edition of this eavesdropping project began with Anne Jacobson Schutte, who brilliantly alerted the press to the opportunity upon reading the French original. Solène Chabanais at Albin Michel offered her kind offices in helping Truman State University Press secure rights to an English translation, while Geneviève Douillard at the Archives départementales de la Haute Garonne generously donated the cover image of a document from the Martin Guerre case. Chandler Davis provided timely expertise and sound counsel throughout the project, for which we are all most grateful. And I wish in particular to thank Orest Ranum, my mentor and friend (as he is Natalie's and Denis's), for setting the stage with his wonderful *avant-propos*. Our appreciation also goes to Nancy Rediger, director and editor-in-chief of the press, and Barbara Smith-Mandell, head copy editor, who so patiently and ably guided the text on to publication. The translation reflects a collaborative effort, as Natalie quite rightly translated her original French into her native English and translated the document on the cover, which she discovered when researching *The Return of Martin Guerre*. She also expanded the text in several places for the benefit of English-language readers. I tackled the translation of Denis's questions and comments, leaning heavily on both him and Natalie for clarification when necessary. Finally, I prepared the accompanying notes, again with much assistance from Natalie, which we hope will help our readers follow and enjoy even more this thrilling conversation.

Michael Wolfe, Editor
Queens, New York
November 2009

Foreword

Orest Ranum

She's done it again! Natalie Zemon Davis places her mind squarely between past and present, and she dares to be her candid, learned, and adventurous self. No other historian is so authoritative and free, so professional and engaged in the research and writing of humanist history.

Denis Crouzet has done what great and very accomplished teachers do: he puts himself in a position of intellectual vulnerability in order to prompt Davis to go deeper and deeper about her nature [*sic*] as a historian. There is no boilerplate in this dialogue. It is truly a dialogue, and it absolutely convinces the reader that Davis is saying exactly what she thinks on all the key questions about method, choice of research topics, and her deeply personal sense of adventure in politics and in practicing history. There is no dumbing down.

Most dialogues involve one person and an imagined other. Not so here. Denis Crouzet is genuinely curious about the mind, life, and writings of Natalie Zemon Davis, and the result is a major addition to the humanist culture of the twenty-first century.

Some individuals can cross oceans and frontiers without any apparent need to reflect on the shifts and exchanges between places and cultures; others are prompted to write, to inventory, to note down the ordinary things in life. Still others are prompted to try to capture vast continental histories and cultures. Natalie Zemon Davis finds these writer-explorer-historians to be her windows onto different times and places. When they fall silent, as Leon the African does when he returns to his native culture, she finds this difficult to accept. But she also understands how these silences have meaning. But what meaning?

Her engagement in feminist history became very strong during the years at Berkeley. Christine de Pizan had deeply interested her as a student, but the subject lacked significance in those years just prior to the rise of feminist history. After the glassworkers of Carmaux, and beyond printers, and beyond peasants who stopped the shipping of grain from their villages, Joan Scott, Natalie Zemon Davis, and Louise Tilly turned to constructing the field in which the life and works of Christine would have the preeminence of a Pico, a Poggio, a Lefebvre d'Étaples. Few historians participate in the creation of a whole new field of history; and without the intense engagement that characterized the earlier work, and without its continuing learned intensity, women's history might not have gained the vitality and legitimacy it has today.

There are occasional seemingly offhand remarks, really categorical statements about how Davis has learned to practice history. While grounded in personal experience, they are in fact *loci,* or commonplaces that, taken together, constitute a body of principles about the practice of researching, analyzing, and writing history. While history brings to the fore diverse modes of existence, these may be either discouraging to a reader or hopeful. Then, on reflection, Davis adds that while past and present human experiences may appear to be the same, they *never* are. For a historian who has sought to interpret historical thinking that is proverbial, the reader may be certain that what seems personal is really a coherent body of principles that are as social-scientific as they are humanist, and that constitute true understanding of *verstehen*. Just how these *loci* are formulated is evident in the exchange about Dipesh Chakrabarty's relativist (my term) questioning of the general scientific and rationalist "system" of proof agreed upon among most historians. Why not let the rationalist and the magical systems of proof coexist! Davis grounds her rejection of this proposal on the principle of exchange, in this instance, exchange between historians. How can there be fruitful debate over the facts of history, she asks, if there is no agreement on the "rules of the game"? The implication that Western historical thought cannot be validly developed about non-Western cultures is rejected, because since antiquity this so-called Western historical thought has constantly incorporated into it the facts not only of non-Western history but also of non-Western systems of validation. After grounding her argument on the need for rules of exchange, Davis then turns to ethics, stating that it is her "duty" to search for consensus about the rules of historical proof.

The process of acceptance and/or rejection of the principal concepts developed by social scientists has culminated in an imaginative, integrated, and personal vision of the human and social. She lays no claims to originality, as she occasionally uses quotation marks to indicate to her readers (e.g., "distance," page 53) that the meaning is technical and goes beyond the usages in Webster's dictionary.

The family members who pull together to help one of their own construct a story that possibly will convince a judge to be lenient, is *not* history, any more than the *procès-verbal* of the court is history. What *is* history is carefully studying the evidence in all surviving sources and constructing a plausible narrative that can be questioned by another historian who has examined the same evidence. The thousands of references that characterize all of Davis's writings awe readers and convince them of the accuracy of her historical narratives.

By now the reader has inferred that, in Davis, the autobiographical is never just that. Her joy in sharing her learning, her enlightening personal history, has no equal in twenty-first-century thought. What may seem casual is certainly the most serious and professional aspect of this dialogue. Davis literally offers her life and her works as exemplary. This primordial (*pace* Geertz!) mode of teaching is as pervasive in twenty-first-century cultures around the world as it was in all ancient societies. Montaigne offers an impressive critique of the ethical status of exemplarity, but he became an *exemplum* in his own lifetime. Huizinga called these role models "historical ideals of life." Recently, they have been particularly effective in African-American and women's movements. Exemplarity is not merely implicit in Davis's writing. In the 1980 interview and also in 2004, she recognizes Eileen Power and Sylvia Thrupp as more than historians whose works she admires: they were an inspiration for her, as would be the life and works of Simone Weil. And yes, naming her children after ancestors and heroines is also characteristic of exemplarity.

Binary types of cultural analysis often lead to superficiality, and what follows is no exception. In the great heritage of radical revolutionary and/or reformist movements centered on the Internationals of the late nineteenth century, two complementary but distinct strategies were proposed for changing the world. One was more quantitative and social-scientific, and it was grounded on studies of increasingly poor working conditions, lower wages for workers, and exploitation of children and indigenous populations across the world. Would a proletarian Spartacus come forth? In her earliest studies of the sixteenth-century printers at Lyon, Natalie Zemon Davis respected but remained unsatisfied with this overly mechanical approach to reform and revolution. Ideas, including radical religious ideas, seemed to be part of the equation.

A second approach, one that also emerged from divisions developed during the Internationalist moment, was more humanistic but no less social-scientific in its analysis of individual and collective motives for action, alike. This approach led to cultural studies with themes articulated through the artistic, the ritualistic, and the historical.

Through her speeches and her talent as an organizer and writer, Rosa Luxemburg worked out a powerful alternative model for revolution and reform that had history, ideology, and heroes, as well as collective and individual leaders to inspire workers to strike and to become politically engaged in workers' parties. The quantitative social-scientific approach was not so much rejected by Luxemburg and her movement as it was subsumed through fostering personal initiative and a deepening sense of the important roles played by union and political-party organizations. All the venerable cultural modalities could be revived to convey messages that had deep social and emotional resonances. Using the saints of the early church as a point of departure, in *The Battleship Potemkin* Sergei Eisenstein created the martyrdom of a sailor killed in a just cause and memorialized by candlelit holiness around his body. In Ariane Mnouchkine's *Molière,* the picnic meal of peasants and actors on the arid Larzac plateau (a sacred site for protesters) was inspired by the ideal of fraternization between workers and artists, or between peasants and actors that was longed for by so many on the cultural Left. In *The Return of Martin Guerre,* when Bertrande learns to sign her name, it is an exemplary historical cultural action on behalf of women's power. Rosa Luxemburg, like Jaurès, showed almost messianic confidence in the powers of history to move minds, history firmly grounded on fact and accessible to general readers. Differences between the ideals and careers of Luxemberg and Natalie Zemon Davis come immediately to mind. Human experiences never are really the same.

Natalie Zemon Davis's professional career as a teacher, historian, advisor for films, and member of university councils and fellowship committees, shares some affinity with the daring marching protester, feminist, and historian that was Luxemburg. In his sketch for Davis's 1980 interview with Judy Coffin and Robert Harding, in *Radical History,* Josh Brown captured her in the guise of Delacroix's famous *Liberty Leading the People*. She holds books in her left arm, as she lifts the tricolor high with the right arm. The Phrygian bonnet and the skirt held up by a sash counterbalance her vision fixed ahead, on the horizon. She does not stumble over the bodies of the dead beneath her bare feet. Pastiche sometimes can be serious play.

Natalie Zemon Davis's joy at being an *exemplum* to the fullest, a living historical ideal of life that inspires her readers, her students, and her friends, leads on and exhorts us to follow her.

Chapter 1

Wonderments

DC: I would like to begin our conversation with a question about the kind of history you write. At times, you stress the joy, the wonder that history brings you; that for you, history is not some cold dispassionate discipline where the historian stands outside what he or she studies. Instead, you allow a place for feeling in your search of the past. How, when, and why did you discover this feeling for the past?

NZD: I felt that wonder at the very start of my studies: I was discovering facts that I never knew existed—discovering a past that at first seemed so different from the present I knew as a high-school girl. It filled me with amazement: "Ah, so that's what it was like in ancient Athens. What ideas they had!" Then I was amazed all the more when I came upon forms of life and institutions that seemed to resemble those of my own time: "Already so long ago, people wanted democracy!" To begin with, it was the great movements of the past rather than particular persons that aroused my sense of wonder. And even as a young girl, I was fascinated by the simple facts of history, the things that people always complain about as boring, that they hated to memorize, that turned them off from history. I didn't find them boring at all. I enjoyed memorizing them, the names of kings, the dates of their succession, the names of presidents as well—I liked the sense of mastery I got from being able to remember and use all that historical information.

I had this pleasure of discovery from the beginning, and it lasted. I felt the same way, if not more, when I was an undergraduate at college and was studying the English revolutions of the seventeenth century, the French Revolution, and the Russian Revolution. This grand history, full of troubles and violence, struck me as an example of the aspirations and tragedies of the human spirit, but also I loved reading about it because I was simply fascinated by the past: "What interesting things happened—all these events, so many of them unexpected and fortuitous!" Later on, I began to have the same feelings about the lives of individual persons and more intimate relations.

DC: It thus all began with a fascination with events and facts, right?

NZD: Yes, the great events of history and the aspirations that I thought of as "democratic," which history seemed to reveal over the centuries. I know now that Athens had many features that weren't democratic at all—slavery, for a start. But I remember how I felt long ago, when I first began to immerse myself in the mysteries of the past: the Athenians wanted to create an equal society, a society founded on the equality of citizens—today, of course, I'd add "male citizens." I was attracted both by the "curious" things in the past and also by similarities and differences between the past and my own day.

DC: You've spoken of the sense of wonderment you felt before these "curiosities." Haven't you also responded with wonder to the stories you've read, even the musty smell of the archives, when you've discovered them?

NZD: Yes, that happened when I began my research in France. But even before I crossed the ocean, there was another dimension to my pleasure. I was starting to read archives—not the real archives, but books with documents from the archives—and also books printed in the sixteenth century. I loved this reading; it drew me closer to the societies and social movements of the past and now even to individuals. I wrote a seminar paper on Christine de Pizan[1]—the first woman I'd ever really examined—and another on Guillaume Budé,[2] the humanist. I began to think hard about issues in personal lives, about the contradictions, conflicts, and tensions between intimate personal life, professional projects, and the social, political, and religious realities of the past. It wasn't yet the "perfume" of the archives themselves, but it gave me a stronger sense for the past. I felt that I was coming to know Christine de Pizan, that I was having an encounter with Guillaume Budé.

But watch out! I'd add today. This passion to know and to understand is positive insofar as it encourages us to explore a mysterious world. But it also brings a danger—that of being possessed by the illusion of greater familiarity with the past than one really has. I hope I was taking precautions against this temptation when I was a student, and I certainly try to take them today. We must always remember to be humble toward this past that we study, this past that beckons us. Never decide things too soon—or rather, never imagine we have the power to understand everything. When we do historical research, we want to be conscious of moving into the past, into a sphere different from our own, and yet maintain an essential detachment.

But to go back to your question—I decided France would be the setting for my doctoral thesis, the social groups of the sixteenth century, artisans, workers, printers, Protestants. And so when I finally crossed the Atlantic, the pleasure of the archives coincided with my first presence in France. France held the taste, the perfume of the archives for me.

DC: What drew you to France?

NZD: Why France? It started with my studying French language, already in high school. So there was a practical aspect to my choice: I could read French. But then, as I heard about France in those years right after World War II, I found it very appealing: stories of the Resistance, the *Antigone* of Anouilh, which I read in college,[3] the writings of Jean-Paul Sartre and the new philosophical movements, and the like.[4] As a young student, I was tantalized by the drama and the romance. And France was also the country of the Enlightenment and the French Revolution, with all their transformations. I was very politically engaged as a student, and I felt that in some sense, this history was *my* history, even though I was a Jewish American.

DC: When did you first come to France?

NZD: I came to France for the first time in 1952. Seven years had passed since the end of the war, but one still felt its traces in Lyon every day. I immediately fell in love with France, the people, their way of living and talking, and with their food, which seemed very different from American food. The French would always say to me, "Ah, you Americans, you don't know anything about cooking." I remember that I even enjoyed the food at the student restaurants I ate at every day. "What good taste people have here," I'd say to myself. I also liked the style of conversation among the French, which resembled my own: a very lively style, where people talked with their hands, very Mediterranean, you could say. I also loved the company of my new French friends, even though I spent most of my hours at the archives and libraries.

DC: So you stayed in Lyon?

NZD: That town was for me a sort of fairyland, as was France itself. I had come to France by boat on this first visit, and then taken the train down to Lyon. I discovered the French countryside looking out the train window. I was very struck by the physiognomy of the fields, so tended, so cared for and demarcated, so different from the vast, spread-out, and even untidy fields I'd see from the car window in the U.S. In a way my love of France began with looking at those landscapes, at the actual territory of France.

Today I still love France, but in a more tempered way. Back then I felt that the country I had chosen for my research was a very special place and I was lucky to be working on it. What undoubtedly reinforced that feeling was that when I returned from France in the fall of 1952, the State Department took away my passport. (I can tell you the reasons for this later on, if you want.) I could no longer leave the United States. For eight years I longed for France and those archives, which I so needed to see. France became for me a sort of dream.

When I finally was able to return in 1960, France still kept for me that image of a fairyland. And at the same time, both in 1952 and later, I had the enormous pleasure, after having to content myself with reading about my sixteenth-century people from afar, with the sources at my disposal in the U.S., to finally have access, if not to their real identities, then at least to a plethora of their words, their phrases in many settings.

DC: The documents thus transported you back in time to lives lived long ago, right?

NZD: Yes, and the fact that the men and women of the past had themselves touched these documents. I always have the feeling when I'm turning the pages of documents in the archives, "Long ago, the men and women whom I'm trying to understand wrote this down. I have before me the human traces of the past." I recall vividly the room in Lyon where this sense of connection first took place—the dark wooden bookcases and the beautiful heavy wooden tables, little lamps that were lit only some of the time because French people were used to conserving electricity. The municipal archives were in one of the rooms of the Palace of the Archbishop of Lyon, right next to the municipal library. It's all very different now, but I still have that feeling of connection whenever I have documents and manuscripts in my hands.

But once again, I say "Danger!" I have the impression that I've met, touched, seized the past. "Watch out, Natalie. You're being taken over by a romantic fantasy." One must always gird oneself with the certainty that one can never reach the living heart of the past from which the documents are speaking. The past always recedes. And yet, while I'm absorbed in the documents, I nonetheless have the sense of being surrounded by the persons I'm discovering, of a kind of ghostly presence.

DC: Don't you frequently use the conditional tense precisely because of the pleasure history gives you, because you're on such friendly terms with men and women in the past? Or when you also decide to intervene in the text in the first person to highlight that you explicitly control the narration of the past's possibilities, a past which you both direct and create? It comes through particularly in your book on Martin Guerre, a character for whom you had very few documents upon which to rely. There are obviously the texts of Jean Coras, such as *L'Arrêt mémorable,* but beyond those there are just mere tidbits of information. Don't readers instead see you fill the evidentiary void with all kinds of rhetorical tricks, such as "I would be inclined to think..."? At the same time, isn't this "I," when you're forced to reveal yourself, the active agent who realizes this sense of wonderment and desire for history that captures the imaginations of those same readers? Isn't this all an intentional subversion of a certain kind of traditional, if not old-fashioned idea of history?

NZD: The use of the conditional is a safeguard for the historian. More and more it seems I have to use it. When I started out studying large social movements, such as the relation between artisanal conflicts and Protestant commitment in Lyon, there were times when I had to venture an interpretation, a kind of guess. That is, there might or might not be a correlation between social aspirations and religious beliefs. But while working on general movements with lots of data, I had fewer instances where it seemed urgent or obligatory for me to use the conditional. And this was still the case in more recent books, such as the ones I wrote on letters of remission and on gifts, where I had lots of examples: I made interpretations, which could be open to challenge, but I could make a flat assertion.

But when I took off in pursuit of the ideas, feelings, conflicts, and dreams of particular persons, I sometimes encountered big gaps in the documentation, especially since I was often tracking people who had left no written traces. So I had to proceed with deductions from related evidence, make speculations, and use words like "perhaps" or "maybe" or "he would have thought" or—and I love the irony of this one—"surely." In fact I enjoy the challenge of finding evidence that can help fill in a gap; the pleasure of discovery in a really difficult situation is extra strong.

Of course, we historians are not just wandering without guidelines here; we have techniques that make it possible to use the conditional, that is, to arrive at a register of alternatives. For example, if one has no precise documentation on a specific person or group or on a specific day or event, one can get evidence about the world around them. One can draw on situations, mentalities, and reactions analogous or close to those one is trying to understand. We seek whatever evidence we can find so as to be able to ask and imagine what might have been *possible* for a precise individual or a particular group or the outcome of a particular event. We spell out the possibilities, and try to figure out what is most likely from the evidence we have.

In my opinion, one of the richest and most fruitful sources for historical analysis is the circle one creates or recreates around the object of analysis—even when one has many texts available, even when one has the diary of the person one is working on. Even with all these sources, the historian has to seek ways to understand the feelings, the conventions, language, words, gestures, and images that define the world around his or her subject, which encircle that subject.

I hope, and I say this with a smile, that my conditionals are well supported by my research. I use all my ingenuity and years of haunting archives and libraries to find evidence that can work. The conditionals are also a way to leave my argument open, to suggest a tension between my interest in my subjects and their own thoughts and desires. And through my conditionals, I'm leaving open to my readers greater freedom to say, "But no..."

DC: Don't you try in a way to have readers discover their own sense of pleasure by inviting them to speak directly with your text, by engaging them in a dialogue with your own inventiveness, one that leads them to share your own relationship with history?

NZD: Why not? If I could share my pleasure with my readers, even a little, it would be a great joy for me. And yet if I hope that my writing might win readers over to my historical enthusiasm, I don't want them simply to be persuaded by the rhetoric, style, detail, or construction of my texts. Rather I want to start a conversation with my readers, a dialogue, even a dispute. I use rhetorical techniques to encourage a double reaction: to agree or not to agree with my approach, my methods, and my interpretation.

DC: In the prologue to one of your major works, *Women on the Margins: Three Seventeenth-Century Lives,* you distinguish an initial level of conversation that puts you into contact with people in the past and thus precedes the kind of relationship you wish to cultivate with your readers. It consists of an imaginary conversation that you broach and then compose with three women from different religions, one Jewish, one Protestant, and the last Catholic. I find it most significant that you call this an "adventure," as if, if I understand you correctly, the historian embarks on a kind of voyage into the past where she is both master and slave of her subject of study because the sources constrain the historian who nevertheless retains the capacity to choose, define, and select which problems to pursue. Above all, the historian defends her right to speak with these specters that almost come to life again in her imagination. It seems obvious that you've pursued this "adventure" throughout your work. You've never fixed on any one subject in your career; instead, you've island-hopped, so to speak, to include even an interest in cinema and the ways it shapes representations of the past. For you, does the historian become a sort of scientist who experiments with encounters and words, places and persons, always shifting, moving, even jumping from one place to another, from one time period to another, from one dialogue to another dialogue, from one "dispute" to another "dispute," as you put it? Is yours a dialogical history in which one interlocutor arrives only to fade away and be replaced by another? Is it a history that craves words, craves "conversation"?

NZD: I must admit that in some ways I'm an impatient person, I'm restless. To be sure, there have been research projects I've put aside because I felt that I had not got to the heart of certain questions I'd posed, that there were certain central issues that I had not figured out. When that happens—as it did with my book on *The Gift*—I put the project on the back burner for a time. Usually I have a different rhythm. When I've explored a subject, perhaps not as thoroughly as one could, but to my own satisfaction, discovered as much I could, and written it up, I have a sense that I've reached the limits of my inquiry. I like to turn toward another subject—in fact, there's usually one there already beckoning me.

I must say there is a contrast between my experience and that of historians who take hold of a big question—say, feudalism in the twelfth century or the humanist world of the sixteenth century—and write marvelous and deeply researched books on these themes their whole life long. I admire their work and their faculty of concentration, but it's not my style. I take a subject and pass to another. It's not that I get bored staying in one place, rather I get attracted by another. It's like a jewel, a diamond that one turns, and suddenly there's a whole other face. It's that new face of history that I want to examine.

So after coming to Lyon to do a type of *social* history and finding the archives appropriate to that approach, I turned to a more *cultural* history, adding charivaris and carnivals to the strikes and trade unions. Next I moved beyond Lyon, an urban and artisanal center, to the countryside and the peasants, inspired, of course, by the studies of other historians. What delight! New archives, new libraries, new settings. And then I started experimenting with other forms of writing and expression, and even imagining I could use film to tell about the past.

But the biggest leap for me has been working on countries other than France. I had long been interested in other countries for purposes of comparison with the French case, but these comparisons were limited and supported by the research of other historians. So it was an exciting moment when I engaged with the three women: the German Jew Glikl; the German Protestant Maria Sibylla Merian, who spent some time in Suriname; and the French Catholic Marie de l'Incarnation, who spent much of her life in Québec. For the first time I used archives outside of France. I had to improve my reading of other languages, and learn to read Yiddish for the first time. That's when I learned what an adventure history can be. I was just amazed at how much one could continue to learn.

DC: Does your dialogue with past lives spring from a personal urge to always amplify and renew the stock of what you know far beyond your own personal experience?

NZD: "Conversation" with people of the past requires a long and ever-renewed apprenticeship. Right now I'm working on Muslims in North Africa. At my advanced age, I've decided that it's no longer possible to really learn Arabic, and so I've decided to use translations and translators to understand the texts in Arabic that concern the man whose real name was al-Hasan al-Wazzān (and not Leo Africanus). Most of the works he left, however, are in Italian or in Latin, especially in Italian, a foreigner's Italian. At my age, simply to have the pleasure of reading not only his writings, but also in translation the great works on Islamic religion and law, the great texts on the history of the Arabs and Arabic literature—this has been an adventure. An adventure, because it's very difficult to step outside of the European world, but it's so interesting, so enriching...

DC: In Leo Africanus, what is it that pleases you beyond the simple contact with writings from the past? Are they the implications that arise for our own world today? Or is it simply restoring a past way to think and live, a way that derives its complexity from Leo Africanus's vagabond life?

NZD: It's both things. I must tell you that I've known "Leo Africanus" under the name given him by Christians since my graduate-student days because the French translation of his celebrated work, *The Description of Africa,* was published in Lyon in 1556 by one of my Protestant printers. I've known this work for a long time, but at first the book seemed important only for its place in European intellectual history and as an edition published by a Protestant in France. Later on, I became interested in the relation between French people and foreigners, especially through my study of Marie de l'Incarnation, and in questions concerning the colonial world. It was only eight years ago that the moment seemed right for me to work on a person like al-Wazzān, a man between two worlds: the world of North Africa and the world of Italy and Europe, between Islam and Christianity. That was in 1995 at a time of intense nationalist passion and rage...

DC: That's the question I wanted to ask you. Isn't looking at the past through a character such as al-Wazzān a way to keep at bay the uncertainties of the present? Or is it a plea against the refusal to acknowledge Otherness, against the illusion of homogeneity?

NZD: Yes, against that nationalist fury, these religious passions, that obsession with frontiers, with fixed and immovable boundaries and borders, which have become so strong in our time and which run so counter to the porousness suggested by documents of the past... and by the figure of al-Wazzān. There's a real need to show that history has not consisted only of exclusions and exclusiveness; in the lives of individuals, of groups, and of nations, the story has been quite otherwise. The will to assign oneself a simplistic single-stranded identity, a "pure" authenticity, is negative and dangerous. So it seemed to me that al-Wazzān alias Leo Africanus was, among other examples—for I have others!—a fascinating person in whom one could explore the creative tension in "mixture," in cultural crossings.

But as I've been working on the project—and I hope I'm on the right track—I've discovered an amusing thing about myself, about my style as a historian. Since *The Return of Martin Guerre,* when I wrote the story of someone who played with his identity, I think I've acquired a sort of style, or at least a habitual way of perceiving situations and people, that is, of always looking for questions about self-fashioning, of fashioning one's inner and outer self, and even of imposture. This is a style that the evidence itself required of me in the case of Martin Guerre, but it continued with the three women, who fashioned and created their lives in unusual directions. I began this study of al-Wazzān without any conscious idea that I was once again going to come upon a case of self-fashioning. And here I am finding it once again. I don't know whether it's just me, my habit of perception, or the evidence that is exuding from this vision. I'd like to believe that it's the documentation, but whatever it is, history is repeating itself.

DC: There's that theme of pleasure again, right? The kind of pleasure when one communes with the objects of one's study to see their different possible identities arising along some sort of set path? Isn't this a way for the historian to find personal reassurance?

NZD: It's true that one can never simply put oneself aside or on the margin of this past with which one has come to live for the moment. But my preferences or my needs, though present, must not determine my historical vision. The historian must be open to the traces of the past, to the voices of the past. That's what must count first of all. This idea of imposture—or rather self-fashioning, for "imposture" is too strong a word for most of my cases—this principle according to which a personality can be crafted leads us to reflect on a kind of game. History is both tragic and ludic at the same time, two aspects that always coexist. My position is halfway between Rabelais[5] and Montaigne:[6] Rabelais for the spirit of play, Montaigne rather for the spirit of tragedy. My preference goes a bit more in the direction of laughter and play. As for the idea of "self-fashioning"—an expression we owe to Montaigne—it includes the activity of a person, like a kind of game or play, in a historical situation where he or she tries somehow to survive, to adapt, to cope, to improvise, to take the best advantage of the possibilities offered. There's perhaps only a small space for comedy here, but that small space, in a world full of sadness, is better than nothing.

DC: Precisely how do you see the relationship between past and present? Do you find in the present world, indeed in yourself, this type of game? Isn't a historian, even the most conscientious one who respects the basic rules of knowledge, still just someone who makes the past into some kind of game? Doesn't a historian put this mask or that one, however knowingly, on the characters she claims to give voice to, be they major or minor figures, based on the sources or not? Isn't a historian thus only a charlatan, a mere trickster, who should leave all of us skeptical about the historian's craft? This is a little like what Cornelius Agrippa of Nettesheim wrote in the 1520s when he said that history is just a pack of fables (most of which recount, he went on, atrocities and acts of violence!).[7] Your heroines, for example, are usually unhappy women who behave in ways that create for them an alternative, closed, and protected space that they can master, where they can exercise power and thus rise above the normative social and gender rules that label them as weak and confine them to certain prescribed roles. Don't you actually realize that they come to you as you wish to see them, thereby avoiding a more complex reality? It's almost as if you wanted to escape from harsh circumstances that threatened your own hopes and dreams by taking refuge in your study of the sixteenth and seventeenth centuries? When it comes to this moment right now, what do you see or want to see?

NZD: Yes and no. In interpreting the past, I have in fact drawn upon insights from my own experience: a family in which my grandparents or great-grandparents were immigrants. That's the American drama, a country of immigrants. My ancestors came to the U.S. in the mid- or late nineteenth century, speaking European languages or Yiddish, and with their own customs. They wanted to create for themselves an American life with a Jewish identity. As for me, I belong to the third generation; on my mother's side, it was the first where the women went to university. I also had to transform myself, to Americanize myself, to find my own identity—but it was a complex matter, because I was very tied to France, the study of France, and to French culture. So self-fashioning was part of my own experience. And then I went on to marry a man with a very different background from my own, another pattern of self-fashioning. This transformative work on the self, my own and that of my family, does provide a link between what I write and the present-day world.

But no, I do not refashion the men and women of the sixteenth and seventeenth century simply from the perspective of my own life or from my own twentieth and now twenty-first century. I am, I must be as faithful, as attentive as possible to all the remains of the past. These papers, these images—I didn't bring them into being. They are legacies from people of long ago, and I am obliged by this gift from the past to take them very seriously. There lies my psychological engagement, my psychological contract, with the people whom I seek to know and understand. If I find things that disappoint me, too bad for me, I've got to make do with them and accept them.

In fact, it turns out that the difficult cases are often the most interesting—full of surprises and the unexpected. I especially had this challenge when I was writing on the three women: the Jewish Glikl and the Catholic Marie de l'Incarnation had each left autobiographies, signs of consciousness of the self. The Protestant Maria Sibylla Merian gave out only a few scraps about herself. So I was forced to question myself and the past about the significance of silence. A condition for a kind of freedom in the seventeenth century? Another form of dissimulation?

These lives of the past have taught me a lot. I think I never clearly perceived the role of self-fashioning in my own life until after I'd reflected on the lives of Martin Guerre, Arnaud du Tilh, and Bertrande de Rols. Elements from the past inform the present, and sometimes we look at the present through the prism of the past. Or to put it another way, a painful or dangerous or vital reality of the present can be examined in light of the past, even though forms and conditions change so much over time: the past offers us ways to reflect on the present with greater nuance, sensitivity, and detachment.

DC: Or more critically?

NZD: Surely—or at least I hope so. The strategies for *métissage,* for mixing, and for self-fashioning of al-Wazzān lead to reflection, they encourage you to look with critical eyes at the issues of religious, racist, or nationalist passion. Throughout the world, in the West and the East, doctrinaire identity movements of this kind are emerging. We need to reflect on other possibilities. Very often the past offers us the memory of possibilities—not models, not possibilities to imitate, but simply other possible worlds, other ways of living that we humans sometimes had here or elsewhere on our globe. The book I wrote on the gift in sixteenth-century France grew out of a fascinating question posed by Marcel Mauss, a question to which both anthropologists and historians have given thought. Why do we live under a religion of the market, which insists on a single mode for exchanging things between people and ignores other possibilities, other modes for the exchange of objects and ideas? I thought such an exploration could open the way to reflection on possibilities...

DC: At the same time, in your books you don't let readers realize the theoretical implications of these calls for reflection. Does that spring from your fear of becoming too didactic?

NZD: A book is not a lesson. I don't know of perfect solutions to all these questions. I have some ideas about solutions, some values that I'd like to see expressed in our world today, but I'm not going to preach them. I have two goals. First, that readers be interested, drawn by a historical account, amused by its comic aspects, saddened by the tragic elements, captured by the possibilities of the past; and second, that readers be aware that there could be another way of looking at things besides the one I offer. I'm not giving a lesson or a sermon, I'm offering a dialogue, as I said before.

Sometimes I imagine a dialogue with my long-dead subjects. For my first book, my husband, Chandler, wrote a poem, which served as a dedication or *envoi*. Already back then, he imagined me wishing for a conversation with the printer's journeymen of sixteenth-century Lyon! I liked this poem very much and was glad to have it as an epigraph to my book since it expressed a wish to know what the printing workers would have thought of what I'd written. Maybe they wouldn't have liked what I'd said at all. Had I caught their "truth" or had I deformed it?

DC: Let's return to al-Wazzān/Leo Africanus. Don't you want to turn this character into a symbol of cultural openness where an individual's power derives from his capacity to be acculturated, to leave off his sense of self or project another one for others to see? Doesn't this raise questions about creative agency?

NZD: Just so. We see here how a person invents procedures for accommodation when he or she is placed in a difficult situation—and I say "difficult" because al-Wazzān/Leo Africanus had been captured by Christian pirates and his arrival in Italy was not voluntary. In this difficult and dangerous situation, he found a way to learn, to gain access to new knowledge, sometimes to amuse himself, and even travel once he'd become a Christian. What especially interested me was how he associated the ideas and features of his education as a Muslim with those of his Christian life, how in some sense he stitched together the diverse threads given him by the vicissitudes of his life. His book on Africa had much success with European readers later on, but it was also a success for him. That book is his own creation, something he might never have achieved if he had not found himself in a tough spot, displaced from his world into another world. And that's important! He became a writer—an author—when he had to write in a foreign language. He shaped himself as a person and writer out of ambivalence: out of attraction to another culture and desire to be differentiated from that culture.

DC: These are the paradoxes of individual destinies, even though he had to endure the shock of a forced dislocation that he coped with by fashioning himself into a writer who invented his own way of trying to describe a homeland he had lost.

NZD: Yes, but when I first started on al-Wazzān's story, I underestimated the cost of uprooting, the toll it could take. Now that I've done research, on him and on other persons I'm studying in this project on cultural crossing, I see that things are not so simple—they never are. To put it briefly, in his book al-Wazzān said that when he returned to his home in North Africa, he wanted to write other works—on Europe and on the travels he claimed to have made in Asia. In my opinion, he would also have wished to rewrite his great work on Africa, composed initially for European readers, in Arabic and make it suitable for Arab readers. Once back in North Africa, he would have had to return to Islam, and then if all had gone as he had once hoped, he would have plunged himself into writing. Now we know he was alive in North Africa in 1532, five years after he had left Italy. But from everything I've been able to discover in Arab manuscript collections and from all my searching in Arabic biographical dictionaries (the *tabaqat,* biographies of illustrious and learned persons, a very important genre in the Arab world), al-Wazzān left nothing after his return, not a single work, not a manuscript.

DC: Were the manuscripts lost or did they simply not exist?

NZD: From what I've been able to ascertain up till now—and it was recently confirmed after conversations with specialists in Morocco, such as Lucette Valensi, Oumelbanine Zhiri, and Faustina Doufikar-Aerts[8]—his hope to continue writing was not realized. And yet, it could have been very interesting, one might think, for inhabitants of North Africa or for the Ottomans to have at their disposal a description of what al-Wazzān had seen in Italy.

DC: For you too!

NZD: For sure! I was left with imagining, with speculating from everything al-Wazzān said in *The Description of Africa* (his manuscript actually had a different title, but the printed work was entitled this way). What to think? I speculated that he was not able to write perhaps because of a lack of readers for or listeners to his story: perhaps his fellow Muslims were suspicious of him and of what he'd done in Italy even though he'd returned to Islam; perhaps he had not been able to find an important patron or protector. In my view, the answer to the question is first of all psychological. To put it succinctly, the leap he made during his nine years in Italy was both intellectual and psychological.

As I see him in Italy, during his time as a Christian, he both remained faithful to his Muslim and Arab origins and at the same time learned a great deal, enlarged his angles of vision and perceptions; he opened out. In his manuscript of his Africa book (though not in the much-edited printed version), there are literary, expository, and rhetorical signs of his state of mind, which we can detect through attentive reading. His exposition indicates a break with an important feature of the Arab and Muslim mental world. There it is expected that the writer acknowledge a line of professional transmission (reverence in regard to my teacher, the teacher of my teacher, etc.). This requirement originated in religious life and pronouncement: to have authority, what one says in the present must always go through a chain of transmission (*isnad*) back to the Prophet or the Companions or wives of the Prophet. Thought is supported by this kind of reference.

Now in al-Wazzān's manuscripts in Italian and Latin, this chain of transmission is suggested sometimes for others, for example, for the great scholar Ibn Rushd (Averroës), but never for himself.[9] He never gives the names of his teachers or the teachers of his teachers. He presents himself to Christian readers as a man educated as a Muslim, who has read many Arabic manuscripts, but who is interpreting his world and the great Muslim figures as an independent observer—cut off, liberated, detached from the chain of transmission. This expository practice, this writing practice is—so I claim—an index of a new sense of self, a new self-consciousness that is precariously solitary.

And then al-Wazzān returns to North Africa. He cuts off his relations with the great but dangerous adventure of his Italian years, years that were for him simultaneously Christian and Muslim. And then he can't put himself back to work. Had his mental uprooting been too extreme? His desire to write seems to have dried up, or at least to write in Arabic. Alas, I am left with some wistfulness. I started this project with the naïve idea, "Ah, here is the creative work of a man in the course of a complicated life." Well, the ending turned out not to be quite the fulfillment of my first hopes.

DC: Shouldn't you really interpret this final speechlessness as a kind of self-criticism of his own making while he was in Italy? Wouldn't it be better to talk about remorse or even estrangement, where distance becomes a necessary condition for such discourse? Remorse or was it nostalgia? Or is it rather a fact that the tools he used—Latin, Italian, printed books—proved most conducive to express this realization? Wouldn't he have lost one of his identities, the one he fashioned to deal with his condition as an alien, when he eventually returned home? Wouldn't he have taken some pleasure in closing this chapter of his life? In the sixteenth century, it seems to me that an individual could choose to deploy any number of different identities; that in fact an individual's identity developed in a plural manner. We'd have to admit that this cultural fact would have required a ceaseless accommodation of the self with respect to others. In this light, the question of contradiction becomes secondary. A person is who a person is as the result of a particular moment in time, space, and the greater human community.

NZD: Perhaps... But above all, I think the life of al-Wazzān/Leo Africanus led me to a criticism of myself. One should never begin with...

DC: Hopes too high...?

NZD: Yes, perhaps it's always like that when one starts out on a research project—one's ideas are too simplistic, optimistic. But I should restrain myself some here, as I'm still in the process of writing this book. Perhaps it was the world to which al-Wazzān came back that accounts for his "speechlessness," as you call it. But I would not follow Bernard Lewis here, according to whom the Muslim world had become a closed world and that would explain why al-Wazzān could no longer be creative after his return.[10] Everything I see about this world indicates this was not true, it was not a closed world, and possibilities were opening for the writing of books.

I'm reminded of an assertion I made about Marie de l'Incarnation. In her situation—that of a seventeenth-century woman who was not at all erudite, who sought her own education and fashioned her own goals—the most important book she wrote on theological matters was not in French, but in Algonquian, produced for the Amerindians. She had written other texts with religious themes, as in her autobiography, but when she wanted to treat theological questions directly, in her *Sacred History,* she did not do it in French. To be sure, she was not authorized to write a theological work: she was not a theologian, she had never studied theology. She had never studied Latin, and claimed that God had "infused" Latin into her head. Thus I find it interesting that it was in Algonquian that she, an unschooled woman, had the audacity to write on learned questions of theology.

This brings me back to your questions about al-Wazzān. Did his audacity in writing a great work on Africa, with its new concept of Africa itself, emerge from the fact that he was writing for Italians? I say "new concept" because though the genres he was deploying—geography, the travel account, history—had existed for centuries in Arabic literature, his concept of Africa, geographical and cultural, had new features to it in relation to the thought of Arabs and Europeans both.

DC: **It's necessary to be "outside of" to be able to...**

NZD: To *do it.* And in a symbolic sense, in another language.

DC: **Overcoming such personal inhibitions would make sense when thrusting oneself, either voluntarily or involuntarily, into another place, another culture, another language. Could you have written a book about American history before you first enlarged your own orbit to encompass the life of al-Wazzān/Leo Africanus?**

NZD: It may be a little bit my own history that I'm approaching through al-Wazzān or Marie de l'Incarnation: to go to a foreign land to be able to write, or for me, first of all to find a past for myself in a foreign land and then to write. I've turned to America and its history only recently. Earlier I sometimes mentioned American themes, as in my study of charivaris. But in my *Slaves on Screen,* a book I published a few years ago about the historical vision of slavery and especially slave revolts and resistance in film, I included three American-made movies: Stanley Kubrick's *Spartacus,*[11] Steven Spielberg's *Amistad,*[12] and Jonathan Demme's *Beloved.*[13] To be able to comment on these films, I had to do lots of research both on filmmaking and on slavery in America.

DC: It was as if America compelled you to examine its history...

NZD: Maybe so. I've certainly found it fascinating. But note that my return has taken place by the path of slavery, revolts, and Africans... I'd like to go back for a moment to al-Wazzān and the significance of his life. I have reservations about having this life end only in a tragedy, in the sorrow of speechlessness. I would like to lead up to a conclusion that is not so clear-cut, even though the story turns out to be more complicated than I had anticipated at first. I want to write a less drastic conclusion, a conclusion in which his intellectual inventiveness, his geographical discovery, and the adventure of his life are not erased by a finish without the creativity I had hoped for or that al-Wazzān must have hoped for himself.

I have a penchant, an appetite for writing lives, even unhappy ones, in the course of which the person holds on to a certain dignity up to the end, in spite of the disappointments, the things unfinished, the suffering...

DC: The life of Arnaud du Tilh, the "fake" Martin Guerre, for example, had been given to his contemporaries to read as a story, if not a fantastic one then at least one with a tragic air, which you certainly presented it as. But, in the end, through the account you reconstruct, one gets the sense that this fake Martin Guerre is almost freed, when he's sentenced to death, from the whole confused affair he began as a game of switched identities, an imposture he slipped into so easily when assuming the character of Martin Guerre, which he then changed and refashioned in a more positive manner that in turn validated in him a new sense of self. His death would thus not be a unique event, just as his life was not (insofar as the fake Martin Guerre possessed a humane sensibility and expressed a love that the real Martin Guerre never had for the wife he had abandoned). Even when all his hopes and dreams finally collapsed, it was if this person lived life in continuous process of self-fashioning, at least as you see it.

NZD: The contemporaries of Martin Guerre envisaged the affair as a tragicomedy rather than a tragedy: after all, the impostor was unmasked and the wife could take up her life again next to her true husband. We're the ones who bring out the tragic elements underlying the story. Yes, Arnaud du Tilh lost, but even to him I wanted to offer a release, or rather I gave him an execution with a certain quality. At the end of his adventure, he could have denounced Bertrande de Rols as his accomplice. Instead he decided to die with some dignity (I didn't make up this ending: it's right there in the documents; but I did stress it and write about it). Arnaud refused to take with him to death and opprobrium the woman with whom he had lived in imposture and perhaps, too, in some happiness...

DC: Was this "dignified" death perhaps tied to the possibility he was a Calvinist or at least open to Jean Calvin's ideas[14] (much as was the author of the *Arrêt mémorable,* Jean de Coras) and that death, for a man converted to the Reformed religion, brings an end to anguish, that it is God's will before which man must surrender humbly and patiently, a test that God sends to him to test the strength of his faith so that he proves all his thoughts are firmly fixed on the hope of Christ, on the rock of Christ? Didn't his self-restraint provide a chance to introduce Christians to Calvin's teachings on Christ's charity and love? Wasn't there a sort of hidden message in the *Arrêt mémorable* about willingly accepting death with calm assurance? Man is certainly a sinner, but his consciousness of sin is regenerated when he places all his hope in divine forgiveness, no?

NZD: Conversion is certainly a strong possibility for Arnaud du Tilh, as I argued in the book, though I haven't got sure proof. I think it very probable that he was part of the Protestant faction in Artigat, in which case your speculation would be justified.

DC: Or rather that Jean de Coras would, in some way, want to insert a subtext into his *Arrêt mémorable,* one about how an exemplary faith led a man to no longer fear death because death made possible his union with Christ. Leaving aside the question of knowing Arnaud du Tilh's faith, didn't Coras want to send an almost subliminal message to his readers? As for al-Wazzān/Leo Africanus, couldn't we surmise that, beyond your own dissatisfaction when confronting his silence, likely his coping mechanism, his return to Islam would have forced or triggered in him a sense of fatalism? Could he really enjoy his silence without a bad conscience somehow lurking in the background? As a historian, you take something of a risk when you emphasize your own sense of disillusionment, thereby forgetting that serenity or wisdom once had other pathways than the ones you

idealize for yourself and for the characters you conjure in your own mind ... Can't a person's silence in fact bespeak their own peace of mind?

NZD: No, I believe that after his years of dissimulation and exploration—and opening out?—in Italy, he may well have been thrown off balance when he returned to Islam. Rather than fatalism, I'd suspect he would have plunged into practices of expiation. We know of other apostates who, in returning to Dar-al-Islam, left for Mecca. Why not a second pilgrimage for al-Wazzān? He himself described the conversion of the great scholar al-Ghazālī, who gave up his professorship of law to become a Sufi mystic, and we can imagine that al-Wazzān, after seeing the splendors of Rome, might have done something similar.[15]

I'd like to tell you about another tool I've been using to interpret this life so full of mysteries. There's an extremely interesting literary tradition in the Arab world, the genre of the *maqāmāt,* that is, the "assemblies," created by two writers, al-Hamadhānī[16] in the late tenth century, and then al-Hariri[17] at the beginning of the twelfth century. The *maqāmāt* were always composed in a rhymed prose, full of alliteration. But it's the hero of the *maqāmāt* who's important here (for some scholars today he's an antihero, but not for me!): a traveler, a vagabond poet, and eloquent speaker, who has adventures everywhere in the Muslim world and who is always in disguise. The *maqāmāt* have a typical form: there's always a narrator, himself a voyager, who travels about as a merchant, a pilgrim, or a judge, and who tells to his friends assembled around him the adventures of the vagabond poet. In each tale, the latter puts on a different disguise, but the narrator always recognizes him at the end, especially when he begins to speak in striking metric verse, sometimes touching on theological questions. The vagabond poet always gets what he's after, whether he's begging or seeking money or some other benefit—he lands on his feet and leaves with his pouches full. You see how I can use this figure, this trope, to interpret my voyager—not in every aspect of his life, but at least in part.

Toward the end of al-Hamadhānī's *maqāmāt,* the tensions and contradictions in the life of this vagabond poet with all his ruses are foregrounded in a dramatic way, followed by an effort at resolution. In the *maqāmāt* entitled "Wine," there's a movement between delicious wine, served by a magnificent hostess, and the mosque.[18] The hero, in disguise as imam, expels the wine-drinkers from the mosque (in the story, the wine-drinkers are the narrator and his buddies); and then as *shaykh* and lover of the beautiful hostess, the hero joins these same friends and drinks in their company. Unmasked and chided for his hypocrisy, he gives a defense in verse for his behavior and his choices. The narrator is not fully persuaded by his argument and leaves the question to God. But he stays with the vagabond poet, rejoicing in his presence. I see here a possible opening toward the celebrated mystical wine-poem of the Sufi Ibn al-Farid,[19] which al-Wazzān recalled often during his Italian years. I would love to have found a text by al-Wazzān where he fit together the different parts of his life as happens in the *maqāmāt* "Wine." In fact, what I'm having to do is conjecture that he could have made use of the verses of the great poet and thinker, the Sufi Ibn al-ʿArabi[20]—that he would have known them and meditated upon them: "My heart is open to all forms." Here was a mystical movement that stayed within Islam, yet opened the heart to other religious sensibilities.

DC: Does this strange journey finally end in a flash of insight that completes an inner conversation giving voice to a mystic?

NZD: Maybe so. I still wish I had a text from al-Wazzān after his return to North Africa: if I could rewrite the past, there would be such a text with some sort of resolution, perhaps with poetic sensibility. As it is, it is Natalie Davis who will be deciding whether to end the life of al-Hasan al-Wazzān with the text of al-Hamadhānī and the poem of Ibn al-ʿArabi.

DC: As a person who's always loved storytelling, haven't you wished at some exact moment in your analysis you could just escape from the confines of history based on sources? Haven't you wanted yourself to write what the primary or secondary sources don't provide you in order to create your own virtual reality? It seems to me that historians become too timid as a result of their attachment, even if unconscious, to this prevailing positivism. Is there some precise stage in writing, when history becomes obscured in shadows, that it's impossible to see how to grab hold of the past, to realize a level of discourse that possesses its own coherence and logic and that develops as a kind of projection of a likely future only set in the past? All history is thus virtual in its essence and by necessity—even if there are historians who say it and assume it, as well as those who don't say it or ignore it. Why don't we once and for all begin to admit what we might call an "imagined" past? Take, for example, the imagined past of Leo Africanus upon his return home after a long absence, returned perhaps to die among his own people, under another sky and on another ground?

NZD: For me, the sources from the past, primary or secondary, are not a prison. They are a magic thread that links me to people long since dead and with situations that have crumbled to dust. The sources set off my reflection and imagination, I stay in dialogue with them, and I love this. This liaison with the past is the heart of my vocation as historian. The sources leave a space for speculation, and I will have to use it sometimes in my book on al-Wazzān. But I must always identify my speculations as such for my readers, and show them the bases for believing a certain thing is possible, probable, or contingent.

DC: It suddenly seems to me that historians often become too timid when faced with contingencies. Why, when a kind of interpretive wall is reached, don't they leap beyond the limits of what their sources tell them and concoct instead a critical space rife with possibilities? It's true that history has tended toward its own sort of marginalized discourse; but apart from the moment where the limits of the past's admissibility are accepted, recorded, and perceived as inevitable constraints, apart from the moment where we can't escape from the realm of the plausible or the admissible unless it's all locked up in a vicious cycle of logical absurdity, all might be possible, for it's this purposeful loss of control, if I can use that expression, which would be interesting to put into practice in order to try to go beyond...

NZD: The sphere of the possible or probable is very large. Indeed, things considered "prodigious," to cite the title of Jean de Coras's book on the Martin Guerre case, actually happen—things considered at the time "monstrous," "beyond nature." I want my speculative jumps to start from a springboard of documentation. And out of respect for my readers and for the past, I must interject my personal voice—"this is what I see." But frankly, al-Wazzān/Leo Africanus is much more interesting than I am; I'm not the important one, he is.

DC: Yes, but he doesn't exist without...

NZD: Without a biographer, without a relation to me—okay, but it's always he who is the subject. I'm not writing an autobiography. I'm doing my best to respect the sources about him, but mysteries remain, more than in more usual historical inquiry. Or to put it another way, I'm not willing to let al-Wazzān go without asking tough questions and they're hard to answer. My voice appears as a murmur now and then, when I acknowledge what I've done.

I actually wish that something similar could be developed in historical films. Serious historical films get made. But filmmakers should also find dramatic and aesthetically appealing means to suggest to viewers what part their own creativity has played in the representation of historical facts, indicate by small signs the role of the filmmaker's invention in the film script and image. Working out how this might be achieved is a future task for the art of historical films. We need something better than the disingenuous "any resemblance to persons living or dead is purely coincidental" disclaimer at the end of the movie, or the naïve "this is based on a true story" at the opening.

DC: You said it yourself: cinema, even when it's obviously fictional, when it uses shortcuts, simplifications, exaggerations, it still helps you formulate a whole series of problems that remain foreign or secondary to formal historical analysis. Gestures such as actions to signal or greet, people's gazes, the colors of clothes and props, the shape of fruit and vegetables... It insists that things be made concrete, that history be comprised of snapshots that taken together form the little moments of life in the past, that recall these moments, even the inconsequential ones that go to the very heart of past lives. The fictional, the fabricated if you'd like, aren't these all just tricks to prompt reflection, to ask questions?

NZD: A good historical film should pose questions to the viewer. But planning and visualizing a historical film are fascinating for the historian or the historically minded filmmaker. So many situations arise for which you would not need to seek evidence if you were writing a prose nonfiction text: conversations, movements, encounters. The imagination is constantly at work here, but as I argued in *Slaves on Screen,* in a good historical film, the imagination will always be informed by historical research into what was possible or likely in a given situation—not just on the traditional matters of costumes and props, but on the deep matters of language, sensibility, the expression of feeling, posture, social intimacy and distance, and the like. Some so-called historical films don't give you any sense of the past at all; they're just full of clichés and recycled stereotypes. But when the filmmaker and those with whom he or she has worked are serious about telling a historical story, the film can bring fresh insight into the past, and be absorbing to watch as well. As for the truth status of such films, I've suggested we think about them as "thought experiments."

DC: What did you think, for example, about the film *La Reine Margot*, set as it is in the middle of your beloved sixteenth century?[21]

NZD: Well, it had some visually beautiful moments, as in the hunting scene and in the court ceremonial. But I found *La Reine Margot* much more expressive of the spirit of France of the nineteenth century, or even the twentieth century, than of the sixteenth century. It is shot through from start to finish with all the fables that make up the "black legend" of the Medici and Queen Margot, a legend well studied by Éliane Viennot.[22] I'd like to know what she thinks of this film! It recreates precisely the repulsive image of absolute monarchy of the sixteenth century, the bad monarchy of the Valois, which was needed by liberals of the 1830s in order to glorify the liberal monarchy of their own time.[23] The massacre of Saint Bartholomew's Day[24] is modeled after the twentieth-century Holocaust. This is what happens with bad films: the strangeness of the past gets remade as today's familiar news.

DC: One rightly senses that this kind of film could be a perfect counterexample to the ways in which one's own personal opinions intrude in the making or remaking of history. It's a film that instead mixes together Alexandre Dumas[25] with Patrice Chéreau,[26] which combines the dark romanticism of a rogue monarchy that uses poison, sex, and murder with the much rawer realism of a Holocaust memoir and the more recent memories of events in Bosnia.[27] The final forms arise from the grafting together of these two approaches, even though they speak with one unified voice as a tragedy, thus leaving the viewer unable to reflect upon facts, unable to think about why even the characters and events are depicted in such stark terms. In this kind of film, there's only a story that unfolds, without any doubt or suspicion, no awareness of relativism, according to its own logic since the goal of the film isn't history but rather to follow the parabolic arc of a narrative. The entire problem turns on the question of reception; its viewers who see history, once and for all, and rare are those of them who suspect that this parabolic path bends history to its own purposes, that it lays hold of history as one would modeling clay. While the promise of history, such as you might make it, would be a dialogue with the reader that allows him to let his imagination course from the most nefarious of the Valois to the most modest in society, which would have been the most enlightening, a dialogue that left room for suspicion ...

NZD: I'd like to mention as a contrast a very good film, Alain Corneau's *Tous les matins du monde*.[28] On the fine details about the music, the court, various objects, I'm not specialist enough to make any judgment. But the film offers much understanding of the Jansenist spirit,[29] the relation between life at the court and life in the country, and the ambivalence aroused by the court, both its appeal and its repellent qualities. There's a French film that imagines the past with rich historical insight, and I certainly learned a lot from it. I'm not so sure, however, that it introduces moments of dialogue with the spectator. For that, we can turn to Ettore Scola's *La Nuit de Varennes*.[30] The construction is completely artificial—all those people, some of them celebrities, crowded together in a coach in 1791—but it's very informative on the different responses contemporaries had toward the French Revolution, and amusing besides. And the film, including its anachronistic ending, when Restif de la Bretonne[31] walks up a flight of stairs into the streets of modern Paris, invites us spectators to react...

DC: I would like for us now to talk a little about a matter I raised a short while ago; namely, when you study a document, be it a letter of pardon, an autobiography, and so on, you look right away for underlying reasons to explain a particular form of writing. You state, for example, that a letter of pardon is a text whose nature is fictional enough but that also, in its means of enunciation, relies on stereotypes that lend it historical meaning because these same stereotypes are purposely structured composites. Doesn't this example epitomize the challenge facing historians who study past fictions? Don't they have to plumb the relationship between what a person says and how he or she says it? Aren't a person's rhetorical choices predicated on his or her particular situation (or that of anyone helping them) and the ends they seek, in this case regaining one's place in society by projecting a sense of self they think others would believe?

NZD: At the beginning, when I was working on the Protestant Reformation and the workers as a pure "social historian," I didn't ask such questions. I was using all kinds of texts: from Calvin, Rabelais, and other humanists to pamphlets intended to be distributed in the streets and taverns and popular songs and stories. I loved this diversity. I knew you had to be careful about the "prejudices" (to use the old word) that might lurk behind these writings, but I didn't worry about or even ask myself about their literary construction. I read the learned texts to discover the point of view of their authors, their opinions, their doctrines, whatever I needed to prop up my argument. For the popular texts, I read them for the point of view on God, on work, on strikes, on women, and the like.

In later years, I never put aside this kind of inquiry, that is, into the modes of thinking and representation embedded in a text, but I asked new questions about ways of writing and the forms and rituals of discourse. I began to look not only at what was stated or declared in a text, but also at what was suggested through expression, through *performance*. This happened for several reasons. First, we're always influenced by our friends and colleagues, and many of my friends in the university milieu were in other disciplines: with Rosalie Colie[32] and Stephen Greenblatt[33] I talked about many "purely" literary matters, but they also turned to history to enlarge their own analyses. Our conversations gave me a new orientation. And then, I got caught up in certain historical topics that took me beyond the usual paths of social history: the history of the book, where the question was not only the content of the book, but also the way in which the book was organized, framed, and formed; the history of oral culture and expression, where the question was not just the moral set forth—"be prudent," "be wary," "be a good neighbor"—but even more the way in which oral expression was given (say, so as to echo an earlier proverb, or to take on the form of an adage). And then especially, feast days, festivities, and rituals. The charivari interested me not just for what was said—for example, "don't beat your husband" or "don't marry a girl too young"—but for its *form*. When I decided to try to make a film or work on a film, I was already captivated by notions of performance.

Those were the practical problems that led me to the account, the narrative, the story. A real turning point for me was in 1979, when I was writing a review of *Montaillou*[34] for the *Annales*. For the fun of it and to learn more about the text Le Roy Ladurie had used, I decided to read the inquisition records of Jacques Fournier, which had been published.[35] Reading this document, I said to myself, "My goodness! We have here not only what these men and women were declaring to the inquisitor—and already this was complicated, because they were speaking in Occitan and it was being translated into Latin and then the Latin read back to them in Occitan for their concurrence—but also the fashion in which they spoke, and specifically the elaboration of each interrogation into a story. 'Fifteen years ago, I was crossing the village square, and carrying a sheepskin…'; or 'Twenty-four years ago, I saw a man in the distance, he had a beard and the color of his clothing was…'" They didn't just give such concrete details about events long ago in this narrative fashion, they also recreated precise conversations, the questions asked and responses given. It was astonishing. I entitled my review "Les conteurs de Montaillou," "The Storytellers of Montaillou," because it seemed to me that this faculty of storytelling was as fascinating as the extraordinary things Le Roy Ladurie told us about the village of Montaillou and its mentalities.

With my interest in rituals, in stories, in performances—and I mean by that the techniques or dramatic modes by means of which persons carry out an action—I have taken another path, or rather I should say, I've enlarged my path, as I've never effaced the practice of social history at all. And furthermore, as you have suggested, I believe strongly that this way of looking at sources from the past does not undermine their value as documents, but rather enhances their value even while going beyond the literal statements they include.

Notes

1. Christine de Pizan (1363–1434) was born in Venice but was brought up at the court of France, where her father was royal astrologer, and spent the rest of her life in France. Poet and moralist, she wrote French manuscripts on many subjects, earning both contemporary acclaim and criticism from her male contemporaries.

2. Guillaume Budé (1467–1540) was a French humanist scholar who served King François I and helped found what in time became the Collège de France and the Bibliothèque Nationale.

3. Jean Anouilh (1910–87) was a dramatist and author of several dozen plays. He published *Antigone* in 1942 during the Nazi occupation of France. The play uses allegory to criticize collaboration with the Nazis.

4. Jean-Paul Sartre (1905–80) was a philosopher, playwright, novelist, screenwriter, political activist, biographer, and literary critic. He was one of the leading figures in twentieth-century philosophy and Existentialism.

5. François Rabelais (1494–1553) was a physician and a major humanist writer of the French Renaissance. His books include *Pantagruel* (1532), *Gargantua* (1534), and the *Tiers Livre* (1546), which won him many readers and the condemnation of the French Faculty of Theology.

6. Michel de Montaigne (1533–92) was among the most influential writers of the French Renaissance, who popularized the self-reflective essay as a new literary genre in his collected *Essais*, first published in 1580.

7. Heinrich Cornelius Agrippa von Nettesheim (1486–1535) was a German magician, occult writer, theologian, astrologer, and alchemist. He made this remark in *De incertitudine et vanitate scientiarum atque artium declamatio invectiva* [Declamation Attacking the Uncertainty and Vanity of the Sciences and the Arts] (1527).

8. Lucette Valensi is a leading expert of the Islamic Mediterranean world and author of several books, most recently (with Gabriel Martinez-Gros) *Islam en dissidence: Genèse d'un affrontement* (2004). Oumelbanine Zhiri is a specialist of French and comparative literature who has published two books on Leo Africanus, *L'Afrique au Miroir de l'Europe: Fortunes de Jean Léon l'Africain à la Renaissance*

(1991) and *Les Sillages de Jean Léon l'Africain du XVIe au XXe siècle* (1995). Faustina Doufikar-Aerts works on medieval Arabic literature.

9. Abū'l-Walīd ibn Rushd (1126–98), known in European languages as Averroës, was a Muslim polymath who lived in Andalusian Spain, writing on philosophy, law, medicine, and poetry. His commentary on the philosophy of Aristotle and defense of rational speculation had great influence throughout the world of Islam and also in Europe.

10. Bernard Lewis (1916–) is a British-American scholar of Middle Eastern history and culture who taught at Princeton University until his retirement in 1986.

11. Stanley Kubrick (1928–99) was a major American film director, producer, and screenwriter. *Spartacus* came out in 1960 and won four Oscars.

12. Steven Spielberg (1946–) is a leading American film producer, director, and screenwriter. *Amistad* debuted in 1997.

13. Robert Jonathan Demme (1944–) is an American filmmaker, producer, and screenwriter. *Beloved* appeared in 1998.

14. Jean Calvin (1509–64) was an influential French theologian during the Protestant Reformation whose vision of reform was laid out in his seminal work, *Institutes of the Christian Religion* (1536), and implemented in Geneva.

15. Abū Hāmid Al-Ghazālī (1058–1111) was an Islamic theologian, jurist, philosopher, and mystic of Persian origin, and remains one of the most celebrated scholars in the history of Sunni Islamic thought. The Sufi movement arose in the seventh century and advocated that believers seek to draw closer to God to realize a closer mystical union with the divine in this life.

16. Badī' al-Zamān al-Hamadhānī (967–1007) was a master of Arabic rhymed prose, whose *maqāmāt* founded a genre of storytelling of importance in Arabic literature in the next centuries.

17. Muhammad al-Qasim ibn Ali ibn Muhammad ibn Uthman al-Hariri (1054–1122) was an Arab poet and scholar best known for his work *Maqāmāt al-Hariri,* an English translation of which appeared in 2008 under the title *Assemblies of al-Hariri.*

18. An English translation of "The Wine" (XLIX) is in *The Maqāmāt of Badī' al-Zamān al-Hamadhānī* (1915).

19. Umar Ibn al-Farid (1181–1235) wrote *qaṣīdah* (odes). An English translation of his poem on wine is in *The Mystical Poems of Ibn al-Fārid* (1956).

20. His full name was Abū 'Abdullāh Muhammad ibn 'Alī ibn Muhammad ibn al-'Arabī al-Hāṭimī al-Tā'ī (1165–1240). He was an Andalusian mystic and philosopher. The quote is from his poem "The Duties of Brotherhood," which can be found in *The Tarjuman Al-Ashwaq: A Collection of Mystical Odes* (1911).

21. *La Reine Margot* was directed by Patrice Chéreau (1944–) and was released in 1994. The title refers to Marguerite de Valois (1553–1615), who was queen of France and Navarre in the late sixteenth century. The House of Valois ruled France from 1328 to 1589.

22. Éliane Viennot (1951–) is a French historian, feminist, and one of the founders of the Société Internationale pour l'Étude des Femmes de l'Ancien Régime. Her book is entitled *Marguerite de Valois: Histoire d'une femme, histoire d'un mythe* (Paris: Payot, 1994).

23. This regime came to power following the Revolution of 1830 and established a constitutional monarchy by King Louis-Philippe d'Orléans. It was overthrown in the 1848 Revolution.

24. The St. Bartholomew's Day Massacre began in Paris on August 24, 1572, and spread to a number of cities across France. Catholic violence claimed the lives of several thousand Protestants as the event marked a major turning point in the French Wars of Religion.

25. Alexandre Dumas (1802–70) was a French writer best known for numerous historical novels, such as *The Three Musketeers* (1844), *The Count of Monte Christo* (1845–46), and *La Reine Margot* (1845).

26. Patrice Chéreau (1944–) is a French opera and theatre director, filmmaker, actor, and producer known for his dramatic, modernized stagings.

27. Armed strife in Bosnia between 1992 and 1995 was especially violent toward civilians following the dissolution of the former Yugoslavia.

28. Alain Corneau (1943–) is a French movie director and writer. His movie, known in

English as *All the World's Mornings*, came out in 1991. It contrasts the superficial life at court of the seventeenth-century composer Marin Marais with that of his teacher, the austere Saint-Colombe, who lives a simple and authentic life in the country.

29. Jansenism was a Catholic movement emphasizing austerity and human depravity that originated after the Council of Trent (1545–63) in the writings of the Dutch theologian Cornelius Otto Jansen (1585–1638). It was condemned by the Catholic Church in 1655.

30. Ettore Scola (1931–) is an Italian screenwriter and director. His film, known in English as *That Night in Varennes*, appeared in 1982. It depicts the attempted flight from France by King Louis XVI and his family in 1791 during the French Revolution. The film follows the debates and intrigues of a group of characters, historical and fictional, as they follow the king in a carriage.

31. Nicolas Edmé Restif de la Bretonne (1734–1806) was a French novelist known for his social commentary and bawdy stories.

32. Rosalie Colie (1924–72) was an expert on early modern European culture. She wrote *Some Thankfulnesse to Constantine* (1956), *Light and Enlightenment* (1957), and *Paradoxia Epidemica* (1966).

33. Stephen Greenblatt (1943–) is a literary critic and scholar of Renaissance literature. One of the founders of the New Historicism, his books include *Renaissance Self-Fashioning: From More to Shakespeare* (1980) and *Marvelous Possessions: The Wonder of the New World* (1992).

34. The full title of this book, in English translation, is *Montaillou: The Promised Land of Error* (1978).

35. Emmanuel Le Roy Ladurie (1929–) is a noted French historian of the Old Regime. The inquisition records, originally in Latin, of Jacques Fournier, Bishop of Pamiers, appeared in a French translation, coedited by Ladurie, as *Le Registre d'Inquisition de Jacques Fournier (Evêque de Pamiers) 1318–1325* (1978).

Chapter 2

Encounters

DC: This now leads us to shift our attention to the fact that wonderment definitely seems a bit like Ariadne's thread which guides us from one curiosity to another. But aren't all our various encounters also a determining factor for the course this journey takes, encounters with persons dead as well as alive? Aren't there, in certain situations, experiences in writing that can't be joined with persons we've met?

NZD: Yes, I made that link in *Women on the Margins,* in the dialogue that opens the book and which I like a lot...

DC: Me too!

NZD: I must say that when I first showed it to my editor at Harvard University Press, she was very dubious about it. She wanted a more "normal" preface...

DC: Maria Sibylla Merian addressed to you words that sound a little reproachful: "I have the impression, Mistress Historian, that it's you who are looking for adventure..."

NZD: [*laughter*] I wanted to make fun of myself and also suggest to my readers the distance between our preoccupations (for instance, on questions of gender) and the perceptions of these women of the past. Here are my stakes in this issue; those of my heroines might be different. I thought the dialogue form would be amusing and accessible, and, besides, my subjects become temporarily alive for a time while I'm working on them—in the shadows, but alive. In the books I've written since then, I haven't used any imagined or direct dialogue, but who knows what I might do in the future?

DC: In your *Fiction in the Archives,* you wrote about letters of pardon and remission that forgave offenses as laboratory instruments that enabled you, as you put it, to retrieve the voices of forgotten people—not just from the lower classes, but also nobles and clergymen ... But it's also true that you start from the principle that these documents have a life of their own and that from these documents you can breathe new life into these actors, actors who above all want to tell a story according their own criteria for explaining change and storytelling. This story is hardly their own, but is rather a story as it's expected to be told, a story that's going to win for them forgiveness! In other words, you simultaneously make your anchor point the individual who faces facts he or she wants to explain, but that this same individual allows you, after a fashion, to take stock of a society in such typical situations.

NZD: In reading letters of remission over the years, I was often astonished by and sometimes even laughed over the curious things I found there. It's the way things are told that makes them so amusing. Who knows whether all the events described in such vivid detail really happened that way? Once I'd read Fournier and the villagers of Montaillou, I realized that the stakes were similar to those in the letters of remission: a situation orchestrated by a notary and limited by the formal and stylistic constraints required for what one must say to ask the king for pardon for a homicide. A person who's committed a homicide must give his or her own version of what happened—extenuating circumstances of one kind or another that will make the homicide excusable—and eventually, if the pardon were to be ratified by the king's judges, he or she would have to repeat the same story in his or her own words. The letter requesting the pardon had to be convincing, plausible, and given at least in part in the words of the pardon-seeker.

Because of these requirements, one can imagine a storyteller practicing his or her art, despite all the obligatory formulas and direction exercised by the notary. I realized that those letters of remission, which I'd been using for social-history material about crime, geographical mobility, and the like, could also let me listen to the voices of peasants, artisans, nobles (not the great aristocrats, but nobles nonetheless), women, traders.

True, there is another possible path toward those voices: the path of the collectors, who, in the sixteenth century and especially in the late seventeenth and eighteenth centuries, collected tales from the countryside. They were followed by the folklorists and anthropologists of the nineteenth and twentieth centuries. I sometimes take this path, but it too presents problems: you're trying to get evidence when there's a time gap of a century or two. In order to "backstream" successfully, that is, to assume some continuity over the centuries, I always use the later narrative as a mere possibility for the past, as a suggestion—and then I look for an earlier sign. This is what I did in my study of Maria Sibylla Merian, in regard to her picture of the great hunting spider of Suriname reaching for the eggs in a hummingbird's nest. I could see she had represented it in the spirit of a natural philosopher from Europe, but I suspected there was also an influence from her African slaves, who told tales of Anansi the spider—the great African tales, still told in the Caribbean today. To establish this hunch, I started with the tales collected about this spider in the nineteenth century, both in Africa and among the slaves in the Caribbean. I was trying to "backstream."

DC: A retrospective history?

NZD: If you like. Happily for me, I found an account of an agent of the Dutch West Indies Company who lived in West Africa in the late seventeenth and early years of the eighteenth—just the period I was working on—who showed that the stories of Anansi the spider were already widespread. So the retrospective jump was confirmed and justified by a document from the time.

But to return to the letters asking pardon, I had before me a historical object from the sixteenth century that was not "pure"—but what historical object ever is "pure"? Here was a situation where a notary was listening to the words of a peasant or an artisan, a notary writing things down according to juridical rules and notarial formulas, but still a situation of fundamental importance: a face-to-face encounter between a person who speaks and a person who writes. The letters did not offer a perfect *mimesis* or imitation, but they gave me the evidence to recreate a living moment of talk. I told my reader exactly what the conditions were for that living moment—I devoted a whole chapter to them.

The book has had considerable impact. I'm not thinking so much about reviews, but about the many persons working on similar texts in different fields, who've told me how helpful they've found it. Over the years I've heard from scholars in law faculties, especially those interested in the rhetoric of law, who teach the book in courses that have nothing to do with sixteenth-century France. Of course, there are those who think only a more traditional kind of history will do and who don't like my work; they simply don't want to use texts the way I do.

DC: There are classic examples of historical research on criminality in which letters of pardon permit us to study the times and places where violence occurred, the social groups more or less implicated in these acts of aggression, the age and sex of the victims and perpetrators... Never mind that every judicial record derives from a particular form of speech that greatly skews the kind of information it provides. And never mind, too, that a document is always a product of a specific situation in which the person who speaks is the object of writing that's simultaneously receptive and coded, and only answers standard kinds of questions that he knows he must respond to in one way and not another!

NZD: Yes, but the classical studies on criminality are important.

DC: There are, however, methods of research that confirm the obvious, that often provide statistical proof of something already found in classic narrative sources, including novels. Some methods even ignoring that a judicial record often becomes skewed by the very ends it serves, that it's a literary work in the sense that it recounts what must be told in very precise circumstances...

NZD: Nonetheless, their social history methods have their use, and my book was not intended to undermine them as such. That is, I did not say that because there were fictional aspects to the narration in letters of pardon, one could draw no conclusions about the location of fights in taverns or about the character of swearing and blasphemy and the like. It's fine if people make such studies, but I wanted to enrich the possibilities in these sources in another way. I must note, in passing, that even now there are scholars who are always suspicious of everything one tries to do to discover the voice of the *menu peuple,* as they were in regard to the history of women in the early days of that field of inquiry, and as they are today in regard to the history of colonized and enslaved peoples. Either they say there are no sources whatsoever, or if you find them, they say that there's nothing authentic in them: you can't learn anything about the way peasants tell stories from a letter of remission because everything there is from the hand of a notary or a lawyer; you can't learn anything about Amerindians from the Jesuit relations or Ursuline letters,[1] because everything there is constructed by the Europeans. They dismiss strategies for finding multiple voices in these documents. It's especially irritating when such a reaction comes from historians who are not even working on the *menu peuple* and are swimming in documents because their subjects are great families, aristocrats, or kings.

DC: Do you find their attacks too reductionist because they ignore the principle of discursive dependency that lies at the center of constructing the story found in a letter of remission?

NZD: Reductionist and naïve in regard to their own body of materials, because in the correspondence and other documents in the archival treasures of the great houses—and it's certainly nice to have such abundance—there are also codes for narration and writing, conventional rules, which can't be ignored. The same analysis should be made here as with the pardon letters. Literary scholars know this well. They remind us that we can't just approach the writings of Rabelais as straightforward witness of the first half of the sixteenth century. We've got to take account of the traditions for writing of his day, the issues of audience and publication, and the many infratexts and hidden intentions that inform the wondrous creativity of the author of *Gargantua*. These problems are present in all kinds of documents.

The idea that persons from a modest background or from an illiterate milieu should have no means to leave traces of themselves bothers me. I can and do sometimes write about great public figures, about queens and kings, but I've never felt that I was truly a historian for them. They've had and have their own historians. It's the others who need me. [*laughter*] I especially felt this in earlier years, when not so many scholars were working on the *menu peuple*, villagers, and outsiders. I hope I've served them well.

DC: In your work, you obviously like to ferret out these vertical intersections in which you discover the shared ideas and signs that together made it possible to create the arts of speaking and writing. But there are also the horizontal intersections between people whom you group together in various ways in your books. When you try to understand, for example, how women were able to find ways to truly "exist" in a world that so stifled their capacity for self-affirmation.

If we return to Leo Africanus, are you going to have him cross paths with other vagabond intellectuals of the sixteenth century? I'm thinking among others about the visionary mystic, Guillaume Postel.[2] Are you going to introduce them to each other?

NZD: Yes, and all the more because Guillaume Postel knew his works: he talks of reading al-Wazzān's manuscript on Arabic grammar. And al-Wazzān himself had contacts with humanists. He taught Arabic to Cardinal Gilles de Viterbo, a great Christian Kabbalist of the sixteenth century,[3] who was one of the godfathers at his baptism. I've been working hard on the various relations between the two men. And then there was Alberto Pio, the prince of Carpi,[4] for whom al-Wazzān transcribed Arabic manuscripts. I've been exploring the humanist circles with which Gilles of Viterbo and Alberto Pio were associated, especially the people in them interested in subjects that al-Wazzān knew about—the Ottomans, for instance, or Egyptian symbolism. This is how I've been trying to imagine the world in which al-Wazzān/Leo Africanus moved. Reading the sources here has been frustrating! Archival documents, diaries, letters, and manuscripts give proof of his captivity, his baptism, and role as a teacher and transcriber of Arabic. And yet some of the people he was in touch with and even dedicated manuscripts to never mention his name—and I've been through page after page in their writings looking for reference to the man they called Giovanni Leone. I figure he was a marginal person.

Here's an amusing fact for you. Manuel, king of Portugal,[5] presented Pope Leo[6] with a white elephant from India. Another captive! That elephant is talked about in numerous places at the time and there are even pictures of him: Raphael[7] drew his picture and painted him. There are fewer contemporary mentions of Giovanni Leone the African than there are of Hannibal, the elephant from India. [*laughter*] So to imagine al-Wazzān's relations with the great figures of his day, I've had to use sources in an indirect way. What did they think of him? What did he think of them? I've had to search hard for clues. One of the most fascinating encounters or crossings for me—perhaps not a personal encounter, but a cultural crossing—is between al-Wazzān and Rabelais. Rabelais is always present in my writing and he'll be an important person at the end of my book. Of course, if I can establish a direct connection between the author of the *Tiers Livre* and al-Wazzān, I'll be delighted.

DC: Do any of the characters found in Rabelais share any resemblance with Leo Africanus?

NZD: That's the case with Panurge. Right now I'm looking to see whether there could be any direct connections. Rabelais spent time in Italy and he and his patron, Cardinal Jean du Bellay,[8] were in contact with Paolo Giovio and other humanists who knew the onetime convert from Islam. Perhaps Rabelais heard people talking about al-Wazzān, perhaps he even saw the manuscript of the Africa book al-Wazzān had left behind when he went back to North Africa, for one or two were in circulation. It had the Italian title *Libro della cosmografia e geografia dell'Africa* (later when it was published, it had the title *Description of Africa*).

But even if there were no direct contact, there are terrific possibilities here. For instance, we can reflect on the treatment of the Ottomans in the celebrated chapter where Panurge tells the story of his escape from his Turkish captor. It's a comic tale, shot through with exaggerations and lies. Rabelais has Panurge claiming that his captor had prepared him for roasting and eating by wrapping him with lard (forbidden, of course, to Muslims), but then Panurge escapes, aided by other Muslims. Two sorts of Muslims appear in the chapter. Panurge, as hero in this episode, knows how to save himself, but he does not behave well at all. I've been wondering if there's an echo of al-Wazzān in these lines—probably not. But I plan to make a comparison between the ruses of al-Wazzān/Leo Africanus and those of Panurge and of Rabelais.

DC: Don't actors like these develop a certain sense of skill and craftiness...?

NZD: Yes, skill and craftiness, but also a sense of play and the use of tricks for truth-telling. Truth-telling is one of the main roles of the trickster. These are personages who practice *mètis*, to use the Greek term for crafty intelligence. I want to compare the games and *mètis* of Panurge with those of al-Wazzān over the course of his life, which for me evoke the ruses of the hero of the *maqāmāt*. I'm hoping to arrive at some cultural affinities, to discern some unity beyond the divisions of the Mediterranean. I see some ludic parallels here. And there's Rabelais's mysticism, the symbolism of wine and the divine bottle in his fifth book. I'd like to put that next to the *maqāmāt* of "The Wine" by Badī' al-Zamān al-Hamadhānī, and the celebrated mystical poem on wine of Ibn al-Farid, both texts important in al-Wazzān's sensibility.

DC: Even so with Rabelais, wine, from the very start, symbolizes the Bible, for it's the Good Book they drink, or that they can finally begin to imbibe after a long dry spell when the humanity of the giants suffered from thirst...

NZD: Exactly. Perhaps I should also reflect on Arab script, the fine calligraphy that was so prized in the Arab world, and other forms of divine symbolism. In any case, the affinities I'm looking for will be suggested not just by texts, but by certain shared ideas, certain ways of looking at the world found in both of these men of the Mediterranean.

DC: In listening to you, I have the impression that the task of analysis is always a work-in-progress beyond the desire for adventure. Of course, one could reproach you for also being in that same uncertain spot where Leo Africanus found himself, and therefore exceeded the limits of what's possible. But isn't it a response to the yearning that always resurfaces to push you to the very edge of overinterpretation? And then is there overinterpretation when plumbing the secrets of a person's inner life? It means for you to not remain fixated on your object of study, for you must discover it in a larger, nearly limitless landscape, because the individual in the Renaissance is a repository of an infinite number of ways of knowing, of interconnections, of personal possibilities, and possible borrowings again and again...

NZD: What you say about "the task of analysis as always a work-in-progress" and about "not remaining fixated on your object of study" are very interesting, though I don't see the possibilities of interpretation as limitless, neither during the Renaissance nor today. But your idea of continual movement during a life makes me think of two things.

First is an affirmation from Eugénie Droz, a very learned Swiss scholar, whom I met in 1960, when she was in her late sixties: "Tout est à faire et à refaire," "Everything is to be done and redone."[9] [*laughter*] Droz was a tough lady, who worked on precise and intricate questions in the history of the book, printing, and bibliography; she turned out valuable articles on the history of religious propaganda in the sixteenth century. One must always remember "Everything is to be done and redone." I say this to myself when I've made a mistake or misunderstood something.

The other association that comes to mind concerns my old age. [*laughter*] I feel fine on the whole and I don't have the sense of being old, and yet I am! Now in the books I've read about old age—books written in the early modern period and today about the stages of life—old age is supposed to be the time when one finds a resolution, intellectual and moral.

One looks at one's life, one hopes for a sense of satisfaction and happiness, but at the very least there's a dominant idea of closure. But I've been discovering that my old age isn't like that at all: it's full of complications, questions, mystification, and uncertainties—the books I read didn't prepare me for this! [*laughter*] I look at the future as a continuing adventure, without a tranquil resting place where I could just be settled and feel that I understood everything. My old age is a reality for me and I accept it, but though I know much more than when I was young, I still have so many question marks. So I say to myself, "Fine. I'll accept this stage of life as an adventure, with many questions still to ask." Perhaps I won't have time to find the answers, but there we are...

DC: **Precisely, to the extent that history is a continual source of adventures, it's necessary, I think, to take account of what historians of your era wrote. First to know that, when you arrived in France, you chose not to embrace the prevailing attempts to realize a totalizing history where one tried, in the confines of a province for example—Languedoc or the Beauvaisis—to capture the entire functional or dysfunctional workings of a social system at the political, cultural, and economic levels. You really had to rein in the scope of your own technique of analysis...**

NZD: When I first came to France, there were no works directly on my topic.

DC: **There were initially very few American historians who were interested in the history of sixteenth-century France, let alone the history of Lyon!**

NZD: That's right. But the most unusual thing perhaps was my coming to the archives, especially the archives of Lyon. Before the Second World War, most American historians working on France based their studies on published sources. Some very important work was done, but in most cases it was not drawn heavily from archives. The medievalist John Mundy,[10] who was a decade older than I, went to Toulouse not long after the war and he had an experience similar to mine: people in Toulouse thought his presence in the archives was bizarre. I heard the same thing in Lyon: "What are you doing here? Why aren't you in the archives in the United States?" [*laughter*]

After having begun my own research, I had read the great work of Richard Gascon, *Grand commerce et vie urbaine au XVIe siècle: Lyon et ses mar-*

chands.[11] It's an excellent economic history, though not centered around the questions of society and Reformation that interested me, questions that linked me rather to Max Weber,[12] Karl Marx,[13] and Henri Hauser.[14] Still I learned much from his book, and Richard Gascon kindly helped me get started in the archives, suggesting useful sources.

In the next years—in the 1960s—I had varied reactions to French historical scholarship. First of all, I loved the books of Pierre Goubert[15] on the Beauvaisis and of Emmanuel Le Roy Ladurie[16] on the Languedoc. Peasants were their focus, and though I was then working on artisans, I felt close to them because we all had the lower classes as our target. I recall so vividly Le Roy Ladurie's pages on the Protestant Reformation in the Languedoc—*Les Paysans du Languedoc* is a marvelous book, one of my favorites among his writings. I invited both of them to North America to give lectures: Goubert came to Toronto and Le Roy Ladurie to Berkeley. What a delight to present them to North American historians.

But initially the French historian closest to what I was doing on artisans was Émile Coornaert,[17] an old gentleman who had published a book on craft guilds in 1940, just as World War II was starting in France, and who then in 1966 published a book on *compagnonnages,* that is, the journeymen's organizations or trade unions that I had been discovering exciting things about in Lyon. For a number of years, many French scholars had stayed away from subjects like this, because the topic seemed traditional and saturated with the Vichyite populism of the German Occupation,[18] but for me, it was part of a new study of working-class culture. Then when I read Maurice Agulhon's[19] book on sociability in southern France—*La sociabilité mériodionale: Confréries et associations*—which also appeared in 1966, I said to myself, "Here's a terrific French scholar whom I admire as much as Le Roy Ladurie, and he's working on the same subject as I and with the same approach." I had not yet met Maurice Agulhon: he was then teaching at Aix and this was his earliest book. But I had a sense of exhilaration to find a comrade in arms. I had the same excitement in 1968, when I read Mikhail Bakhtin's *Rabelais and His World.*[20] I came to it after I had written the first version of my essay on charivaris, and now I felt, "Here's someone who cares about carnivals the way I do." Bakhtin was a literary scholar, not a historian, but I still had such a sense of connection with him.

My experience is common to other historians. There are two forms of association or transmission among us. One is a vertical form linked with teaching: the professor-master, surrounded by his or her students, who go on one day to have their own students. I'm not so much a partisan of this as the privileged form of transmission, in part because I never had a real "master" myself. That is, I never had a real "doctor-father" at my university: while I was in residence there, no one among the faculty was much interested in my approach or my topic on religion and social class; and then for political reasons, I was in absentia during the actual writing of the thesis.

The other form of association or transmission grows up around the subject we're working on: a network of people perhaps from diverse backgrounds who are drawn together by a common interest in the same questions. So for a certain length of time, sometimes a long while, you stay in contact with this informal network—exchanging ideas and bibliography about carnival or proverbs or gifts, to name only a few topics that have brought me into networks of scholarly friendship. Nowadays with the Internet, these networks are easy to establish and commonplace. But when I was young and over the decades until the 1990s, such communication was established by letter-writing and get-togethers at scholarly conferences. These communities have been very important in my own development, and have often outlasted a specific interest.

Both forms of transmission and association must exist, and alternate with each other in our lives. I certainly feel grateful to those who helped me: for instance, the literary scholar Rosalie Colie, who was not my professor in any formal sense, but who played the role of a mentor when I was the mother of young children, trying to finish my doctoral thesis and teaching a course at night school. She would be a figure in my line of transmission; and I feel very proud of my students as well. Still, I like the idea of changing groups to which one belongs: for example, you and I were drawn together by our interest in the sources and rites of violence in the sixteenth century, as was Barbara Diefendorf[21] and also scholars studying peasant violence in the seventeenth century.

DC: Yves-Marie Bercé?[22]

NZD: Yes, his work on peasant uprisings also drew us together. These informal communities seem to me at the heart of intellectual endeavor.

DC: We are all confronted, sadly too rarely, with a certain number of works that shock us, that mix reading pleasure with intellectual feeling.

Which historians have most influenced you, and they needn't be French?

NZD: I'd begin with the historians who influenced me when I was an undergraduate. I'll never forget how enthralled I was by Giambattista Vico's *New Science,*[23] especially by the way he fit the different parts of a society together, its forms of expression and values together with its economy and political structure. About the same time I read Werner Jaeger's *Paideia*[24] and was struck similarly by how he portrayed connections, here between the educational aspirations and ideals of the Greeks and other features of their city life. Interested in Marxism as I was, I wanted to pursue such connections in the early modern period, but not in the mechanical way of those historians who reduced everything to narrow class interest. Then I read two works that pointed the way: Charles Trinkaus's *Adversity's Noblemen,*[25] which suggested that the precarious social status of the Italian humanists informed their claims for the importance of humane letters, and Edgar Zilsel's "Sociological Roots of Modern Science,"[26] which showed the essential contribution of hands-on artisanal observation to the development of natural science. These delicate and nondeterministic treatments of "experience" were a real boon for me; they shaped the way I rethought the relation between social class and religious choice in my doctoral dissertation later on.

My last two years at Smith, I also started reading in the French school of historians, especially books in Henri Berr's great series *L'évolution de l'humanité.*[27] What a joy of discovery this was—and it climaxed when I read Marc Bloch's *Société féodale.*[28] The Smith College Library had the first edition published just at the beginning of World War II. I loved the book and I so admired him, his life as a great and learned historian and as a man engaged in public issues. And he was Jewish, like me.

DC: He would be for you *the* greatest person, *the* most attractive ... ?

NZD: Well, a very great figure. His *Strange Defeat* explaining the fall of France [in June 1940], his recreation of that medieval feudal world, with all its social and cultural features so linked, and his beautiful style—even though I wasn't French, I was charmed by the way he wrote history.[29] And then his heroic end, killed by the Nazis for his role in the Resistance. I read other French historians at the time, but he was my hero.

A few years later, of course, I came upon the publications of Henri Hauser, your great-grandfather, who opened the doors to my doctoral dissertation, especially in his 1898 book *Ouvriers du temps passé*. I had never known that such documents existed on journeymen and strikes, and I realized I could follow them up and make my own study of what he had called "the Reformation and the popular classes." Back in the early 1950s, I shared to some extent his view about the sixteenth century as the beginning of "modernity," and with my social concerns, I was on his wavelength. Today my views about modernity are different, but I still have that feeling of affinity to him that I had when I was young. [*laughter*] I read more French historians in the 1960s: Goubert, Le Roy Ladurie, and Agulhon, whom I already mentioned, and also Philippe Ariès.[30]

DC: On death?

NZD: Ariès's book on death was interesting, but it was his earlier book on childhood that caught my attention. He was a pioneer in making children and youth a subject of historical inquiry, but he was also one of the targets for my essay on charivaris: I really didn't agree with him that there were no separate age-categories for children and adolescents before the seventeenth and eighteenth centuries. These categories existed in the Middle Ages and sixteenth century—the youth groups I was writing about in my "Reasons of Misrule" were one of the examples—but they were defined somewhat differently. Still I found his discussion fascinating, even if I didn't adopt his overall theory. Later, when I met him personally, I found him a delightful and generous person. His political culture was on the right: he was a royalist, but very open in spirit. He liked people for what they were. As he said, he had "red" friends—and that would include me—and "white" friends. A few years before he died, he brought us all together for dinner and fine wine on a boat ride on the Seine.

But why am I not speaking of women? It's partly because there weren't any books by women historians in my fields of interest during the decades when I was getting started that could play the same role as, say, Bloch's *Société Féodale*. But yes—Eileen Power[31] had already published her innovative studies in medieval social and economic history by the 1920s and had been an inspiration for Sylvia Thrupp,[32] who was coming into her own in the 1960s. I included both of them in my presidential address to the American Historical Association years later to pay tribute to them. My women teachers at Smith College were more important as role models than for their historical vision. But I've always had many women as scholarly friends, starting off with Rosalie Colie in the 1950s. Her portrait of literary culture and of intellectual networks taught me much, and I loved her playful and learned book on paradoxes in the seventeenth century. I took the first draft of my charivari paper to her to read in 1967, and she was the person who first told me of Bakhtin. Nancy Roelker[33] was another dear friend during those years, and we used to talk, really gossip about sixteenth-century France—she was then doing her edition of Pierre de l'Estoile's journal of Paris life and I was deep in the printing shops of Lyon.[34] Printing history drew me to Elizabeth Armstrong,[35] whose book on Robert Estienne I so admired and whom I visited at Somerville College during my first trip to England. And Françoise Weil[36] and I began talking about publishing history and politics in the Geneva archives in 1960; we still email each other petitions and statements about what's going on in Israel/Palestine and other world events. By the early 1970s, I'd become friends with Michelle Perrot[37] and Christiane Klapisch-Zuber[38] in Paris, and Jill Ker Conway[39] and I had begun to teach the history of women in Toronto. And this was just the start of my friendships with women scholars. All of these relations have been multifaceted: we'd talk about our research and about our families and about the politics of being women in what was in those days a male-dominated profession.

I also felt a special complicity with some of my male colleagues in different lands, by which I mean that I believed we had common goals, however different our books, either writing about people in the "lower orders" and working classes or trying to change historical practice in similar ways. Such were Le Roy Ladurie in France and Carlo Ginzburg and Giovanni Levi[40] in Italy. I read Bronisław Geremek's[41] study of artisans and the labor market when it first appeared in French in 1968 and felt an immediate kinship with him—we had both emerged from an early interest in Marxism; I finally met him when I visited Warsaw in 1973. We shared many themes in our early works: marginal people, poverty. Several years afterward, during his first visit to the United States, I invited him to give a lecture at Princeton, and we all sat enthralled at my dinner table listening to him talk of hopes that he would later fulfill with Solidarność.[42] In England, there was Keith Thomas[43]—our early articles had appeared in consecutive numbers of the *Journal of the History of Ideas* in 1959 to 1960, his on "The Double Standard," mine on "Sixteenth-Century French Arithmetics on the Business Life"—and the young Peter Burke[44] and, of course, Edward P. Thompson,[45] whose book on *The Making of the English Working Class* had such an impact. I was trying to make sense of the charivari at the very same moment that Edward was looking at its English variant, the skimmington or rough music. Independently we were examining the very same subject.

DC: Isn't this an example of these encounters that work because they share a thematic interest that you like to cite?

NZD: Yes, a coincidence in the intellectual world of us historians. Around 1968 or 1969, when I finished my charivari essay, I sent it to *Past and Present,* and Edward read it—he must have been on the board of editors at the time, or one of the editors asked him to review it. He wrote me about what an astonishing coincidence this was—he was just then writing his celebrated article on the skimmington ride. My "Reasons of Misrule" appeared in *Past and Present* in 1971, his "Charivari Anglais" in the *Annales* in 1972. These things happen in our intellectual universe: despite the distance between us, we simultaneously hit on the same subject. It's true that Thompson's article is more somber than mine. I had stressed the comic aspect of the charivari, I suppose that's a typical habit of mine, and his reading was tougher. For Edward, the English skimmington led primarily to exclusion, the humiliated persons being ridden out of town; for me the French charivari led more often to inclusion, the reintegration of the humiliated persons back into the community after they'd paid their penalty. There are evidently real differences between the two countries, not just different interpretations.

So often one thinks one is the only person working on a topic, and then it turns out not to be the case.

DC: But is it only a coincidence? Isn't it limiting to see this conjuncture of interests only from this perspective?

NZD: Of course, you're right—it's only a seeming coincidence. These similar questions are connected with big questions or events in the air at the time: the late 1960s were a period of the carnivalesque turning of the world upside down of the student movements *and* the time of resistance against the Vietnam War. And in the history profession, some of us wanted to explore forms of popular action that had not been taken seriously by earlier scholars of resistance movements, who thought them archaic or folkloric.

DC: This brings us back to the question of your own personal journey.

Why the rites of charivari during the late 1960s? What's most remarkable, moreover, is that you opened the way on the American side for a powerful new school interested in the history of sixteenth-century France, since you had been to some extent the person through whom, in a manner more or less direct, these interests came to the next generation of scholars, such as Barbara Diefendorf, Mack P. Holt,[46] Philip Benedict[47] to only cite the most well known. This profusion of intellectual talent has contributed so much to rediscovering the complexities of sixteenth-century France.

NZD: I'm certainly happy to think that I might have played this role and been of use to such formidable historians as the three you mention. Barbara Diefendorf was actually my doctoral student, and I have been much impressed by the books she's written on the religious, social, and political life of France in the sixteenth and seventeenth centuries—giving us a new understanding of both Catholics and Protestants.

Why the rites of charivari in the late 1960s? I was quite involved in the antiwar movements of the time, as well as in the efforts to restructure the university. I had charivaris going on around me. And also I had begun to read in anthropological literature. I've told you about some of the historians who influenced my thinking, but by the late 1960s, anthropologists were especially important for me—that is, for my understanding of French history. The first one I read was the old-time ethnographer Arnold van Gennep.[48]

DC: Isn't it somewhat paradoxical to first learn anthropology through the biases of the author of the *Manuel de folklore français,*[49] when American anthropology was in full flower?

NZD: That may seem odd, but the *Manuel* was just what I needed at the time. I was not flailing around for grand theory, I was trying to make sense of a specific ritual carried on by Lyon printing workers and other artisans, a noisy masked demonstration often directed against men beaten by their wives. "What is going on here?" I kept asking myself. "What does this mean?" The social history of my day had no answers here: the people weren't complaining about their wages or the price of bread or taxes. The *Manuel* opened the doors for me, with its ethnographic studies from all over France and its frequent use of historical documents.

DC: How did you discover Arnold van Gennep?

NZD: I had never heard of him from historians. One day I asked an anthropologist friend at the University of Toronto about the charivari, and I think it was he that told me of Arnold van Gennep. I found the many volumes of the *Manuel* in the University of Toronto library. What a surprise! The charivari was a widespread practice going back centuries, performed by groups of young men in the countryside who used it against marriages when there was a great disparity of age between the partners and against other violations of village norms. This was just a start for reading that took me across Europe and into other uses of the charivari, both for family matters and political matters, and into other forms of festive behavior. I discovered how important age categories were, and stages of life. That may seem obvious nowadays, but it wasn't to a historian back then. [*laughter*] Van Gennep's main contribution to theory concerned rites of passage, and it was relevant to these youth groups or "Misrule Abbeys" (Abbayes de Maugouvert), as they were called in France.

Then, in fact, I did turn to the American anthropologists and began to read Victor Turner[50] and Clifford Geertz.[51] I read Victor Turner's *Ritual Process* after my paper had first appeared in *Past and Present,* and immediately added his beautiful insights to a new version of the essay.[52] Meanwhile, he had learned of my work and invited me to a colloquium with anthropologists. It was my first colloquium with anthropologists and I was thrilled. We each talked of a ritual of inversion, of some form of the world upside down. I spoke of gender inversion, the paper that became "Women on Top."

DC: The rituals of inversion happen in real life when the social order becomes disturbed and thus in need of corrective action, right?

NZD: That's certainly part of it, but they also have wider uses for playfulness, social definitions, and changes from one status in life to another. Turner talked more broadly of the liminal quality in rites of passage and inversion—he saw the pilgrimage as an example. I was dazzled by his ideas and by the debates inspired by them.

Another great encounter for me was Clifford Geertz. I read his collection of essays, *The Interpretation of Cultures,* right after they appeared in 1973, and I found them deeply engrossing. (In passing, I'm remembering the first time I spoke of his work to the historians at the École des Hautes Études en Sciences Sociales and my listeners asked me "Why is Clifford Geertz so important?" Later on, they understood...) For me, Geertz's work was essential, not so much for what I was doing on carnivals and festivity, but for my efforts to interpret religion. I very much liked his perception of religion as a cultural system—a system that, on the one hand, shapes our perceptions, experiences, and mentalities, and that, on the other hand, is also shaped by them. There's a process of exchange here, which contrasts with the old one-way Marxist model of the material infrastructure determining the superstructure of consciousness. With Geertz, there's always an exchange between experience and ideas, a principle of back and forth. Later, when I came to Princeton, I taught a seminar with Clifford Geertz, and we talked much about the relations between history and anthropology. It was a great experience.

But I can't leave the anthropologists without mentioning Mary Douglas[53] from England. I read her *Purity and Danger* several times over in 1972 when I was writing my essay "The Rites of Violence." What she had to say about the dangers of pollution helped me make sense of the rhetoric of violence in the sixteenth-century religious texts and the destructive and murderous practices of "cleansing" that took place during their religious riots. Later on, she came to Princeton to teach for a year and I had the delight of hearing her lecture and talking with her.

I want to stress, though, that as a historian, I never take the ideas of an anthropologist and just *apply* them to the historical past. Mary Douglas's writings about our sense of the limits of our bodies and of our selves, about the dangers of pollution and our desire for protection—all that yields mere possibilities for interpretation, new questions to ask of the evidence, say, about violence. That last is a topic on which you have enlarged our field of vision, and I've learned much from that, too.

DC: Staying with the vantage point of an approach to history by mining the suggestive potential that other methods and ways of knowing offer, which discipline seems to you actually the most dynamic, the most adept at problem-solving to guide your own reflections? Don't you find that anthropology has today become too narrow and it seeks to devise systems of explanation less global or encompassing than twenty-five years ago? But perhaps, before going into this, you might wish to talk about the contributions of French anthropologists?

NZD: I've received much stimulation from the ideas and books of French anthropologists. I read Claude Lévi-Strauss early along, and had students read *Tristes Tropiques* in my courses.[54] His structuralism is often too rigid and abstract for us historians, but there have been times when he's offered me real leads for my own research. While I was writing my book on women on the margins, I was led via Marie de l'Incarnation to the people she wanted to convert: the Amerindians, especially the Amerindian women of seventeenth-century Québec. How could I understand their ideas and their ways of talking? I was facing a version of the same problem I had with the peasants in the world of Martin Guerre—how was I going to get access to the language, the speech of peasants? I wanted to imagine a possible conversation between Marie de l'Incarnation and one of the young women she hoped to make a Christian. Now I had available nineteenth-century collections of Amerindian legends, but I wanted guidance for the seventeenth century—I wanted some clues as to how an Amerindian woman of that period might tell a story, especially on a topic that would be interesting to Marie de l'Incarnation as well. You're probably wondering what all this has to do with Claude Lévi-Strauss.

DC: I didn't say anything!

NZD: Claude Lévi-Strauss gave me the clues I needed. In his *Histoire de lynx* and elsewhere, he had systematically examined Amerindian stories about abduction, specifically, the abduction of a woman by an animal; among the Iroquoian people, it was often a bear.[55] He had described the different outcomes of the abduction and the woman's relation with her husband: you ended up with a "tale-type," as the folklorists call it, and a sense of Amerindian style. He also suggested a connection between bear-abduction stories told to the Amerindians by French fur-traders in the seventeenth century and those current in parts of France. Well, I knew that abduction was a theme dear to the heart of Marie de l'Incarnation, since her cousin had been abducted in France by a noble army officer, and Marie was worried about the abduction of her converts by non-Christian husbands. So through Lévi-Strauss's stories, I saw the path to take. I could not simply reconstitute a conversation, but I could use some of Marie de l'Incarnation's texts and compare them with the Amerindian ones. His writing gave me possible ways of imagining an exchange.

DC: You thus promote, when all is said and done, an intuitive approach to history where the variables don't dictate a particular way to think about the past and people's mind-sets, but which instead treats history as a set of possibilities that sets it along a path not bound by the signposts of the sources. Couldn't we speak of formulating a historical inquiry that's cross-pollinated by other scholarly disciplines that, without taking them up wholesale, still serve as fertile sources of creativity, of inventiveness? Isn't your manner of thinking, insofar as it's a technique that proceeds as a round of questions and answers, much like the historical subjects you study? Doesn't it rely upon a technique of mixing and blending?

NZD: I don't think of my approach as "intuitive," because I take the signposts from the past very seriously indeed. But I do think we often miss those signposts, and that we can get ideas about where to look for them from other disciplines. We set up a back and forth between our sources and these new sets of questions—yes, a kind of cross-fertilization.

You ask me about French anthropologists. Others have been important to me as well. Around 1980, I became very attracted by the life and writings of Marcel Mauss.[56] I approached the whole question of the gift in sixteenth-century France through his great 1925 study, the *Essai sur le don,* and throughout my work on that subject, I was in dialogue with him. And then, I was interested in him as a Jewish intellectual in France: I followed his fate in the archives as a Jew "retired by the Collège de France" and in hiding in Paris during the German Occupation.

And to give another example, I was struck by the work of Maurice Godelier[57] on the charivari. Jacques Le Goff[58] and Jean-Claude Schmitt[59] organized a colloquium on the charivari in 1977 at the École des hautes etudes en sciences sociales, and brought together historians and anthropologists.[60] Godelier's paper on noisy demonstrations in societies very different from those in Europe opened a new perspective for me. I hope that exchange with historians has been equally beneficial for the anthropologists. I know that Clifford Geertz, who has been interested in change and transformation since his early inquiries, had found such exchange very fruitful. Do you think that's the case with the new generation of French anthropologists?

DC: Don't scholarly disciplines tend to become more and more parochial? When a historian is invited to an anthropology conference, he or she seems to me like an odd duck, almost a test subject to determine whether anthropology's study of "otherness" extends to the past as well as the here and now. It's in this sense that I asked you the preceding question: don't you have the impression that anthropology has long since lost its allure for historians? Even in your latest books, we see that

your references are often more literary than sociological...

NZD: Actually, in regard to my current research on Islam, I must say that some anthropologists, including Clifford Geertz and Jacques Berque,[61] have done major work. Their writings are immensely useful for analyzing certain issues concerning al-Wazzān. But along with anthropology, my most important guides right now are coming from literary studies, including specialists in Arabic literature. It turns out that one of the best tests for understanding al-Wazzān is his style and habits of writing. He tells a lot about himself and his travels, but in some areas of his personal life and feeling—say, in regard to his marriage or his feeling about conversion to Christianity—he is silent. But I can use his ways of writing as a useful index: by reading the specialists in Arabic literature, I can learn about the ordinary strategies for writing, the possible ways of writing and themes found in the genres al-Wazzān chose, and then see what's original about the way he wrote in Italian, the Italian he'd learned as a foreigner. Fascinating things have been turning up, even on matters as seemingly small as whether he uses the pronoun "I" or not.

To go back to your query about anthropology: I'd say that at least American and Canadian anthropology are going in several directions. There has been a split between those who stress the material and economic domain as the proper one for anthropological inquiry and those who stress "culture." Moreover, for practical and political reasons, there are many anthropologists who are taking Europe or North America as the subject of their inquiry. There are no more ethnologically pristine islands in the Pacific to set oneself down in. And often postcolonial governments don't readily welcome anthropologists from the West. [*laughter*] So these various factors together have increased the collaboration between anthropologists and historians: once you're working on, say, American towns or urban settings, it's impossible to ignore the past, to ignore history. Of course, it shouldn't be ignored for Pacific communities either, as Renato Rosaldo[62] long since told us for the Philippine Ilongot...

DC: You often refer to Michel de Certeau[63] as someone who definitely played a role in your work, that he always reinvigorated and recast your historical approach...

NZD: I miss, we all miss Michel de Certeau, but his works are a patrimony, our legacy. He was a man who went beyond the usual categories:

a historian, an anthropologist, and a man of letters with a vision of the world both sacred and profane at the same time. His perspectives were very original and not always easy to grasp: his writing was intricate and very finely wrought, and one must make a real effort to understand the significance of what's there on the pages of his books and essays. I loved his choice of subjects, a choice that I might call democratic, as with the possessed Ursuline sisters of Loudun. He treated these women with great respect, not reducing them to mere hysterics or dismissing them as mentally ill. On the contrary, he always tried to find significant meaning in what the women were saying and affirming.

As I recalled my appreciation for the life of Marc Bloch, so, too, I had much admiration for the experience, for the experiment, in Certeau's life: his decision to become a Jesuit and the way he lived that life both within and without the brotherhood, his interest in China, his work with the Indians in South America, his great erudition and yet his opening toward the students during 1968 and afterward. He possessed an authentic simplicity, a flexibility, a way of being a historian through and through and yet being easy and relaxed... I recall one day when we had lunch in Paris in a popular non-fancy neighborhood—I go back to that restaurant from time to time in memory of him. We talked of learned matters, historical questions. He was totally unstuffy, very pleasant, and courteous toward the waitress, whom he knew because he came there often.

I could not be present at the funeral, but friends told me about it. "What boldness," I thought, "along with the church ceremony to request that Edith Piaf's 'Non, je ne regrette rien' be sung."[64] I rushed right out and bought the record, and listened to it thinking of his choice. I've spoken of Certeau at length, as I did of Marc Bloch, because there are sometimes persons who add a remarkable human quality to the work of a whole life.

DC: Let's return to the problems of communication and exchange with other scholarly disciplines to find inspiration. Do you think that history can today retain the same dynamism?

NZD: I think there are many possibilities for creative interchange within history itself—between social, cultural, and political history. At the moment fascinating things are going on in the history of science (physics, mathematics, etc.) and in the history of scientific knowledge. Specialists are examining the way in which "truth" is established in natural science, or rather the technologies for the production of truth that contemporaries recognize as truth. Lots of possibilities in this area of intellectual history. Also very interesting developments in the history of law. Legal scholars are turning to us for approaches in cultural history and the history of women, and are eager to reflect on the literary and social aspects of legal texts and legal events. This is different from the much older collaboration between historians and historians of law on matters such as the history of hospitals, welfare, charity, and gifts. Today it's a question of sharing approaches, not just of looking at the history of the legal status of certain institutions or practices.

DC: These connections have become weakened in France for largely political reasons.

NZD: I don't know this situation in France. But I would make another comment regarding collaboration. In earlier decades, works published by historians of the law, however excellent, were usually composed in very technical language: they often included the texts of laws and ordinances, but in their discussion of the evolution and interpretation of the law, they stuck closely to the language of the legal specialist. Reading on the history of the laws regarding gifts and contracts, I found the discussion very difficult, sometimes impenetrable. But today, there are changes, at least in North America. In all the important law faculties, there are young—and not so young—scholars who are studying rhetorical aspects of the law and of civil and criminal cases, and looking at the cases as "performative" acts. They are still deeply steeped in the juridical questions, but they are considering relations between systems of legal writing and expression and other systems of expression. As I mentioned a few moments ago, I tried to do the same thing with letters of remission, putting them in relation to other forms of storytelling. This new generation of legal scholars will be of great help to us historians.

DC: In light of your ability to find alternative ways to investigate historical situations and persons by stressing the need to think differently about how we pose questions, hasn't this approach negated the initial premise that a distance really exists between you and the sixteenth century? As you noted in one of your works, when you arrived in France, you noticed that the sixteenth century was split between Catholics and Protestants, and that for a long time French historiography had been one of conflict between Catholic historians and Protestant historians, that even if their disputes over religion had quieted, they remained almost presumed or embedded in the ways these historians did history. However you, coming from another culture, from another religious world altogether, you had some distance from what was at stake in these disputes but could instead contemplate the Catholic and Protestant worldviews in the sixteenth century through a lens that avoided these exaggerated, woolly arguments that sometimes had seduced historians...

NZD: You've certainly caught something of my sensibility as a young historian. There was indeed a confessionalization of studies on the Protestant Reformation and the Catholic Counter-Reformation both in France and in the United States. Historians in those days were writing religious history from within their own religious frame. Protestants wrote on the history of Protestantism and published in Protestant periodicals...

DC: Didn't departments of theology in the United States, which don't exist in France, also come into play?

NZD: Yes, that is part of the story. And Catholics wrote on the history of Catholicism and published in Catholic periodicals. I don't know whether I had read Lucien Febvre's book on *Martin Luther* when I began my own studies, but I must say in passing that his book is exemplary of historical analysis written by someone born and baptized as a Catholic, but absolutely secular—*laïque*—in spirit: already in 1928, he was approaching Luther without any confessional commitment or presuppositions.[65] In any case, when I came to Lyon in 1952, I was Jewish, not especially a practitioner of Jewish laws and liturgy and not a believer in the supernatural, but still identified with Jewish culture and upbringing. I did not have religious stakes to defend in the conflicts between Catholics and Protestants of Lyon in the sixteenth century. This gave me, indeed, what you've called "distance." To be sure, without being a full-blown Marxist, I did have at that time some Marxist sensibilities. That is, I was attached to a view of history in which "progressive" movements were in struggle with "traditional" movements, and if I was going to favor one side rather than the other, it was the Protestants. In that regard, I resembled Henri Hauser: in his early essays on the Reformation, he clearly had a preference for the innovating Protestants.

DC: He saw Protestants as the trailblazers of republican democracy.

NZD: For him as for me, the Protestants represented the forces of resistance against the established order. At that period, I still thought about historical movement in terms of evolutionary schemes, which I have long since abandoned. Nonetheless, I tried to maintain distance from the two sides in the religious conflict. This was made all the easier since the Protestants soon developed an establishment of their own.

DC: You had, however, around 1975, a controversy with the Protestant historian, Janine Garrisson, which actually reflected her sympathetic engagement with respect to Protestant martyrs.[66] We very well see in this controversy how the point of view you defended is a step removed from the charged emotions and identity politics inherited from the past, and how Janine Garrisson—and I don't mean this as a criticism—wished to advance a set of interpretations closely related to the struggles of the "Protestants of the Midi" in the sixteenth century out of which emerged an attitude that could be described as modern.

NZD: Though we disagreed, I want to start by saying how much I appreciate Janine Garrisson's scholarship. Our debate concerned questions of violence, the sources and character of the violence of the Saint Bartholomew's Day massacres and the bloody uprisings that preceded it. In my view, Garrisson did not attend to the meanings of *religion* and symbolic action in this violence and diverted the socioreligious dimension of violence into the familiar socioeconomic one: popular Catholic crowds, often angry about the high cost of grain, assaulting rich Huguenots. In contrast, I saw the Catholic fear of pollution by the Huguenot "vermin" as emerging from the threats to sacred values and the power structures and identities embedded in them.

By 1972, when I wrote my "Rites of Violence," I had already put aside my earlier evolutionary perspective and I wanted very much to understand the horrendous violence from a double point of view: not just to look at enraged Catholics killing poor Protestant victims, but to examine and compare the shape of violence on both sides, to make sense of what people said and why they behaved the way they did. Two things had changed my views. One was the impact of my reading in anthropology on my understanding of religion—not just reading, but also attending different religious services in Lyon, visiting pilgrimage sites, watching processions, etc. I began to understand Catholic sensibility and liturgy more clearly and see both Catholicism and Protestantism in a new light. Rather than a "progressive"

Protestantism and a "conservative" Catholicism, I saw two alternate styles of religious life, two different "languages" I called them, for describing the world. Each of them had the capacity for change in the early modern period. (Some of John Bossy's writings on the modern features of sixteenth- and seventeenth-century Catholic structures of power were very helpful to me here as well.)[67]

The second thing that moved me away from a narrow evolutionary perspective was my work on the history of women. Serious research on that topic quickly disabuses you not only of an old-fashioned view of linear progress, [*laughter*] but also of the notion that there is any *single* site that is always better for women or always the source for improvement of their status. If the Calvinist Reformation opened certain paths for women in its early decades—the call to biblical reading, the reevaluation of marriage—it also held on to hierarchies and eliminated the Catholic celibate option, a female setting that offered space for exploration and institutional authority. There were trade-offs; each religion had its openings and limits. Each religion seemed a possible path to "modernity." I wrote about these matters in some essays, and I didn't change my mind when I began to add Jews to the story, as later on in my *Women on the Margins.*

DC: Among the three women you met and invoked, the one I find most fascinating is Glikl bas Judah Leib, the one woman whose writings in Yiddish you could not at first understand. I asked myself if, in the way you brought her back to life, she and you didn't share some kind of elective affinity. How was it that among these three women, it was Glikl whom, as a reader, I preferred? Wasn't it because you yourself preferred her over the others, whether you realized it or not? Wasn't it because, in writing her life you involuntarily inserted in her an extra measure of virtue the other two lacked? And this despite your protests that you have never favored one of your "women on the margins" over another!

It's her I prefer, because I see her acquire or, better yet, fashion for herself the most charismatic personality, the one who most embodied our own view of humanity in her disappointments and happiness. Aren't you found out by the fact that the reader, at last...

NZD: ...will be the one who decides, who senses the affinity...

DC: Yes, who decides that you, Natalie Zemon Davis, like one of them more than another. Aren't you also found out because you're capable of

sharing a memory in common and empathizing with your historical subject?

NZD: Well, I suppose that's possible. But from a conscious point of view—not that of my unconscious or subconscious [*laughter*]—I like all three and treat them in the same manner. I have no favorite. In fact, Glikl is not the first Jew who has crossed my path in my historical research. By 1971 I had started to add the history of the Jews to my studies and to my teaching, especially in my courses on women and gender. I wanted to enlarge the range of comparison in those courses, and so I assigned an English translation of Glikl's Yiddish autobiography and an excerpt from the fascinating autobiography of Leon Modena, rabbi of Venice in the seventeenth century.[68] So through reading Glikl and Leon Modena along with Christian memoirs, the students could learn about different modes of representation, Catholic, Protestant, and Jewish.

And then after 1978, when I came to Princeton, I taught a course with Mark Cohen on early modern Jewish history—Mark is a specialist in medieval Jewish history—and we decided to edit an edition of Leon Modena's autobiography, with a translation from the Hebrew made by him.[69] I wrote one of the introductory essays for the volume; it was a first effort to do what I later did with Glikl. That is, with Leon Modena's autobiography we had a text with certain features particular to the Jewish situation, which had to be linked to Jewish practices of self-description, but which also had to be restored to the European cultural world of the time. That was my strategy, important to me personally and as a historian: to portray Leon Modena both as a Jew and a European. So I compared his self-presentation with that of Michel de Montaigne and especially with the *Life* of Girolamo Cardano,[70] who was both learned and a gambler like Leon. That essay meant a great deal to me. When I came to writing *Women on the Margin* about three women whom I knew initially through my teaching, I had in some ways a preexisting model. I said to myself, "I can now make a real comparison between three forms of European life." Thus, my goal was not to show Glikl as the "best" of the three women, even though studying her gave me much pleasure.

DC: Not the "best," but the most alive, the most human ...

NZD: I did not feel that way about her at the time. It is true that the woman who I felt was most different from myself was Marie de l'Incarnation, with her ascetic style and excess of mortification of the flesh. As for her desire to convert the Amerindians, I could connect with it because it was fueled by eschatology, by her messianic hopes[71]—and I had had a dash of such hopes when I was young, albeit not as part of Catholic spirituality. I was also impressed by Marie's audacity and energy when she decided to leave France for Canada and set up an Ursuline house there. As a mother myself, I was very amused by the relations of all three women with their children and enjoyed making comparisons among them. And then if Glikl loved to tell stories—and I'm the same way—Maria Sibylla Merian was the most intellectual of the three. Thus, from a personal point of view, there were traits that I admired or found interesting in all three women, and this may have been in part because I sensed some resemblance between them and me. But I want to stress very strongly here that good history-writing cannot be based on perceived resemblance. Our task is to understand our subjects in their own terms and language, and not simply to read them through resemblance.

DC: But isn't Glikl the least extreme of the three?

NZD: In the rhythm of her life as a merchant woman, wife, and widow, who moved from the Jewish community in Hamburg to the Jewish community in Metz, she is typical of other Jewish women at the time. And I'd have to say that Marie de l'Incarnation and Maria Sibylla Merian, who left her husband, joined a radical Protestant sect, and then went off to Suriname to study its insects, were well beyond Glikl in terms of audacity and the spirit of adventure. Glikl's originality lay in the innovative structure she gave to her Yiddish autobiography. But, I repeat, what was important to me was not only Glikl as a woman and a Jew, but Glikl and the Jews as part of the history of Europe. In the wake of Nazism and the barbarism that wanted to efface the role of the Jews and their existence in Europe, it was vital for me to show that Jews *belong* to that history. I had both this personal goal and a goal as a historian: one's personal goals must not get in the way of one's role as a historian, but I don't think that happened here. I had good evidence to show that her love of storytelling was not only a Jewish trait, but a widespread interest in seventeenth-century Europe—even the stories she told in Yiddish were widely shared in other languages.

I also wanted to show through the three women that there is not one way to be "European" in the seventeenth century. There's not one style that should be singled out as "progressive" or "good" or "authentic." There are always multiple paths, then and now, though today the models are different from the Jewish, Catholic, and Protestant in my book. In regard to the three models in the book, I must mention the response of one of my readers. She asked why I had put the three women in the order that I did. It wasn't strictly chronological, for though they all overlapped to some extent, Marie de l'Incarnation lived earlier in the century than the other two. I put Glikl first because the Jewish Bible, the Old Testament, was the book that informed her life and writing. And then the Catholic Marie and the Protestant Maria Sibylla, because of the historical timing of their religions. But my friend pointed out that this ordering could give the impression that I was setting out a "progress." That was not my intention at all. In any case, it gave me great pleasure to work on this book, both as a person and a historian; I'm moved to remember how much it meant to me.

Notes

1. The Jesuit relations were annual reports that the head of the Order of Jesus in New France sent back to Paris during the seventeenth and early eighteenth centuries. The Ursulines are a Catholic religious order founded by Saint Angela de Merici in 1535; it is devoted to the education of girls and care for the sick and elderly.

2. Guillaume Postel (1510–81) was a French humanist scholar adept at ancient and Near Eastern languages who advocated a universal world religion to unite the major faiths.

3. Gilles of Viterbo (1465–1532) was a cardinal of the Catholic Church, famous preacher, and scholar of the Hebrew language and Kabbala, which he used to support Christian teaching.

4. Alberto III Pio, Prince of Carpi (1472–1530), was a Renaissance Italian prince celebrated for his promotion of humanism and for his role as diplomat to Rome of the king of France and Emperor Maximilian.

5. Manuel I, King of Portugal (1469–1521), promoted overseas exploration and commercial expansion into the Atlantic and Indian Oceans and the conversion of conquered peoples to Christianity.

6. Pope Leo X (1475–1521) was a member of the Medici family and the last nonpriest elected as pope. His efforts to raise money through the sale of indulgences prompted Martin Luther's challenge to the church. He was celebrated for his patronage of poets and artists.

7. Raffaello Sanzio da Urbino (1483–1520), better known as Raphael, was an Italian artist and architect of the High Renaissance.

8. Jean du Bellay (1493–1560) was a French cardinal and diplomat.

9. Eugénie Droz (1893–1976) was born in Neuchâtel, Switzerland, and was a graduate of the École des Hautes Études in Paris. She opened the publishing house Librairie Droz in Paris in 1924, which she transferred to Geneva and ran until 1963. She founded the journal *Humanisme et Renaissance* in 1934. Her own numerous publications deal with fifteenth-century literature, the French Renaissance and Reformation, and typography.

10. John H. Mundy (1917–2004) was a prominent medieval historian. The book emerging from his postwar doctoral studies in Toulouse was *Liberty and Political Power in Toulouse, 1150–1230* (1954).

11. Richard Gascon (1913–82) was a French economic and social historian. His two-volume study on commerce and urban life in sixteenth-century Lyon came out in 1971.

12. Max Weber (1864–1920) was a German sociologist and political economist who profoundly reshaped the social sciences through his study of reason and religion as well as the rise of the state and capitalism.

13. Karl Marx (1818–83) was a German philosopher and political economist whose ideas established the foundations of modern revolutionary communism.

14. Henri Hauser (1866–1946) was a French economic historian and author, among many works, of *Ouvriers des temps passés* [Workers from Past Times] (1898).

15. Pierre Goubert (1915–) is a pioneering French social historian of the Annales school and author of many books, including *Beauvais et le Beauvaisis de 1600 à 1730: Contribution à l'histoire sociale de la France du XVIIe siècle* [Beauvais and Its Region from 1600 to 1730: A Contribution to the Social History of France in the Seventeenth Century] (1958) mentioned here.

16. The book mentioned here came out in 1966.

17. Émile Coornaert (1886–1980) was a French economic historian, early member of the Annales school, and member of the French Resistance during World War II. The book mentioned here is *Corporations en France avant 1789* [Guilds in France before 1789] (1941).

18. Vichy France or the Vichy regime refers to the government under Marshal Philippe Pétain between July 1940 and August 1944 that collaborated with Nazi Germany to rule those portions of France not under direct German Occupation following the French defeat in June 1940.

19. Maurice Agulhon (1926–) is a French social historian noted for his work on eighteenth- and nineteenth-century republicanism. The full title of the book mentioned here is *La sociabilité méridionale: Confréries et associations dans la vie collective en Provence orientale à la fin du XVIIIe siècle* [Southern Sociability: Religious Fraternities and Associations in Communities in Eastern Provence at the End of the Eighteenth Century] (1966).

20. Mikhail Bakhtin (1895–1975) was an innovative Russian philosopher, literary scholar, and theoretician of culture. He wrote the work mentioned here as a dissertation during World War II. It was not published until 1965, however.

21. Barbara Diefendorf (1946–) is a historian of early modern France. Her most recent book is *From Penitence to Charity: Pious Women and the Catholic Reformation in Paris* (2006). The book alluded to here is *Beneath the Cross: Catholics and Huguenots in Sixteenth-Century Paris* (1991).

22. Yves-Marie Bercé (1936–) is a French historian of the early modern period best known for his work on popular revolts. See in particular his *Revolt and Revolution in Early Modern Europe: An Essay on the History of Political Violence* (1987).

23. Giambattista Vico (1668–1744) was an Italian philosopher, historian, and scholar of rhetoric. In his most important work, *The New Science* (1725), he developed a new way of conceptualizing the philosophy of history and described the different ages of humankind, with each age marked by different forms of reasoning, laws, poetry and expression, and government.

24. Werner Jaeger (1888–1961) was a German classicist who emigrated to the United States in 1936. The full title of the three-volume study mentioned here is *Paideia: The Ideals of Greek Culture* (1933–47).

25. Charles Trinkaus (1912–99) was a historian of Renaissance Italy. His books include *Adversity's Noblemen: The Italian Humanists on Happiness* (1966) and *In Our Image and Likeness: Humanity and Divinity in Italian Humanist Thought* (1970).

26. Edgar Zilsel (1891–1944) was an Austrian historian and philosopher of science who emigrated to the United States after Austria was annexed by Nazi Germany in 1938. This essay originally appeared in *The American Journal of Sociology* 47 (1942): 544–62.

27. Henri Berr (1963–54) was a French philosopher and historian who founded the influential journal *Revue du synthèse* in 1900. The book mentioned here was published in Paris in 1920.

28. Marc Bloch (1886–1944) was a prominent French medieval historian who founded, along with Lucien Febvre, the Annales school. His book was a two-volume study originally published in Paris in 1939 and 1940. It appeared in English as *Feudal Society* (1964).

29. Bloch composed his memoir in September 1940 but it only appeared posthumously after the war in 1946 as *Étrange défaite* and a subsequent English translation, *Strange Defeat: A Statement of Evidence Written in 1940* (1949).

30. Philippe Ariès (1914–84) was a French demographer and historian of the family and childhood. His major works include *Centuries of Childhood* (1962) and *The Hour of Our Death* (1981).

31. Eileen Power (1889–1940) was a British medievalist and economic historian. Among her

most important books are *Medieval People* (1924) and *The Wool Trade in English Medieval History* (1941).

32. Sylvia Thrupp (1903–97) was a medieval historian who wrote *A Short History of the Worshipful Company of Bakers of London* (1933) and *The Merchant Class of Medieval London* (1948). In 1958, she founded the interdisciplinary journal *Comparative Studies in Society and History.*

33. Nancy L. Roelker (1915–93) was a distinguished historian of early modern France who wrote *Queen of Navarre: Jean d'Albret* (1968) and *One King, One Faith: The Parlement of Paris and the Religious Reformations of the Sixteenth Century* (1996).

34. This book is entitled *The Paris of Henry of Navarre as Seen by Pierre de l'Estoile* (1958).

35. Elizabeth Armstrong (1917–2002) was a scholar of sixteenth-century literature and a historian of the book at Somerville College, Oxford. Among her books is *Robert Estienne, Royal Printer: An Historical Study of the Elder Stephanus* (1954; 2nd edition, 1986).

36. Françoise Weil (1922–) is a scholar of eighteenth-century French letters, book-history, and censorship, and has been director of research libraries in Dijon and Paris. She has published *L'interdiction du roman et la librairie 1728–1750* (1986).

37. Michelle Perrot (1928–) is a major French historian and feminist. Her many books include *Les ouvriers en grève, France 1871–1890* (1974), translated into English as *Workers on Strike 1871–1890* (1987), and *Les femmes ou les silences de l'histoire* [Women or the Silences of History] (1998). Together with the late Georges Duby, she edited the many volumes of *A History of Women in the West* (1992–1994).

38. Christiane Klapisch-Zuber (1936–) is an innovative historian of women and the family who focuses on the late Middle Ages and Renaissance in France and Italy. Among her works are *Women, Family and Ritual in Renaissance Florence* (1985) and, together with the late David Herlihy, *Tuscans and Their Families: A Study of the Florentine Catasto of 1427* (1985). She served as editor of volume 2 of *A History of Women in the West.*

39. Jill Ker Conway (1934–) has been an important figure in the study of the history of women and in women's education in North America. Among her publications are *The Female Experience in Eighteenth- and Nineteenth-Century America: A Guide to the History of American Women* (1982), *The First Generation of American Women Graduates* (1989), and her best-selling memoir *Road from Coorain* (1989). In 1975 she became the first woman president of Smith College.

40. Carlo Ginzburg (1939–) is a noted historian and pioneer of microhistory best known for his groundbreaking work *The Cheese and the Worms: The Cosmos of a Sixteenth Century Miller* (1976; English ed., 1980). Giovanni Levi (1939–) is a social and economic historian, and founder of the Italian journal *Microhistoria.*

41. Bronisław Geremek (1932–2008) was a Polish social historian and politician. The book referred to here is *The Margins of Society in Late Medieval Paris* (1987).

42. Solidarność is an independent Polish trade union federation led by Lech Walesa that opposed the Communist government in the 1980s and helped usher in the first post-Communist regime in 1989 when Walesa was elected president.

43. Keith Thomas (1933–) is a Welsh historian best known for his books *Religion and the Decline of Magic* (1971) and *Man and the Natural World* (1984). The article referenced here appeared in *History of Ideas* 20, no. 2 (April 1959): 195–216.

44. Peter Burke (1937–) is a prolific British historian who specializes in social and cultural history.

45. Edward P. Thompson (1924–93) was a British historian and political activist who specialized in the history of British radical movements. The landmark book referred to here appeared in 1963.

46. Mack P. Holt (1949–) is a specialist of early modern France whose books include *The French Wars of Religion, 1562–1629,* 2nd edition (2005), and *The Duke of Anjou and the Politique Struggle during the Wars of Religion* (1986).

47. Philip Benedict (1949–) is a leading expert on early modern Calvinism. Among his books are *Rouen during the Wars of Religion* (1981), *Christ's Churches Purely Reformed: A Social History of Calvinism* (2002), and, most recently, *Graphic History: The "Wars, Massacres and Troubles" of Tortorel and Perrissin* (2008).

48. Arnold van Gennep (1873–1957) was a French ethnographer and folklorist famous for his

study, *The Rites of Passage* (1909), which examined the rituals that mark significant transitions in human lives.

49. The full title of the journal is *Le Manuel de folklore français contemporain* (1937–58).

50. Victor Turner (1920–83) was a cultural anthropologist best known for his work on symbols, rituals, and rites of passage. Among his many books are *The Ritual Process: Structure and Anti-Structure* (1969) and *Dramas, Fields, and Metaphors: Symbolic Action in Human Society* (1974).

51. Clifford Geertz (1926–2006) was an anthropologist and ethnographer known for his innovative work in symbolic anthropology and the study of meaning. His many books include *The Religion of Java* (1960), *Islam Observed: Religious Development in Morocco and Indonesia* (1968), *Negara: The Theatre State in Nineteenth-Century Bali* (1980), as well as collections of essays, such as the widely read *Interpretation of Cultures* (1973).

52. The version of this essay appeared in *Society and Culture in Early Modern France,* chapter 4.

53. Mary Douglas (1921–2007) was a British cultural anthropologist known for her work on symbolism as articulated in many books such as *Purity and Danger: An Analysis of Concepts of Pollution and Taboo* (1966) and *Risk and Blame: Essays in Cultural Theory* (1992).

54. Claude Lévi-Strauss (1908–2009) was a French anthropologist and ethnologist who became a central figure in the structuralist school of thought that posited the existence of common patterns underlying all forms of human symbolization. *Tristes Tropiques* (1955) appeared in an English translation as *A World on the Wane* in 1973.

55. An English translation appeared in 1996. *Histoire de lynx* was first published in 1991.

56. Marcel Mauss (1872–1950) was a French sociologist and anthropologist, who brought a new approach to the study of religion, sacrifice, and forms of exchange. His influential *Essai sur le don* was published in 1925, and is available in English as *The Gift: The Form and Reason for Exchange in Archaic Societies* (1990).

57. Maurice Godelier (1934–) is a French anthropologist who specializes in the societies of Oceania.

58. Jacques Le Goff (1924–) is a French medieval historian who headed the École des hautes études en sciences sociales from 1972 to 1977 and whose many books reshaped medieval social and cultural history.

59. Jean-Claude Schmitt (1946–) is a French medieval historian known for his use of anthropological and art historical methods in his research. Among his books is *Le saint lévrier: Guinefort, guérisseur d'enfants depuis le 13e siècle* (1979), translated into English as *The Holy Greyhound: Guinefort, Healer of Children since the Thirteenth Century* (1983).

60. Godelier's "Charivari chez les Baruya de Nouvelle-Guinée (le 6 octobre 1968)" appeared in the conference proceedings edited by Le Goff and Schmitt entitled *Le charivari* (1981), pp. 347–51. Godelier was director of the École des hautes études en sciences sociales at the time.

61. Jacques Berque (1910–95) was a French historical sociologist and scholar of Islam, the Arab world, and North Africa, writing both about the past and the period of decolonization.

62. Renato Rosaldo (1941–) is an anthropologist writing both about the Philippines and the practice of anthropology. The reference here is to his book, *Ilongot Headhunting, 1883–1974: A Study in History and Society* (1980).

63. Michel de Certeau (1925–86) was a French Jesuit and scholar whose work combined history, psychoanalysis, philosophy, and the social sciences, as well as commentary on contemporary politics and culture. His books include *The Possession at Loudun* (2000; French edition, 1970), *The Practice of Everyday Life* (1984; French edition, 1980), and *The Mystic Fable* (1992; French edition, 1982).

64. Edith Piaf (1915–63) was a popular French cabaret singer and cultural icon. The song is known as "No Regrets" in English and was recorded by Piaf in 1960.

65. Lucien Febvre (1878–1956) was a renowned French historian best known for his role in founding, together with Marc Bloch, the French Annales school of historical interpretation. His book, *Martin Luther: Un destin* (1928), appeared in English translation in 1929.

66. Janine Garrisson (1932–) is a specialist of early modern French Protestantism. The exchange with Natalie Zemon Davis can be found in *Past and Present* 67 (1975): 127–35.

67. John Bossy (1933–) is a specialist of early modern England and European Catholicism and is the author, among other studies, of *The English Catholic Community, 1570–1850* (1975) and *Christianity and the West, 1400–1700* (1985), which are being referred to here.

68. Leon Modena (1571–1648) was a learned and eloquent rabbi of Venice, author of numerous works in Hebrew and an Italian description of the rites and customs of the Jews, translated after his death into English as *The History of the Rites, Customes, and Manner of Life of the Present Jews, Throughout the World* (1650).

69. Mark R. Cohen, ed., *The Autobiography of a Seventeenth-Century Venetian Rabbi: Leon Modena's Life of Judah* (1988).

70. Girolamo Cardano (1501–76) was an Italian Renaissance mathematician, physician, and astrologer. An English translation of his autobiography appeared as *The Book of My Life* (2002).

71. Eschatology investigates the theological nature of what are believed will be the final events in the history of the world. Millenarianism is the Christian belief in an imminent major transformation of the world resulting from the second coming of Christ.

Chapter 3

Fashionings

DC: Let's leave off for the time being the various characters you encountered and shift our discussion now to a related dimension in this history of your life as a historian. I would briefly like to return to this impulse to direct your historical writing to consider how the horrors of the twentieth century, in effect, represented a rejection of history as well as fed your interest in confessional violence in Lyon from the early 1540s to the Saint Bartholomew's Day Massacre in Lyon. Were you recalling, when you worked on the Holocaust, all the heartbreaking tragedies that gave it such poignancy, and don't we touch here on the beginning of your own self-fashioning?

NZD: Ah, yes ...

DC: But at the same time—and I believe it's the power of this kind of analysis—we don't immediately see that you write with these memories in the back of your mind. It's up to the reader, again, to intuit it in your writing and even realize that danger, for you, is not unique to the tragedies of the twentieth century but is rather also latent in other historical periods when societies fell prey to the most horrible slaughter. Surely, you write history as a way to search for hope.

NZD: It is certain, even many decades afterward, that the Holocaust, the mass murders, and extraordinary violence of the 1930s and 1940s influenced me. The Holocaust has always been at the back of my mind, and it was there when in 1970 to 1971, I began the reflection that led to "The Rites of Violence." But, curiously enough, I'd stress the *back* of my mind, for the events up front that aroused most immediately my thinking about religious violence in the sixteenth century were those of the 1960s and early 1970s. There was the Vietnam War, with all its horrors, the resistance against that war, in which I participated, and the debates within the Left and opposition movements. I was troubled by the violence, including even that sometimes unleashed in our own demonstrations. I kept asking myself, "What does this mean?" And that opened the path for me to thinking about the character of violence during the Holocaust...

DC: **Your analysis of sixteenth-century religious sedition has led you to signal the importance of the crowd which, according to you, sometimes appropriated the state's rites of punishment to legitimate to the broader public its own aggression and desire to eliminate the "pollution" caused by its adversaries in order to restore the world to its lost pristine purity. However, these are not the same techniques as those used in the Holocaust where the vast bulk of the violence was the work of machines within the closed confines of the camps, nowhere more than in the enclosures of the gas chambers... In Lyon or in Paris around 1562, the Protestants died in public in a ritualistic spectacle in words and images that formed a language to explain why, in the minds of the torturers, it was necessary to put them to death so theatrically and also why they lacked humanity and thus worth.**

NZD: Of course, there are many differences between the ideology and practices of the Nazis and those of violent religious crowds in the sixteenth century: among others, the technological and bureaucratic character of Nazi extermination in the gas chambers is different from the multiple forms of destruction, assault, and murder carried out by Protestant and Catholic rioters. But there are what you might call structural similarities, forms of ritual and symbolic behavior, that seem to appear whenever we humans engage in extreme violence connected with deep issues of boundaries and identity. The repetitive practices in the concentration camps—the queues, the removal of all clothes, and the rest—are not just bureaucratic routine; they have a ritual quality, dehumanizing the Jews and the political enemies of Nazism and investing the murderers with power. In the Nazi films, Jews are "rats"; in the Catholic tracts, Protestant heretics are "vermin" (albeit "vermin" who can return to humanity by conversion). In some places in Eastern Europe, the villagers executed their Jewish neighbors themselves, accompanying them with rituals of humiliation, as Huguenots did to priests before killing them.

Right after I wrote this essay, I had the students read it in one of my undergraduate classes at Berkeley. We had quite a debate in class—

and its theme is still a current one today, with all that's going on around al-Qaeda... I had wanted to propose an explanation for violence: not a pardon or justification, but a social and cultural explanation for such extreme forms of aggression. I did not want to attribute them to a demonic force lying in human beings, and that was very important to me. I recall that one of my students—she was Jewish like me—was very bitter about the Nazi murders, for which she saw Zionism as the only solution. She announced, "The purely demonic acts in history, without any explanation. There are evil people, people possessed." For me the idea that the final explanation for an event is absolute evil is *unacceptable*.

DC: This anecdote raises the question of knowing whether the demonic can be reduced simply to irrationality and if irrationality can actually be considered a causal factor in history, especially of reason unhinged by our own desire for rationality...

NZD: Irrationality can be a way of finding an explanation, for example, by having recourse to psychoanalysis. There is an explanatory role for the irrational in history. But the affirmation of the demonic, the claim that there are some people simply possessed by evil, constitutes for me a path toward exclusion and genocide. It is too cruel to prejudge that there are people so possessed. History is full of atrocious actions, but they are perpetrated by people born (as Pico della Mirandola[1] said five hundred years ago) with the potentiality for good or for evil. The historian seeks either some way to explain that choice or some way to narrate it.

DC: Finally, I would tend to think that the concept of evil shouldn't be invoked in history except with a great deal of prudence. Victims as well as everyone else are caught up—involuntarily for the former, voluntarily for the latter—in the sociocultural dynamics of panic, that history is quite rightly a sad pursuit because of this terrible logic that requires, in certain situations, that everything be overturned by the desire for exclusion. There are moments that go beyond all normality because individuals suffer and express their suffering of who they are and wish to be by slipping into violence, by destroying everything that might increase their sense of helplessness and anguish or could be the cause of their suffering, for the time being and in the immediate future. Sadly, evil forms part of a whole logic. That's why when I worked, after you, on sedition during the French Reformation, I underscored the importance of eschatology as a factor. There

seemed to me to be a kind of cycle under way from the 1480s to the 1520s in which the Last Judgment appeared extremely close at hand. Every Christian had to live in tense expectation of an event that would bring history to an end, pursuing penitence and self-improvement with the feeling that at any moment he could find himself face-to-face with God who would excuse no fault, no sin, or any residue of doubt. This sense of guilt arose and drew strength from preaching as well as the circulation of astrological leaflets. *Ira dei super nos.*[2] To a degree more or less conscious, a sense of disquietude upset people's imaginations and led Christians to doubt themselves and their capacity to live up to the demands of a wrathful God. Evangelical reform powerfully responded to this anguish by assuaging it. I hypothesized that those persons who refused to become mired in this sense of guilt found in Calvinism an outlet, an inner place free of anguish because the return to evangelical purity was finally at hand after so many centuries of darkness and neglect of the Truth, because the destruction of papal Babylon was imminent. I further hypothesized that the individuals who remained in the grips of this panic over the end times became even more obsessed with it the more they saw those they called Lutherans as false prophets of the Apocalypse whom God commanded them to chase and destroy. Moreover, those who remained faithful to traditional religion became set on edge by the image of the eschatological monstrousness of the "heretic," so much that they hardly hesitated to eradicate and annihilate them to appease a wrathful God, whereas those who joined the evangelical faith aimed to bring down the Roman Church, to wipe out all those tonsured heads, the priests. Each side sought confrontation as the moment of God's supreme test... Wasn't there in this historical case a demonstration of how history sometimes becomes caught up in an antagonism's very logic that arises out of a sense of anguish, the reduction or assuagement of which is the motor force of history itself, a force all the stronger because it encourages the very conditions for the total negation of another person. Apparently not that violence should play a necessary role because history is absolutely contingent, but rather to underscore the emergence of a state of breaking norms, of transgression that might convert horrible acts into expressions of liberation, to contend that after a certain moment misfortune can loom up in history to animate people like marionettes. In point of fact, misfortune is simultaneously a common fear of history and a desire shared with history... Anyway, a "human" history—rather than a "humanist" one, a hackneyed term for sure—mustn't it aim to understand in human terms this misfortune, along a spectrum that would consider some criminals and others as victims? Doesn't history produce and resolve anguish, create misfortune, lead some to play the role of victims and others to become executioners? Not that history aims to pass judgment, that it tries to weigh this transgression for all the participants in their respective roles as victims and executioners?

NZD: Your description of the spiral of religious violence in the sixteenth century is extraordinary in its psychological richness, and moving and persuasive. And it's an interpretation, an effort at explanation that does not divide the world into black and white, bad and good. If you divide the world into the demons and the others, there's no room left for responsibility. Your path, which I hope is also my own, tries to explain or interpret the facts: the idea of a tragic history that you can examine attentively and get some diagnosis as a *human* history. It doesn't necessarily give you any perfect assurance about being able to change things, but it does bring some perspective for today: it allows one to recognize the force and grandeur of eschatological hopes and the extreme dangers inherent in them. Tragic history, sorrowful history is important for us, because it reminds us that we are all human beings, in danger...

DC: Do you defend history because you see it as a source of social or ethical utility, in the sense it could help orient us in history...

NZD: I would say "useful" in a very special sense. What human beings have done in the past, the enormous range in ways of living and possible actions, is a source both of hope and despair. How fascinating it is to consider this variety in human events. We can draw hope from it in the sense that if things have been different in the past, perhaps we're in a position to make them a little different today [*laughter*]—at least a little bit different. When I say "usefulness," I don't mean that history offers us models that we can apply—the details of different situations are too unlike each other. History offers us ideas, points of view, perspectives, landmarks, indices—possibilities.

DC: Yes, history as an introduction to an epistemology of difference, of diversity. Let's return to this crisis of religion in France in the middle of the sixteenth century. You suggest that acts of violence had been extraordinarily intense in terms of the treatment of bodies, in the presentation of bodies to crowds, and in the depiction of the gestures of the persons who tortured them. You show it very well: there's a seductive quality about horror that must come into play in order to cut down an adversary and those who share his faith. It's for that reason that I thought about a "history of misfortune": these journeymen printers whom you saw in the 1550s and 1560s as Calvinists and who all truly shared a hope in the coming at last of a godly kingdom on earth after a long period of blindness under the Roman Church. Later we rediscover these same men, at least those who didn't choose the path of exile, in the 1580s and 1590s back in the bosom of the church, just as if violence had succeeded in turning them away from their dreams, to the point where they next fell prey to similar fantasies such as the eschatology of the Catholic League.[3] It's quite striking to see how history can be not only a great leveler of dreams, but also a form of discourse that notes the irony of events and sets of beliefs.

NZD: This is true of all movements for historical transformation. You can see this in connection with revolutions, and even in connection with a simple change in government. One hopes for, even expects all kinds of improvement, even on the morrow of an ordinary election ... and then one perceives how difficult it is to change the order of things. The moment of hope, the happy sense of full possibility, lasts for about two hours. [*laughter*] But we must rejoice in those two hours, savor and remember the feeling of possibility. The vision is never fulfilled; things never work out in the grand manner; the future is full of difficulty and sometimes terrible consequences and disappointments. But without the memory of the dream, nothing hoped for would happen at all.

People respond to such disappointment in different ways—an ironic stance, as you say, but there are other possibilities. I've often thought it would be interesting for someone to make a systematic study of French Protestants who abjured their faith and returned to Catholicism in the last part of the sixteenth and early seventeenth century. As far as I know, this hasn't been done. I wonder what one would find if one looked at patterns of marriage, networks, friendships, and sensibilities; I should think that the Protestant years would have left their mark. I'm not thinking so much of Jansenism, which has been much discussed, but of what such people may have brought to the various Catholic positions of the time. Interesting studies have been made of Jews converted to Catholicism and Protestantism in Europe, marriage patterns, associations, and the like.[4] There's been speculation about the extent to which earlier Jewish tradition may have influenced some of these converts. Teresa of Avila,[5] for example: could there have been any influence from the Jewish past of her family on her mystic sensibility? What's been done for these Jewish converts—even those who stayed within the Christian fold—could be done for the French Protestants returning to the Mother Church.

DC: Some have tried to make this kind of analysis for the former members of the Catholic League by examining how, in the early seventeenth century, they reinvested their involvement with a sacrificial faith in the practice of pious foundations. There again, it seems, the dominant impression would be that of extremely varied and variable experiences that merge together but can never be fully explained in isolation from each other.

NZD: That shows the care one must use in making generalizations.

DC: At the same time, there exists on both sides a desire not to remain in a state of lifelessness, to not be erased away... To return to the Protestants, there's one character about whom you've written sublimely by endowing him with such personal complexity. It's Jean de Coras. I had the impression that with Jean de Coras you had touched upon what constitutes the core of Protestant subjectivity or the embrace of Protestantism, in other words an approach to a crisis of identity, of the reality an individual can give himself and others, during a precise time in which the immediate aspects of one's self-image disintegrate. Where is the reality of the self? That's the question that Jean de Coras, a convert to the new thinking, seems to confront when staring at the Janus-faced man with two potential identities, Arnaud du Tilh/Martin Guerre. A past, repudiated identity and another stolen and assumed. Couldn't you have gone further, in the end, by asking if the Reformation offered a response to the desire to cut free from one's sense of self, a subjectivity yearning toward a dream of escape? In your book on gifts, you explain very well how Calvin created a destructive critique of the whole system of reciprocity upon which, in society, identity operates but only insofar as it's a social identity.

NZD: You ask me a complex question there. I don't think the Reformation offered a response to the desire to be cut free from one's sense of self, but rather offered ways to change that sense and relieve the self from endless anxiety and obligation. You'll notice I'm using "self" and "sense of self" here rather than "identity": "identity" is a later word and when we use it for the sixteenth century, I think we should confine it to external marks that are part of social relations—he is a noble, she is a Savoyarde, I am a goldsmith, you are my cousin—rather than extend it, as we do today, to cover inner issues of subjectivity. The crisis of the self in the first half of the sixteenth century was "overdetermined"—a term from psychoanalysis, I think—by which I mean there were multiple pressures on the self at the same time across the social spectrum, in family life, in intimate life, in social life, especially in situations where there was social mobility, pressing toward obligation, duties, achievement, including sexual achievement, control for some, fertility for others. This endless taking on of obligation was acted out in the obsessive performance of Catholic devotion and liturgy: it provided the formative model for understanding and shaping social life. (As in Clifford Geertz's definition, religion both shapes and is shaped by social experience.) And this situation was important for the person's sense of self not only in relation to other people, but also in the supremely important relation with God: "How do I situate myself in relation to God?"

There are different ways of getting around the guilt and anxiety aroused by such pressure, the "works-righteousness" that Luther decried. One way is to open up the self so widely that the individual boundary disappears—the mystic seeking union with God, the fusion of a collective eschatological movement. I talked about this option in my book on the gift. This would be the closest to your "desire to be cut free from one's sense of self." But it's not something that many people can follow, and it's not something that can last very long. The quest for fusion finally founders on the existence of the individual soul: God gives it to each person and it lasts in the next world till the end of time. (I made this point some years ago in response to Stephen Greenblatt's claim that my Martin Guerre book demonstrated that identity and the self were totally social constructs in the sixteenth century; the belief in the existence of the soul and its relation to God puts a limit on that idea.)

The major solutions were the Protestant and Catholic reforms, which at their best relieved the pressure in different ways and offered persons different subjective states in regard to God. An especially interesting contrast, I think, is the different role allotted to other persons and to hierarchical relations in the arrival at a sense of self in relation to God. If I may simplify here and use a kind of Weberian ideal type: the individual Catholic is willing to place himself or herself in a dependent relation with figures who carry both maternal and paternal features and to open intimate subjectivity to another person; the individual Protestant has the Bible and his or her pastors or preachers for guidance, but finally holds the doors of the subjective self open only to God. We have two different models of the boundaries of the self here, and in both religions, they would have different implications for men and for women in the sixteenth century.

DC: Yet when all is said and done, if you were to offer an explanation for the religious split in the sixteenth century, would you first see it in existential terms? Is self-fashioning, as you describe it, the need to fashion a sense of self already in crisis, one that suggests or is open to suggesting in that moment alternative paths with respect to the one earlier taken?

NZD: I would rather save the phrase "self-fashioning" for the social relations people had, especially those associated with geographical or social mobility, and use more collectively infused language to talk about religious change and the negotiations concerning the soul. I suppose you can call a conversion experience or joining the Jesuit or Ursuline orders a kind of self-fashioning, but these changes are so guided by rules for performance that it's probably better not to put them all under the same rubric.

I've described a possible existential or psychological source for the religious split and alternate solutions to a crisis of the self. Let me say a word about the social side of the same story: at the heart of the split are the privileged position of the Catholic clergy and the theology of merit, works, and the possibility of perfect sanctification associated with it, including the possibility of celibacy and the full control of sexuality. This is a world where the socioemotional axis of clergy and laity is as important as the socioeconomic one of noble and commoner, and where political power is tied up in both sets of relations. Pressures built up across the clergy/laity axis, due among other things to the exorbitant demands of the clergy for exclusive obedience from the laity (perhaps connected with associated demands from parents on their children—but that would have to be researched); extravagant demands that some individual Christians placed on their bodies and sentiments; and, of course, the aspirations of kings and other political authorities. And the gulf opened between what the ecclesiastical authorities were requiring be put into practice—say, in regard to the way charity was expressed in Christian life—and what the faithful could see was being done. At this juncture (and I return to the image of overdetermination, all these pressures and perceptions *at once*), you have a real crisis of credibility. (The credibility gap reminds me of what we saw in 1989, with the fall of the Communist regimes, especially in the Soviet Union.)

Out of this pressure, both psychological and social, on the Catholic system emerged two forms of Christian faith and religious practice, both viable. To give an example, the Protestant system accepts the presence of sexuality as a permanent desire in men and women and insists that pastors and preachers marry. The reformed Catholic system affirms the possibility and superiority of the celibate state, but reduces the distance between it and the "pollution" of sexuality and marriage, in several ways, including the greater prestige accorded Joseph, Mary's husband, and the greater spiritual role accorded to widows.

DC: But don't you think that, in this context, an individual reacts—as you have shown—through his social experience as part of a group to which he belongs and that permits him to share common values, or is it rather that at the end of the day the individual is alone in his choice? In effect, in your studies, there's often this shift back and forth between a social experience that defines a group and a biographical impulse that renders the individual alone when he sets about to write or faces his judge, a solitude that you recount.

NZD: The contingent qualities particular to an individual life can always come into play and lead to surprising decisions by an individual, unexpected by those around him or her. But even then, the constraints the person has to face and the resources available for fashioning that surprising decision come from the surrounding culture. There's a movement between social experience and what you've called the "biographical impulse."

Michel de Montaigne provides a nice example of individual choice within a cultural field... and by the way, I should mention that he talks of the omnipresence and dangers of "self-fashioning" [*se façonner*] in his day with great sharpness. In my book on the gift, I distinguished three forms of human exchange: contractual modes, where in principle all the obligations are clearly spelled out; coercive modes, where services and goods are taken by force or constraint; and gift modes, where things pass in principle with polite ambiguity via networks of reciprocity or outward waves of gratitude.

Now Montaigne knew the world of political gift and favor perfectly: he was a judge, and mayor of Bordeaux, and diplomatic go-between during the Wars of Religion; but in his *Essais,* he rejects that mode. His friendship with his beloved late friend La Boétie[6] is "beyond gifts," so close were they. In more ordinary circumstances, he says he finds the fulsome language accompanying gift presentation and the quest for favor hypocritical. But even more, he doesn't want his conscience to be caught in the unceasing obligations of gratitude and honor that come when one receives a gift. "I'd rather buy a [royal] office than be given one, for buying it, I just give money. In the other case, I give myself." He'd rather be throttled by a notary than by his own conscience. Though Montaigne himself went right ahead in the world of gifting, he put his finger on a major danger of his time.

DC: Yes. I find that, for historians, Montaigne is an extremely difficult writer to decipher, even more than Erasmus.[7] He's in fact the most difficult when writing about the history of subjectivity because his interior life was so complex it could not be readily articulated in thought or words.

NZD: He's an extraordinary figure.

DC: Because he goes right to the edge, to the crisis point of the contradictory, often quite negative tensions that had been worked out and reflected upon in the Christian West since the 1490s, first in Italy then France, the Holy Roman Empire, and England. Montaigne succeeded in "domesticating" these tensions through a sort of experimental method of self-definition, even in the use of paradox or recourse to what resembles, without truly being it, a mode of skepticism. He goes far beyond Calvin and Rabelais in his invention of a conscious reflexivity, always in flux, always in search of its own displacement. Forming identity in the sixteenth century was analogous to the process used in developing a photograph. A person's subjectivity needed some kind of fixing agent. Some found it in the different religious faiths, while others strove to create their own personal systems of belief.

NZD: That's what's so prodigious about him: you think at one moment that you've got completely hold of his thought, and then a minute later, as you read on, he's slipped away and turned the argument on its head. But I think Rabelais is close to his achievement, while choosing another form of fashioning, that is, the comic mode—also elusive but endlessly rich. Between the two of them, the reader is constantly led into new vistas.

DC: There are chameleons who certainly write different chronologies, but who play with this sense of mobility, resorting to techniques where the senses and subjects shift back and forth to better lose the reader in the labyrinth of their writing, who cast a spell over their imaginations, in order to make a person better understand the need to avoid, no matter what, the tyranny of firmly held beliefs.

NZD: I respect them as superb observers of their own times, differing in some ways, alike in others. Whenever I have an idea about something happening in sixteenth-century France, or an interpretation of some event or expression, I run it by Rabelais and Montaigne. Usually I find some sign of what I'm looking for. If I get no whiff of it from them, I'll rethink and recheck what I'm doing—between them, they hardly miss a thing. Since I'm interested in the history of women, I've also put Marguerite de Navarre in that category of privileged witness to her times, not only as a woman observer (albeit highly placed as the sister of King François I[8]), but also as author of a genre in which you hear women and men in discussion. In the *Heptameron,* each story is told by one of her well-born travelers, caught as they are by floods in the Pyrénées. But then each tale is followed by a conversation between the women and men about what they've just heard. They're not in agreement—including the women, who argue among themselves even on such matters as unfaithful husbands. Such debates are not found in Boccaccio's *Decameron*[9] or other earlier collections of tales; Marguerite was the innovator here. She's a terrific witness for the range of attitudes in her day.

DC: This brings us back to the fact that, in the whole history of the sixteenth and seventeenth centuries, which is basically a long shift from unity to division as well as the erection of confessional communities to which men and women end up belonging for better or worse, the historian is almost led to the individual, to a model inherently biographical. From Martin Guerre to the lives of three *Women on the Margin* and Leo Africanus, the individual is there. But is he only there as an animating device because it's easier, in terms of documentation, to recreate a unique experience? Or because, for you, it's an ideal way to reconnoiter a society, its tensions, and its dreams, to investigate those particular places where it's most vivid and establishes a sense of control?

NZD: I do savor the individual persons I write about, but I'm probably more interested in the way the individual life is an opening toward the society around him or her. Even while trying to make everything I've learned about them work for my story, I never have the feeling that I'm writing a *biography.*

DC: Don't you write what I would call reticent biographies in the sense that you only look at your subject from a certain angle, rather than research it in all its fullness and linearity?

NZD: I have enormous respect for the life of my subjects, but my interest in them is always triggered by some prior question that I think I can fathom better through their lives. In a "pure" biography, I believe there's a quest for exhaustiveness, with the stages of life itself the central narrative thread. Even in my *Women on the Margins,* where I tried to find everything about the women's lives from birth to death, I was using the lives to illustrate varieties of women's experience and adventure. With Judge Jean de Coras, I put what I discovered about him—his intellectual precocity, his movement into the world of ennobled judges, his attraction to Protestantism, and his affectionate relations with his wife—to work for matters of identity: that is, the possibility of his drawing some resonance from the imposture of the talented peasant Arnaud du Tilh and Arnaud's intimacy with Bertrande de Rols for his own self-fashioning. As for al-Wazzān, whom I'm writing about right now, any scrap I find about his life is precious, but it and the extensive manuscripts I have located are especially being used to explore how a person moves between cultural worlds.

DC: But shouldn't we turn the problem around? Wouldn't "true" biography disclaim to be totalizing, that it would instead strive to be abiographical in the sense that it would eschew any linear or integrative goal?

NZD: I'm not one to pronounce on a single correct form for writing a life. The classic biography itself ordinarily has an interpretive edge, and it is surely better when it's acknowledged. The main thing is to encourage a range of writing about lives and to welcome new forms.

DC: Why then have you gone outside the French framework?

NZD: It was my work on the Amerindians of Québec, whom Marie de l'Incarnation wanted to convert, and the African and Indian slaves of Suriname, whom Maria Sibylla Merian used as her helpers and informants in her search for insects and plants, that set me off in this direction. At the same time I was writing that book, I was reading scholars in postcolonial countries, especially India. They were pointing out that the new national histories being written there remained "European," even though their cast of characters were Indians and the narrative thread was the quest for and achievement of independence. The histories, it was claimed, were still using the same categories, posing the same questions, using the same frames as European and North American historians. Now all this suggested to me that I try for a real shift in my consciousness. I was telling my story from the point of view of these European women, and I wanted at least for some pages to see the whole thing from the non-European point of view, indeed, even imagine non-European forms of narration.

I participated recently in a colloquium with Dipesh Chakrabarty, one of the founders of the school of Subaltern Studies in India.[10] He has taught in India and Australia and is now a professor at the University of Chicago. In his book *Provincializing Europe: Postcolonial Thought and Historical Difference,* which appeared in 2000, he shows the limits of European historical thought, especially in regard to the use of its ideas of "modernity" as a system of universal description. The European model for modernization is taken as the standard, and other countries' history is written—including by historians within that country—in terms of "catch-up" or "not-yet." Europe always gets there first. Chakrabarty acknowledges willingly the importance of European historical philosophers for his own thinking—including Karl Marx on capital—but challenges their claim to universality. They must be reconsidered and reformulated in terms of experiences elsewhere. He even raises the question of different modes for extracting evidence and acknowledging truth that grow out of the Indian experience and that are at odds with Western systems of social science.

It's a very interesting book, and my own earlier work on the European subaltern classes—artisans, printing workers, peasants, women—prepared me for his approach. I had already taken issue with the assessment of charivaris and journeymen's *compagnonnages* [associations] as simply pre-political forms that needed to catch up to be meaningful—rather than understanding how they worked in their own day and noting how they continued as a mode of relevant action. And I've already mentioned my critique of evolutionary theories about the Reformation. So I felt I had started out on Chakrabarty's route. When I told him this, he laughed and said once again, I was claiming that the West got there first. Anyway, from his perspective, it's not enough simply to add non-European or non-Western countries to the agenda: we must decenter the West—make it one example among many as a pattern of change—and enlarge our field of vision to include categories and modes of thought used by people in these other lands. It's very difficult, but that's what I mean when I say that I no longer feel myself a "historian of Europe." The transformation is in the way one locates oneself: even when I'm writing about Europe, I try not to perceive myself as centered in Europe. Rather I locate myself sometimes close to Europe, sometimes far from Europe.

DC: **How do you think you can acquire or fashion the tools necessary to illuminate this dual perspective?**

NZD: Of course, that's the major problem, including all the languages and other background one must acquire. One can't just suddenly become a master of all learning, especially when you're as old as I am. We all have our limits, but still we must do as much as we can, and use translations if that's all that's possible.

DC: **Aren't translations already directed to alter this exterior aspect as a result of linguistic bias? What you propose is attractive, but the tools that you use are fragile, no? Wouldn't you lapse into a false comforting myth to believe you can slip into the worldview of another? Even words are the enemies of such epistemological projects, aren't they?**

NZD: Surely, one must be wary of translations, and we hear many warnings about the "violence" that translations can do to a text. I've felt this acutely in my current research on al-Wazzān. To start with, I've followed his repeated struggle with Italian words as he tried to describe his North African world to Europeans: for instance, he ended up using "*sacerdote*" or "priest" for "*imam,*" which gives the wrong impression of the role of the Muslim leader who directs men in prayer. I've learned to recognize Arabic letters and individual words and have a good Arabic-English dictionary always at hand; but for the most part I depend on translators and translations. Most of al-Wazzān's writings are in Italian or Latin, else I would not have taken him on. But to read the books he read and cited and the authors and texts that shaped his vision, I have depended on translations—which are fortunately very plentiful. The great Orientalists of the past have done their work, especially in France, and today there are multilingual people from Arab lands preparing translations in English and French. Once I get hold of a reliable translation, made by someone close to the culture, I use it as a model for others. At the very least, these translations serve as an entry into the worlds in which the original works were once written. One reads them knowing one's limitations and reminds oneself how difficult it is "to slip into the worldview of another." We know that it's already difficult enough to do this for sixteenth-century France!

One of the best ways to face this difficulty is through collective work with historians from other backgrounds—that is, to read their accounts of their own lands and of our lands and to collaborate with them in different forms. Let me give an example of a book that I thought a very good start, though it needed to go farther to live up to Chakrabarty's criteria. When I was in Tokyo in 1997, I visited the museum of the Edo dynasty. It's an immense and wonderful museum, where among other things a whole quarter for printing and bookselling has been recreated. I immediately thought of the printing industry in our France, the printer's quarter of Lyon in the sixteenth and seventeenth centuries. Then I went to a performance of Kabuki theatre, and besides marveling at it from start to finish, I thought of Molière,[11] especially during the comic interludes—though, of course, there were differences as well. Upon my return to North America, I came across a recent book, *Edo and Paris: Urban Life and the State in the Early Modern Era,* an excellent collection of essays by historians from the United States, France, and Japan making the precise comparison between Edo Japan of the seventeenth century and the France of Louis XIV.[12] In terms of country, the West was not given pride of place; both histories were treated with respect. But the problematic of the book, the questions posed, seemed all to emerge from the historiography of France in the seventeenth century: the organization of government, resistance to government. Edo Japan was presented according to that problematic. I wondered what would happen if some of the questions structuring the book, both the presentation of Japan and France, had emerged from writing and perception distinctive first to Japan. For instance, Japanese literature and woodcuts of the Edo period offer a fascinating portrait of what is called "the floating world"—a world gravitating around artists, geishas, theatres, intellectuals. What if you started off with the questions inspired by the floating world? That problematic generated by the Japanese experience and writing might lead to new insight into urban life and politics.

DC: But at the same time, don't you believe that the Western way of writing history has changed a lot, and extremely quickly, and can despite all its shortcomings continue to change? Don't you consider it possible that this kind of history can serve as a tool to unlock mysteries that the Japanese or Indians, for example, wouldn't even be aware of but for the influence on them of the English, French, and American schools of historiography? We

can no longer put our heads in the sand. Aren't the multiple methods of understanding identity from a historical standpoint that you call for a by-product of this same Western historiography due to its inherently critical stance? Wouldn't this all in the end simply be a hermeneutical illusion?

NZD: Of course, Western historiography has changed in many directions, and I'm not in any sense speaking against the central rules of my craft or its potential for continuing growth in research strategies and narrative expressiveness. And, of course, non-Western scholars have learned from our schools of historical scholarship, in some cases while receiving their doctoral training in Europe or North America. Chakrabarty expresses his gratitude to David Hume,[13] Hegel,[14] and Heidegger,[15] along with Marx. But some of the transformations in Western historiography have come precisely through the experience of conquest and the histories of colonized peoples, and from contact with non-Western traditions and scholars from non-Western countries. The exchange of "tools to unlock mysteries" is two-way.

DC: It's always been cross-fertilized. Xenophon[16] and Thucydides[17] always exercised a powerful influence over Roman history, and this cross-fertilization in Greco-Roman history has, in turn, influenced the writing of history in the Renaissance...

NZD: Cultural mixture, intellectual *métissage,* has a long history behind it. In recent decades, there was a period where this side of encounters between colonized people and the colonizers or between conquered peoples and their conquerors was downplayed in favor of theories of incomprehensibility and opacity. One focused on violence and resistance, but not exchange or crossovers. And yet violence itself is a form of communication. Ideas, objects, languages, customs get picked up, adapted, and transformed, even in the most tragic of circumstances. The historian should be attentive to relations of power and relations of exchange both.

Chakrabarty makes one critique of universal theories that I don't think is fruitful for cross-fertilization in historical practice. It has to do with systems of proof in Western historiography: he challenges the universal application of "scientific" and "rational" methods of proof, and argues for the coexistence of "rational" and "magical" paths to proof. Now as choice for personal life, let it happen; I'm not addressing that here. As a path to establishing truth for, say, healers, from shamanic to psychoanalytic, fine—there are different languages and intuitions, and "truth" can be arrived at in various ways, especially if the healer knows his or her community or subject well.

But for *historians trying to find agreement about our craft*, I don't think it's good advice. I say this even while being fully in accord with Steven Shapin's[18] views on the social factors that shape acceptance of "truth" in science, and with due recognition of the power of accepted paradigms in persuading us what's "true" in a given situation. Historians throughout the world can extend our notions ever wider about what constitutes sources or objects or evidence from the past and how to interpret them—including magical practices; we can argue about what the evidence means, we can carry along different interpretations about, say, the spread of slavery and many other disagreements, but we should have a common *goal* in regard to how we might accept a conclusion as established. If you say, "I want to establish a picture here through the incidence of legal prohibitions," and I say, "I want to establish a picture here through marriage patterns," we have a common language to use to argue about it. We may not agree, but we still seek common rules for how to prove a historical case that allows the argument to go on. If you affirm you have a form of proof from a realm into which I cannot enter (your special "magic" as compared to our shared "reason"), then there's no ground for us to debate as historians.

DC: Don't you think that, despite all this, we still come close to the edge of an abyss? History as it's generally developed to the present day has often wanted to be, often without always declaring it overtly, a school of freedom. It's a school because the historian exercises her critical freedom to seek understanding, that is, to make and unmake the past. She knows she should strive to stifle in herself every tendency to be reductive, to simplify, or to overly generalize. It's a school because, as you've said, it's always necessary to seek out new methods of questioning the past. It thus relies on a logic that refuses to accept received opinions, definitions, and goals. It's not all positive on the outside. I think about what can happen today in certain Muslim countries where history cannot be written except along prescribed theological and teleological lines, where anything can be said so long as it conforms to this preordained way of thinking, even to the point of using the *Protocols of the Elders of Zion*[19] as a way to prove one's case... Can't another's different way of looking at history thus be more troubling than stimulating, or isn't it at least becoming so? Wouldn't we

therefore run a risk if we wished to think like a different person?

NZD: From what I've just said, it's clear that I'm advocating critical freedom in researching and writing about the past. And learning about various forms of popular or polemical writing about the past—which we see in textbooks all over the world and which provides us evidence for, say, political movements and governmental policy—is not the same thing as taking seriously the different forms of historical thought generated in different cultures. In the same Arab lands where some extremists are using the forged *Protocols of the Elders of Zion* to make outrageous claims, important new conceptualizations are emerging about the late medieval philosopher Ibn Khaldun;[20] just as in Israel, where extremists are claiming that the Jews have always had the legal right to the land from the Jordan River to the sea since God gave it to them, innovative writing is being done about forms of religious exchange among Jews, Christians, and Muslims in the medieval and modern period.

Let me give another example of the difference between a historical source and a historical proof. Chakrabarty discusses the role that dreams have in India as proof. In fact, dreams have played such a role in many other settings. The Indians of North America took their dreams seriously as a form of reality and as carriers of commands for their future actions. Jewish and Christian prophets used them in a similar way. The boundary between a dream and a vision was porous. The dreams certainly provide a way to talk about the self and the world, and Jean-Claude Schmitt has shown us beautifully how we can use them as sources for medieval discourse.

To give another example that comes to my mind as we speak: in the history of American memoirs written by slaves or former slaves, there are relatively few writings that give much full detail on the Middle Passage, the Atlantic crossing between Africa and the Americas and the Caribbean. The suffering was immense, as we know from other sources (boat lists, captains' journals, and the like): with many deaths, desperation, degradation, sometimes uprisings—an experience of trauma. In the nineteenth century, that experience was more often expressed through dance, legends, songs, and stories, animal tales. It was Toni Morrison,[21] the great novelist, who first talked to me about this; her novel *Beloved* was partly a symbolization of the Middle Passage, as the mysterious Beloved emerges out of the sea with strange memories. But earlier, in his 1953 novel *In the Castle of My Skin,* the Barbadian writer George Lamming[22] broached the

Middle Passage through an old man talking in his sleep. After World War II, the Afro-American poet Robert Hayden[23] interspersed poems about the Holocaust with those about the Middle Passage.

So here we have an important body of sources, including dreams and dance, that can be explicated to understand the impact of slavery, traces of the past, and expressions of sensibility. We use them as such.

DC: It's what poets known as the *grands rhétoriqueurs* did at the end of the fifteenth and the early sixteenth centuries. They told a story by turning it into a dream. For example, a funeral lament for the Constable de Bourbon[24] became thus recast after his death before the walls of Rome for his sister, the Duchess of Lorraine.[25] As the story went, the chronicler, while dozing in his bed (evidently, it's a convenient fiction), dreamed that the recently deceased constable came to him covered with luminous, brilliant jewels. One dream arises out of another, since the chronicler's own dream enabled him to enter into the supposedly "real" dream about the life and afterlife of the dead hero. Life returns and everything happens in such a way that what the constable couldn't express while alive now becomes distinct the moment he ceased to exist. The Constable de Bourbon tells the chronicler, in effect, that after his death he was led away by Mercury, the symbol of reason and language, to hell. But this hell is not the hell of Virgil[26] or Dante[27] but rather a succession of desolate places with hideous old women who represent worldly sins, such as envy, avarice, and so on. Charles III of Bourbon descends all the way to the cave of Pluto, king of the underworld. It's there that the literary strategy of the false dream becomes interesting. In reality, Bourbon presents here his description of François I's court, a place of vice and passion. His dream is a huge allegory about why he left the court and why he refused to remain obedient to his king and instead joined the service of Charles V.[28] He wanted to become the man who refused to submit to passion, the pure man who resisted all compromises in order to obey God. Next, after his journey to these dark, dank, and noisy reaches ended, he came to the Island of the Fortunate in the middle of the Atlantic Ocean where he was welcomed by the Famous Lady who promoted him to become her lieutenant for all eternity. The dream allowed the poet to make sense of a make-believe purity that would have ruled the constable's life, to almost make live again the truth of a person's inner self haunted by the search for an honor that derived from the will to obey God, to accomplish his designs. But this inner self would not have spoken of it, because a gentleman in the Renaissance speaks by his actions and not his words. Thus, the techniques of writing or rather the revealing of history through a dream became bound up in certain moments with historiography... But we're in the literary realm of a made-up dream, for sure.

NZD: A splendid tale: your poet/chronicler constructs a dream setting in which an allegorical interpretation of the Constable de Bourbon's actions is put into the constable's mouth. And you and I can take it seriously as a sixteenth-century *source* and discuss the constable through its lens.

DC: Just as dance is a theatrical allegory, the dream itself takes form through a succession of allegories. But, as I've indicated, here we're dealing with a kind of writing whose main conventions depict the dream as a means of transference in the psychoanalytical sense. The deceased person returns and articulates what he could not say during his life through the power of the chronicler who dreamed of him. We're now dealing with a system of multilayered representations in 1527, the year this funeral lament was composed, in which the subject, even when living, was not supposed to speak about himself or even have others speak on his behalf. It thus fell to the chronicler, through whom the subject returned to fashion, in this dreamlike fiction, the final verdict about himself. It's all a game that plays with the truth and reality established by the dream, a game of illusions in which the ego cannot be realized through its own voice but rather only by the intervention of another person... But the truth and reality of people in the sixteenth century is not the same as those of historians in the early twenty-first century! Individual identity comes through the discourse of another person and history thus obeys particular constraints. It's by another person that one can begin to come into touch with oneself, that the other person is the central vector for self-fashioning. The "proof" thus acquires a specific status...

NZD: I surely agree that the "truth and reality of people in the sixteenth century" are not the same as they are for us historians at the opening of the twenty-first century. We must develop the best methods we can, stretch our scholarship and imagination to be able to discover, understand, and describe their sense of "the true and the real." But we must not abandon our practices of proof. We can be open to new definitions of what constitutes a proof, but we must stay faithful to the ideal of proof, that is, to the ideal possibility—always receding, never fully achieved—of forms of common knowledge in this world of differences, a shared knowledge. If you had a dream that the Constable de Bourbon had spoken to you, it would give me knowledge about you, but I'd want a sixteenth-century source for further knowledge about him. The imaginary dialogue that opens my *Women on the Margins* was to give my readers information about me and a chance to reflect on my intentions; it might lead my readers to think a little about my three women, but it offered no *proof* about them.

DC: But from this perspective, your method always remains trapped by the idea that, in a given society, prevailing verities matter less when explaining change than the questions that often arise along that society's margins. These questions may be dimly evident at the time and only become more crucial much later on. Isn't the historian's quandary to investigate questions that become more essential, even in an ontological sense, the more they seem peripheral and lacking significance to mainstream historical approaches? Doesn't the historian have to accept, sometimes by seeming to be naïve, to work on subjects that lack historical determinacy but that still can, despite their hidden or misleading nature, open up the critical places and moments when an entire era and society changes?

NZD: Sometimes you can find revelation at the margins, sometimes at the center, sometimes in "subjects that lack historical determinacy" (whatever you mean by them), sometimes in subjects classically clear. It depends on the historian, the sources sought, the interpretations put to work. To me an important entry into a period is through its arguments and debates, the unresolved questions that keep being tossed about, the issues on which a consensus seems impossible. Central conflicts or axial debates are great markers or signposts for a period. For the Old Regime in France, it has seemed to me that a central debate, one that stirred up passions and arguments for three or four centuries, was whether one advanced in the world by merit, personal qualities, and virtue; or by friendship and favor, important people you knew; or simply by purchasing advance, buying it. I followed this especially in regard to the argument about royal offices, when I was working on gifts, but the argument goes well beyond offices. It reached out to many other areas, symbolic and social. You can see the connection with religious conflict: how do you advance in God's eyes?

I don't think we formulate the issue today in these early modern terms, or at least, I don't think it's as central, as axial. For early modern

France, rather than saying "this is a society that believed absolutely in hierarchy and was founded upon it," you could say "this is a society for which the central question was quarreling about hierarchy." Central disagreements are a good way to characterize a society or a time period.

This recalls a disagreement I had with Michel Foucault.[29] Clearly there's much we all drew from his writings, but I was not in accord with his concept of an unconscious and consensual episteme on which every period is based and that he as a philosopher somehow could extract and describe. (He just gave examples from western Europe, of course.) I raised this question in a talk at a memorial service for him at NYU right after he died, even while speaking of him with admiration and affection. To give one example, if you looked at how some women wrote about ways of knowing and ways of ordering in the seventeenth century, you'd find profoundly divergent views expressed from those he saw as epistemic. There are always these deep discords; the "unity" comes from being bound together in an argument. I've even wondered about this in regard to Thomas Kuhn's celebrated paradigms, which, to be sure, he limited to the way knowledge moves in the history of science.[30] But even there, I've wondered whether there aren't always serious disagreements pushing at the edges of paradigms or gnawing from within, and whether the force of the paradigm and its potential for change doesn't come from an ever-present simmering discord rather than a sudden breakdown when the paradigm is perceived to have lost its explanatory power.

I suppose these views of mine are part of my habits developed when I began as a student of the lower orders. Even when there are issues on which everyone seems in agreement and even though there is exchange across the lines of social class, conflicts and contestation persist. And I suppose, too, that this habit of looking for points of difference goes back to my girlhood as a Jew in a world where I shared many of the views, practices, and customs of those around me, but still felt that I was positioned in it differently and had my own critical views. Perhaps this youthful experience predisposed me to expect that not everyone was in agreement with a seemingly dominant view and that one should seek the points of friction.

DC: Did this critical dissent you felt only focus on the Jewish middle class to which you belonged, or did it have other targets?

NZD: [*laughter*] There was, indeed, a Jewish middle class, a Jewish bourgeoisie, in Detroit, whose penchant for speaking mostly about automobiles or clothing and the like led me to critical dissent. But here I was speaking of the impact of a larger experience: that of being Jewish in a community that was primarily Christian and with which I did not see eye-to-eye. This kind of experience prepares the way for a different perception from that of Foucault, who, except perhaps in his last work on sexuality in antiquity, focused so on the principle of domination that he lost sight in his writing—if not in his actual life—of the facts of resistance, of a refusal ever to bend.

DC: In these acts of resistance, these refusals of the conscience, you seem to distinguish two forms: first a theatrical one that is open, violent, collective, and another made up of processes revolving around symbols, which can go from a burning desire to write to adopting alienated yet highly singular modes of behavior...

NZD: Yes, I make the distinction between outer social forms of resistance and those that are interior or particular to the individual life. And thinking of the interior life, I'd make the same suggestion about it as I have about historical periods. Rather than always looking for the way power and domination are reinscribed in the individual consciousness the way Foucault does, I think we should look for subjective conflicts. Because we certainly have subjective conflicts. [*laughter*] Rather than seeking the overall unity in a life, we can see it as marked by interior conflict—sometimes unresolved until death. Surely that's the drama in the lives of great spiritual figures.

DC: They remain almost attached to the self. Even among those who appear to have realized a way of living that gives them the greatest stability, the greatest assurance. Calvin would attest to it, for the reformer compared himself to a vigilant sentinel watching to prevent the faithful from succumbing to the repeated assaults of Satan, ceaselessly denouncing the sins that could return in them, speaking and writing ferociously against vice. Calvin thus lived a life of obsessive struggle, committed before God never to bend, never to stop speaking out. Calvin was almost tragically forced to surrender every moment of his life, from early morning to late at night, to the apostolic mission he knew God had willed for him, to never interrupt his watch. Calvin, who seemed intensely strong, exclusive, even totalitarian—if I may use that anachronistic term—and who hid his immense fragility, his anxiety that became all the more tragic because it concerned not only his own salvation, but that of the new children of Israel

called by God, after centuries of corruption of the faith, to return to him. But didn't these debates he had with himself, consciously or not, shape his entire life because they remained unresolved? Aren't contradiction and the questions it raised in the sixteenth century, beyond even what Lucien Febvre wrote about them as instruments rather than urges to understand and to know, the sources of the self's creative energy and thus the motor force of history? This question of creative energy goes right to the heart, in my opinion, of an analysis centered on individual existence. What is it that makes a person act, think, and escape the confines of thought and action in which he or she is supposed to remain? And this in the sixteenth and seventeenth centuries, to remain in the time period you prefer?

NZD: I very much like what you say about creative energy and innovation having its source in inner conflict. It's hard to give a general theory about what makes a person escape the confines of thought and action in which they're supposed to remain. Whenever I've come across this in the figures I've written about—and they mostly end up escaping some kind of confine—I've tried to look for a conjuncture between cultural resources around them from which they could draw and elements in their own life or situation that allowed or encouraged a creative use of those resources.

You refer in passing to Lucien Febvre's writings about what was possible and impossible to think in sixteenth-century notions of God and the universe. I've actually given some thought to conflicts and creative energy in Lucien Febvre's own life and also in that of Marc Bloch. I wrote about how they tried to situate themselves both at the creative margins and the powerful center, to think of new directions from both positions. In some ways I think it's true of me as well, a back and forth between margin and center. This is a psychological state that is both fruitful and uncertain.

DC: My question is perhaps absurd: would you prefer Lucien Febvre or Marc Bloch? You have been a bit hard on Lucien Febvre... I have myself always been very skeptical when reading Lucien Febvre, who has seemed to me, since my student days, to have become less readable over the years and weighed down more by a somewhat turgid, dated style. Moreover, people suspected his ambivalence toward Marc Bloch during the war or even the nastiness that often came through in his writings, a nastiness that I now actually find fairly refreshing... When re-reading him, I ask myself if Febvre's position can't be explained by identifying him with his subjects,

Rabelais and then Erasmus, if in fact he didn't become another Erasmus or Rabelais by refusing to enter the fray, by preferring to work for the survival of intelligence in barbarous times, by preferring thus to write and join in another kind of possible resistance.

NZD: My personal identification, as I suggested earlier, is with Marc Bloch, but I've tried to understand both men and their goals. Febvre wanted to be a fighter and saw himself as such, a strong fighter for cultural reform. He was not a megalomaniac, but some of his projects were grandiose. On the one hand, his book on Martin Luther was truly innovative when he published it in 1928, as I mentioned earlier—trying to *understand* Luther in a German urban milieu. And his *Problème de l'incroyance au XVIe siècle* (*The Problem of Unbelief in the Sixteenth Century*), published first in 1942, right in the midst of the German Occupation, was very important. It's true that he underestimated the possibilities for denying the presence of God in the sixteenth century, but his effort to paint the mental universe of sixteenth-century people and their categories for understanding the world was pioneering. He opened a historical-anthropological route for inquiry. On the other hand, his tone became pompous, and a project like the *Encylopédie,* which he started with Anatole de Monzie[31] to synthesize all human knowledge, was grandiose.[32]

DC: It's somewhat maddening that he wasted his time in this almost mystical endeavor and that he did not write the other volumes of *L'Évolution de l'humanité* that he had envisioned...

NZD: I see two sides to Lucien Febvre. The first, the *Encylopédie,* founded in 1932 under the aegis of Monzie, the Minister of National Education, an effort to reform culture from the center. The second, the *Annales,* co-founded in 1929 with Marc Bloch, an audacious and innovative periodical, which provided a genuine challenge from the margins. Regarding his conduct during the Occupation, I think he was sincere in believing that "one must keep a French voice alive" during the German Occupation through publishing the *Annales,* even if it meant removing the name of the Jewish Marc Bloch from the cover: it was a way to show that the Germans had not succeeded in silencing the French. And after much disagreement between the two men, Bloch finally agreed and, as I was able to show from Bloch's correspondence, Bloch even said that the *Annales* issues being published during the Occupation were "a fine success" ("un beau succès"). Articles by Bloch were published under a pseudonym, and he sometimes blew his cover by referring to his own *Feudal Society*. But for Bloch, this was not the only way to oppose the Germans and he finally became part of the Resistance. Febvre was more timid. He liked to think of himself as a fighter and he had ambitious ideas, but he was also very prudent and fearful...

DC: He was, we mustn't hesitate to say, a true believer that history was a science that enabled a person not only to think about himself in terms of his past, but also to gain gradual access to an idea of universality that transcended violence and strife. Does this mystical dimension account for this ambivalence?

NZD: Possibly that's a key. In his *Problème de l'incroyance,* Febvre presented an Erasmian defense of keeping quiet when necessary and of adapting one's expression to the necessities of a situation of repression—as the Erasmians and Rabelais had done in the sixteenth century, so he believed, and as he liked to think of himself as doing during the Occupation.[33] But this didn't come without some inner turmoil for him. Also his personal life was full of conflict: his romantic affair with the refugee historian Lucie Varga and his efforts to make it up with his wife, to whom in 1944 he dedicated his book on Marguerite de Navarre's *Heptameron,* a gift to ask for forgiveness.[34] And I think he was truly torn apart by Marc Bloch's death at the hands of the Nazis. There were so many years of friendship between them: one can see it in their correspondence, those letters of friendship, sometimes teasing, but honest. He surely took Marc Bloch's death as a hero of the Resistance as a kind of reproach to himself, to his own claimed "Erasmian path." Lucien Febvre was a human being with his weaknesses and his strengths. Bloch is easier to admire: he had fewer pretensions, was enormously creative, found a way to resist after he was banned from teaching as a Jew. Febvre was professor at the Collège de France to the end.

DC: Febvre truly had a sense of mission that recalls the mission of the religious reformers in the sixteenth century...

NZD: But it was an intellectual mission—through the writing of history, to which he may have given a more grandiose role than history books can play by themselves.

DC: Yes, we discover in him a form of language that's almost mystical, or at least idealistic. The speech he gave in 1941 to the École normale supérieure on the Rue d'Ulm is over the top—when we look at it today—in its enthusiasm for history. It's history that will save the world from its difficulties, horrors, and conflicts. And when he founded the *Cahiers d'histoire mondiale* in 1953, which seemed like the beginning of a new idea of history, the notion that guides him is still that of humanity's future reconciliation ...

NZD: Whereas in 1940, following his military service, Bloch wrote *Strange Defeat* (*L'Étrange Défaite*)—a work oriented toward practice and action, a realistic analysis of why France had lost so easily to the Germans.

DC: While Febvre never literally spoke of defeat, he spoke about misfortunes that were shattering and tragic. Wouldn't he have assumed an Erasmian stance in order to avoid talking about what really happened?

NZD: Erasmus himself wrote directly on political matters: think of his writing on peace and the satire of his *Praise of Folly*. Febvre was certainly very interested in current politics, but it is not centered in his writing, even in his correspondence. In his book on Rabelais, Febvre praised the prudence of the Erasmians of the 1550s, who knew how to be quiet when necessary and, when possible, expressed critical ideas in ways that could get by the censors. I think that's what he thought he was doing during the Occupation.

DC: At the same time, the *Cahiers d'histoire mondiale* became conceived as a laboratory that could create the conditions for peace among the people of the world, which thus elevated history into a discourse about peace ...

NZD: In that sense Febvre was following an Erasmian hope, but he never had Erasmus's sense of humor.

DC: That's why we must, in the end, read and re-read Febvre more than one does today. You've shown the reasons why, in his case, we must avoid the risks of overstatement. He can serve for us as a transition point insofar as he was the sort of individual historian who assumes the identity of the past he studies and writes about when, say, dealing with Erasmus or Rabelais, and because he confronted the demands of his own times by using these historical figures as his models. He understood them so much better because he leaned on them when analyzing them.

Notes

1. Pico della Mirandola (1463-94) was an Italian Renaissance philosopher best known for the work referenced here, *The Oration on the Dignity of Man* (1486).

2. "God's wrath is upon us."

3. The Catholic Holy League was a major faction in the French Wars of Religion (1561-98) formed by Duke Henry of Guise (1550-88) in 1576 to oppose the spread of Calvinism in France.

4. For example, Todd Endelman, *Radical Assimilation in English Jewish History, 1656–1945* (1990); Elisheva Carlebach, *Divided Souls: Converts from Judaism in Germany, 1500–1700* (2001); and Deborah Hertz, *How Jews Became Germans* (2007).

5. Teresa of Avila (1515-82), born into a Jewish *converso* family, was a prominent Spanish mystic and reformer of the Carmelite Order. Author of the widely read autobiography, *Libro de la Vida,* she was canonized as a saint in 1622.

6. Étienne de La Boétie (1530-63) was a French judge and political philosopher who wrote the *Discourse on Voluntary Servitude* in the early 1550s, but it did not appear in print until 1576.

7. Desiderius Erasmus (1466/69-1536) was born in the Netherlands and became the greatest figure in Christian humanism in the sixteenth century, writing on religious reform and doctrine, literature and language, moral conduct, peace and social welfare among other contributions.

8. François I (1494-1547) is considered France's first Renaissance king. He patronized the arts, initiated new building projects across the kingdom, and challenged the Hapsburgs for domination in western Europe.

9. Giovanni Boccaccio (1313-75) was an early Italian Renaissance humanist and writer whose works include the *Decameron,* a collection of tales completed around 1353.

10. Dipesh Chakrabarty (1948-) is a historian, born in Bengal and now teaching in the United States, who has made major contributions to the field of postcolonial studies. Subaltern theory developed in the 1970s and focuses on the historical experiences and perceptions of persons who are politically, culturally, and geographically outside the dominant power structures.

11. Molière was the stage name for Jean-Baptiste Poquelin (1622-73). He was a French playwright and actor best known for his satirical comedies performed in Paris and other French cities and at the court of Louis XIV.

12. John L. McClain, John M. Merriman, and Ugawa Kaoru, eds., *Edo and Paris: Urban Life and the State in the Early Modern Era* (1997).

13. David Hume (1711-76) was a Scottish philosopher and major figure in the Enlightenment who expressed profound skepticism about the power of reason to provide knowledge about human experience.

14. Georg Wilhelm Friedrich Hegel (1770-1831) was a prominent German philosopher and one of the creators of German Idealism who developed a comprehensive philosophical system predicated on the notion of dialectical change.

15. Martin Heidegger (1889-1976) was an influential German philosopher known for revisionist work on the question of being (ontology) and phenomenology.

16. Xenophon (430-354 BCE) was a soldier and admirer of Socrates who composed histories of his own time based on his personal experiences.

17. Thucydides (460-395 BCE) was an Athenian general and pioneering historian who wrote *History of the Peloponnesian War.*

18. Steven Shapin (1943-) is a historian and sociologist of science. His works include *A Social History of Truth: Civility and Science in Seventeenth-Century England* (1994) and *The Scientific Life: A Moral History of a Late Modern Vocation* (2008).

19. The *Protocols of the Elders of Zion* is an anti-Semitic literary forgery that first appeared in print in Russia in 1903 and purported to present a Jewish plan to take over the world.

20. Ibn Khaldun (1332-1406) was a learned Islamic scholar and jurist, whose most important work was a world history entitled *The Book of Examples.* Its opening volume is the *Muqaddimah* (known as the *Prolegomenon* in the West).

21. Toni Morrison (1931-) is a major American writer and professor who won the Nobel Prize

in Literature in 1993. Her book *Beloved* was published in 1987 and won the Pulitzer Prize for Fiction.

22. George Lamming (1927–) is a novelist and poet from Barbados who has lived in England and the United States. *In the Castle of My Skin* was the first of the seven books he wrote.

23. Robert Hayden (1913–80) was an American poet, essayist, and educator named Poet Laureate by Congress in 1976. His poem "Middle Passage" was inspired by the events surrounding the *United States* v. *The Amistad* affair in 1841. Among his most prominent poems on the Holocaust is "From the Corpse Woodpiles, from the Ashes" (*Poems* 46).

24. Charles III, Duke of Bourbon (1490–1527), was appointed constable by King François I in 1515 but later defied the king by entering the service of his enemy, Emperor Charles V. See Denis Crouzet, *Charles de Bourbon, connétable de France* (2003), and Vincent J. Pitt, *The Man Who Sacked Rome: Charles de Bourbon, Constable of France* (1994).

25. His sister was actually Louise, Duchess of Montpensier (1482–1561).

26. Publius Vergilius Maro or Virgil (70–19 BCE) was a classical Roman poet best known for his works the *Ecologues,* the *Georgics,* and the *Aeneid.* Virgil describes hell in book 6 of the *Aeneid.*

27. Dante Alighieri (1265–1321) was an Italian poet of the Middle Ages known best for his *Divine Comedy,* book 1 of which is the *Inferno.*

28. Charles V (1500–58) was the leader of the Hapsburg dynasty, ruling the Holy Roman Empire from 1519 and the Spanish realms from 1516 until his abdication in 1556.

29. Michel Foucault (1926–84) was a French philosopher, sociologist, and historian known for his critical studies of social institutions, such as hospitals and prisons, as forms of knowledge and control, and the history of sexuality. His theory of the episteme is developed in *Les mots et les choses* (1966), translated into English as *The Order of Things: An Archaeology of the Human Sciences* (1970).

30. Thomas Kuhn (1922–96) was trained as a physicist and became a leading historian of science. His argument that science undergoes periodic revolutions or paradigm shifts is set forth in his book, *The Structure of Scientific Revolutions* (1962).

31. Anatole de Monzie (1876–1947) was a French politician and scholar involved in education reform. He served as minister of education from 1932 to 1938, and had a controversial role during the Vichy government of the early 1940s.

32. Febvre and Monzie began work on the *Encyclopédie française* in 1932. It eventually appeared in print in twenty volumes between 1935 and 1966.

33. An English translation appeared as *The Problem of Unbelief in the Sixteenth Century: The Religion of Rabelais* (1985).

34. Lucie Varga (1904–41) was a historian and ethnographer. Born in Austria into a Jewish family, she took refuge in France in the mid-1930s as anti-Semitism rose. She worked on the rise of National Socialism in Germany and Austria, and was the first woman to be published in the journal *Annales.* The full title of Febvre's book is *Autour de l'Heptaméron: Amour sacré, amour profane* (1944). Febvre's wife was Suzanne Dognon, a former student he met as a young instructor in Strasbourg. They married in 1921. See Natalie Zemon Davis, "Women and the World of the *Annales,*" *History Workshop Journal* 33 (1992): 121–37.

Chapter 4

Memories

DC: You earlier emphasized that your familial, religious, and social origins have all shaped the course of your intellectual life, and you've said you remain quite attached to all of them. Does your past explain for you why you look at history in certain ways? Can you now reconstruct your family tree, beyond what personal memories and what others have told you, because I've read that secrets were hidden from you during your childhood? Your mother spoke Yiddish so you couldn't understand her.

NZD: I come from a family of immigrants. I belong to the third, or in one instance, the fourth generation. Mine is a typically North American story. The grandparents and parents don't speak of their past, or if they do, it's only among themselves, not to the next generation. Letters arrive from Europe written in Cyrillic or Hebrew characters, which the children couldn't read ... In my family, there was no tradition of telling stories about their past in the old country or even about the first years of their arrival in the United States. Today, when so many families are seeking roots, that may no longer be the case. But for my own generation and that right after mine, when the Holocaust complicated everything, one often had to seek the family's past or pasts by oneself.

DC: Wouldn't the mystery of this past have directed you toward the historical profession and have given you this method of questioning that always seeks to unlock other enigmas?

NZD: My turn to history may have been partly due to the sense of being deprived of a concrete past. My ancestors arrived in America in the nineteenth century, one branch in the middle of the century, the rest toward the end. And because we were Jews, the history of America that I learned at school did not seem my history. Although I'm American, it nonetheless seemed the history of others. [*laughter*] I learned my family history only later, little by little, and some I've discovered only recently as the cousins on both sides piece the story together.

On my father's side, I have ancestors who came to Michigan from northeastern Poland a few years after the Civil War. Who knows why? Probably there was someone in their town who had already come to Michigan... Whatever the case, by the 1870s Solomon Goldman moved from Detroit with his wife, Gussie, to Elk Rapids, Michigan. Elk Rapids is not exactly a household name in France or even in the United States: European settlers arrived to live there among the Ontario Indians around 1850 and, located in the midst of the Michigan forests, Elk Rapids soon became the center of an active timber industry. There, with another Polish Jew, Solomon Goldman opened a general store, selling the usual mixture of hardware, soaps, garments, dry goods, and so on. After several years, the partners must have quarreled—a custom among Jews [*laughter*]—and for a while there were two general stores across the street from each other. I have a photograph of my great-grandmother, looking very American. And I inherited from her a diamond broach, which coincidentally is in the form of the Eiffel Tower! I guess the family had become somewhat prosperous. Anyway my grandmother Mary Goldman was born in Elk Rapids in 1878 and was a schoolgirl there for a decade till they moved back to Detroit. I was pretty amazed to find my great-grandfather buying land from and having other business with the Ojibwe Indians (today they're known as the Anishinabek).

DC: So it was in Elk Rapids that he came into contact with Native American peoples.

NZD: Yes. And I learned of his transactions in the late nineteenth century at the very time I was working on Marie de l'Incarnation, who lived among Algonquians and Iroquoians in the seventeenth century. Québec is not next door to Elk Rapids, but the two places are part of a northern world of indigenous peoples. "Wow," I thought to myself, "Marie de l'Incarnation had relations with American Indians and so did my own great-grandfather." It blew my mind: I had never imagined that anything in my family history could have any resemblance to the people whose past I was studying. And yet here was Solomon Goldman trading with the Ojibwe! [*laughter*]

Anyway, Solomon Goldman finally moved his wife and children to Detroit, where eventually my paternal grandfather, David Zemon, became part of the family. David Zemon came from Lithuania to Michigan in 1891, when he was only fifteen or sixteen: again an example of a Jew who didn't go to a big center like New York. There are two types of Jewish immigrants in the late nineteenth century (perhaps this is true of other groups as well): those who head for the great urban centers, where there are already many Jews, and those, like my ancestors, who go to places where there are very few coreligionists, perhaps only one or two from their village or town. That's how it was for my grandfather. I have a photograph of him at around eighteen years old, which shows the transformation he was undergoing. He was peddling goods in central and northern Michigan: he is completely shaved and dressed in very snappy clothes. He was something of a dandy. He looks very different from a drawing I have of his father, who stayed in Vilnius and who was somewhat modernized, but nevertheless, still had a beard.

DC: Did you know what his father did in Lithuania?

NZD: No, I've never found out. He was definitely not a rabbi; perhaps he was in business or trade. I know that my grandfather's brother Moses Ziman (that's how the name was spelled in the old country) became an important physician in Białystok, where in 1919, he was one of the founders of the Białystok Hebrew Lyceum; a few years later he moved to Palestine.

DC: Has there always been a branch of the family in Israel?

NZD: On my father's side, this was the only branch. Moses Ziman presumably had descendants there, though I don't know anything about them. But to return to my grandfather, I think his marriage to Mary Goldman was something of a social ascension for him. Often Jewish immigrants, like other immigrants, marry among themselves. But Mary Goldman, born in Elk Rapids, married David Zemon, born in Prienne: you'll note that this is where the Zemon comes from, which I always insert into my name when I publish. Here's another story relevant to the assimilation of immigrants. Mary Goldman did well at Central High School in Detroit—I have her school yearbook—and she wanted very much to go the University of Michigan, along with her best friend, also Jewish, who did study there. But her parents opposed it as inappropriate for a woman. Later when she saw me with my head stuck in a book all the time, she said to my aunt (who later laughed about it with me), "That girl reads too much for her own good."

So Mary Goldman married David Zemon, who went on to do very well in business in Detroit. To start off, he had a small factory, manufacturing cloaks and suits. He was quite an admirer of Henry Ford, who was starting his automobile manufacture at the same time—ironic when you think of how anti-Semitic Ford later became. According to my father, what led David Zemon to turn away from manufacture were the demands of his workers—what a story for me, on the left! He sold his factory and went into real estate, where he prospered—not a great fortune, but wealthy.

DC: Did they always live in Detroit?

NZD: Yes, they did. David Zemon was very active in the Jewish community there. He was a pillar of his synagogue, Shaarey Zedek, a Conservative synagogue. (You don't have the same organization of Jewish congregations in France as we do in the U.S. We have three—the Orthodox, the Conservative, and the Reformed.) He was a major figure in a Detroit organization that you'll recognize from its Christian variants: the Hebrew Free Loan, which made loans without interest to Jewish immigrants to help them get started. A Jewish Mons Pietatis.[1] [*laughter*] He and my grandmother also loved American technology. They were the first in their neighborhood to have automobiles, he one with gas fuel, she an electric car. I even have an electric machine that my grandmother used to make milk shakes, one of the earliest manufactured.

That's the family of my father, Julian Zemon. He went to the University of Michigan just after World War I. His sister, many years younger than he, went there as well in the 1930s, the first woman in the family to attend university. My father also wanted to go into the theatre: it was his dream. He even went to Harvard for a year to study Shakespeare under the great George Lyman Kittredge.[2] I think he would have really loved to become one of those Jews who wrote Broadway musicals, like his contemporaries Rodgers and Hart.[3] He did write some songs—but perhaps he didn't have their talent...

DC: There was thus, prior to you and your passion for history, an aspiration to write in your family. Do you feel any connection with him, especially because you've sometimes had a theatrical idea about reconstituting the stories from the past that you've analyzed, for example with the letters

of pardon?

NZD: Yes, I do feel a connection. But let me comment further on his dream: for him it was a Jewish dream. First there was Irving Berlin[4] and all his songs, and then George and Ira Gershwin.[5] All these Jews who assimilated to America through the world of music and theatre and also contributed to the transformative ferment of those years.

DC: And in exalting and recasting the great American myths?

NZD: For sure. Just think of *Porgy and Bess,* which the Gershwins wrote together with DuBose Heyward, and what it meant for the Afro-American story and presence on the American stage.[6] As for my father, he became a businessman in the wholesale textile firm of my mother's family, but he always kept his attachment to the theatre as an avocation. He wrote, directed, and acted in popular revues for the clubs he belonged to, like the Rotary Club and his country club. During the Second World War, he had a United Services Organization troupe, which performed his plays and reviews for American soldiers still based in the States. I remember his typewriter clacking away and his excitement about the performances. His dream surely marked me.

DC: On several occasions, you've said you finally realized that cinema was a tool, that it was a means of making history. As you've explained it, does a trace of your father's own aspirations resurface here?

NZD: Probably. When I was an undergraduate, my initial hope was to make documentary films. I followed the path of becoming a university professor, mostly because I married Chandler—but it's also true that I tried twice to become an apprentice with documentary film companies, once as an undergraduate, and once just before I entered graduate school, and was not accepted. And as far as I knew at the time—the late 1940s—there weren't good film schools. So it was years before I could return to that interest.

DC: And your mother?

NZD: I want to add a last detail on my father's experience, since I think it's typical of his generation of American Jews born in the U.S. My father, like his brother and my mother's brother, was very good at tennis. They were all champions. (I have good tennis genes, or at least I ought to have them; unfortunately, my game was just middling.) One of my family's stories concerns my father's years at the University of Michigan, where he was part of the tennis team. The main tennis coach did not want to accept him formally on the top team and present him with his *M* (for Michigan), despite his talent, because he was Jewish. So in a typically American twist, there was intervention from a Jewish athlete who had already been accepted on the University of Michigan football team, where he was a star—we're talking of an event that took place around 1920 to 1921. He went to the coach and persuaded him to give Julian Zemon his *M*. The *M* finally passed to me, and I gave it to one of my grandsons, also a fine athlete. [*laughter*] What I take from this story is my father's determination to succeed as an American, but also sustain that Jewish identity. Despite my very different path, his double goal certainly influenced me.

DC: **A desire to be integrated into the fabric of society by signs that show the individual the ways to embrace common values...**

NZD: Well, yes, but it is connected with a desire to hold on to certain distinctions from the common values, or at least a distinctive way to connect with them. This is perhaps a routine story in the lives of all immigrant families, or minority families. But there are different solutions adopted. In France, you have the mode of resolution provided by the Third Republic: one is a Jew at home, one is French in public. In America, there was and is more overlap: the Jewish side is more public, less secret.

DC: **And your mother's family?**

NZD: Their story is similar to that of Solomon Goldman and David Zemon. The Lamports, my mother's family, came from Belarus to Vermont. The first to arrive was Nathan Lamport, who came to Franklin Falls, New York, in 1877, peddled up and down Lake Champlain, and then in 1884 made Burlington, Vermont, his base. He brought over his sister and brothers and their families, including my grandfather Moses Lamport. Like Solomon Goldman, the Lamports were among the first Jews in their town. Nathan was one of the founders of Burlington's first synagogue, and in 1900 my grandfather Moses, now known as a merchant, was one of the charter members of a Jewish lodge of the Knights of Pythias.[7] Jewish firsts. [*laughter*] When I visited the Ohavi Zedek synagogue while I was giving lectures at the University of Vermont, I was welcomed as a Lamport descendant.

DC: **Do you know what part of Belarus they came from?**

NZD: Nathan was born in Navahrudak, but his father had been a rabbi in Nesvizh and other relatives spoke of Minsk and Slutsk. These places are very near each other, and not far from the Lithuanian birthplaces of the Zemons and the Polish birthplaces of the Goldmans. Nathan Lamport had been a Jewish wunderkind, a young genius rabbi in the old country, and continued his sermons and even circumcising among the peddlers' families in the New World. My mother said to me one day with some indignation: "But there were never shoemakers in our family!" And I asked myself, "What did she mean by that?" I think this must have been a kind of adage, a way of saying we're above the artisanal status—as there were certainly shoemakers among the Jews. My mother must have heard this said to her in Yiddish.

I've tried to learn about the family of my maternal grandmother, Ethel Herzog, who also came from Belarus. I heard nothing from my mother, who perhaps knew very little—she was born in Burlington—or at least she didn't pass on to me what she knew. As for my grandmother, she spoke English very poorly. Despite all those decades in the United States, she preferred Yiddish, and then for some years (and I'll come back to this), she lived in Palestine.

When I visited Israel for the first time, in 1976, I met one of my Herzog cousins, Naftali Herzog, who was then quite elderly. Naftali showed Chandler and me family photographs and told us something of the family's past. The pattern was typical of Jews in the Russian Empire: one branch departed for Palestine, one branch stayed in Belarus, one branch came to America. Naftali had taken the first path, studying engineering in Berlin before going to Palestine. He told me about a nineteenth-century ancestor celebrated in the family, Alexander Sender Herzog, a merchant of peat from Nesvizh—"the tsar of peat," Naftali called him—who was also a fiery preacher. He carried both bricks of peat and Talmuds on his travels and preached from his cart. Chandler wrote a lovely poem after that about my roots, my mixed origins: he contrasted me with Alexander Sender Herzog, "a giant with an archangelic beard, / selling his Talmuds from his horse-drawn cart. / A mitzvah. You've harked back and deeply known / his old faith. But you know it more than are it. / It kindlier shines through your eyes than his own."

DC: Did you pursue this research into the question of origins because you were a historian, because you didn't want to lose the history of your ancestors, because you knew better than anyone else the French women and men of the sixteenth and seventeenth centuries? Or was it because you felt a more personal need, for yourself, to rediscover these traces of lives far removed, quite different and distant from your own, but by the light of which you hoped to try to understand or appreciate a piece of yourself, about why you made your choices, your refusals, and your commitments?

NZD: It was a combination of personal and historical curiosity, aroused in me rather late in life. When I find a crossover between the Ojibwe of Michigan with which my ancestor had dealings and the Algonquins of Marie de l'Incarnation, I'm tickled pink, as I mentioned. Sometimes it's just interesting for a historian to see how families work, that is, to see how my relatives express patterns found among Ashkenazic Jews.[8] For instance, my cousin from Belarus is Naftali, I'm Natalie from Detroit, both of us linked to some deceased Nathan.

But to get back to my mother's family—the Lamports installed themselves in Burlington. My grandparents Moses and Ethel had eight children, five boys and three girls, some born in Belarus, some in Vermont. My mother, Helen, was the youngest, born in 1904. The five sons all went to university; the three daughters, all very intelligent, did not. My grandmother thought her daughters should help with the family business, to which she herself was very committed. A little like Glikl Hamel, [*laughter*] but unfortunately, she didn't leave any memoirs the way Glikl did.

DC: It is exactly what I would ask you: weren't there written biographical testimonials that helped you in your investigation?

NZD: No, everything passed by oral transmission, and between her and her children, the language was Yiddish. Of the three daughters, my aunt Anna was the most learned in Jewish matters; she was a businesswoman, and when she wasn't at the family store, she was at the synagogue, and when she wasn't at the synagogue, she was at a Zionist meeting. And she was managing her Jewish household as well. If I had role models for female activity in the world when I was growing up, they were my aunt Gertrude Zemon, who went to the University of Michigan in the 1930s, and my aunt Anna, who was so politically engaged: she even took her children to visit Palestine in the '30s. Though my politics went in a different direction from hers, including in regard to Zionism, her activity impressed me.

DC: Can you say some words about your maternal grandmother?

NZD: Ethel Herzog Lamport joined her husband in Burlington in the 1890s, and continued to have children and run a kosher household, even while helping her husband with the dry goods business. In 1912, her husband, Moses, died at age fifty, and the family began to disperse. In fact, Moses's older brother Nathan had already left for New York because one of his daughters was dating a Christian and he wanted to be sure to have a pool of Jewish husbands. Or so the story goes—who knows whether this is the whole truth? But that's what was passed down. As for Ethel, she was now widowed with six children aged fourteen and under. She and her eldest son, Alexander, took the business in hand—it became known as Alexander Lamport and Brothers Textiles—and Ethel and her son decided where people would live. Alexander went off to New York with one brother; Ethel took the younger children to Detroit where she opened an office, and when sons got old enough, they were sent off to Cleveland or Chicago.

DC: **Isn't there a slight resemblance to Glikl as you describe her here? Or rather wasn't Glikl perhaps a way to pay homage to your grandmother through your artful recreation of her character?**

NZD: I'm probably reading my Grandma Lamport through Glikl! Both of them active businesswomen and Jewish mothers widowed in their forties with young children still at home. And, of course, the Yiddish that Ethel spoke with her daughters and that I was never taught—a mysterious family language that I learned only when I started working on Glikl's autobiography so many years later.

In any case, Ethel moved to Detroit, and there my mother had a very American youth: she went to Central High School, she enjoyed her *goyishe* girl friends, and she was an excellent athlete. She loved horseback riding—not exactly a sport that a Jewish girl growing up in Slutsk would have engaged in. One of my father's first poems written while he was courting her was about her as an equestrienne and her favorite horse. She did not attend university, because (as I said) Ethel Lamport kept her daughters close to home, while sending her sons to university. My mother met my father through her brother, who played tennis with him at the University of Michigan. They were married in 1926; it was a grand affair in the style of the twenties.

My father decided to abandon his project to become a great writer for the American theatre. He did not follow his own father into real estate, but rather became a salesman for the Lamport textiles firm, which especially supplied the Detroit auto industry. My parents did not live in the Jewish neighborhoods in Detroit. They had a very strong sentiment of being Jews, to be sure, but they decided to move to a newer part of town. Very few Jews were in my grade school in the 1930s, and it was the same at my high school in the early 1940s. A source for my sense of difference! For high school, my parents decided to send me to Kingswood School, Cranbrook, a private school on the outskirts of the city, where most of the girls came from wealthy families. The buildings and grounds were beautiful—the school had been designed by the great Finnish architect Saarinen[9]—and the teaching was really excellent. I loved my courses in literature and Latin and history, and I still remember all my teachers and classes. I especially recall Miss Manchester, who taught European history and who was rather conservative in her politics. She had a different take from mine on the Enlightenment and the French Revolution, but that didn't matter to me. Her argumentative style appealed to me. I was completely fascinated with history.

DC: **Were there history books in your house? Did you read history before receiving this training?**

NZD: Our house was full of books, but not many, if any, history books. My father owned lots of theatre books, Shakespeare and Ibsen and many more, and interesting novels. I remember seeing James Joyce's *Ulysses* in a beautiful edition on our library shelf, published sometime after the prohibition of the book had been lifted in the U.S.[10] I held it in my hands because the binding was so special, but I was much too young to read it. As for my mother, she especially read women's magazines and the *Reader's Digest*, which I sometimes read myself as a girl.[11]

DC: **I'm struck by how much the move to the New World seems to be accompanied by a sort of break with history, and how, to the contrary, your own commitment as a historian has consisted of trying to return to the past, to find again the lost threads of history, the threads that reconnect you, however indirectly, with your grandparents and great-grandparents...**

NZD: That break was true in many families. I recall only one relative actually recounting to me something of her past life while I was growing up: a relative of my grandfather Zemon, whom he helped bring over with her husband from Białystok as the dangerous years began: she told me with considerable pride of her years of study at the Lyceum in Białystok.

She really thought it better than anything her son was getting in America. Still, my desire to connect with the past began first with my search for a cultural and political path with which I could identify—already in high school—and the quest for family links came only years later.

DC: After the war, when the horrors of the Nazi extermination camps became known, did anyone in your family talk about it or, even at that time, was there silence?

NZD: I was in my last year of high school when the first news and pictures of the concentration camps appeared, and I recall discussing it in my current events class at Kingswood. It's odd that I have no memory of discussing it within my family. There was certainly talk of the dangers of Hitler in the preceding years. I wrote a poem for my Sunday School—"Fellow Jews in foreign lands / whose lives are in a monster's hands," it began—and I recall that my family was proud of me for that. I certainly read the newspapers that came into my house, so I had access to news if not dinner-table discussion about it. I left for Smith College in September 1945, and most of my political discussion, which was very extensive, took place there.

DC: Why do you think there was so little discussion of the Holocaust within your family?

NZD: During the war itself, they may have wanted to protect my brother and me from frightening news. Earlier, in connection with the outbreak of the war in Europe, I remember seeing a huge headline in *The Detroit News* and running screaming "war" to my mother, who then tried to calm me down. I certainly was afraid that Hitler was going to come and get us Jews in the United States, but I don't think I ever told my parents about this fear. This lack of discussion may go back to the habit I mentioned from the earlier generation—about not describing troubles in the old country, because now we were living in a "land of hope." And then, there was discussion of Palestine and Zionism, especially when my aunt Anna was around.

Oddly enough, my daughter Hannah told me not long ago that I hardly ever discussed the Holocaust with her when she was growing up, that I would simply bite my lip and look troubled. It was very difficult to believe this when she told me, as Nazism and the murder of Jews and millions of others in Europe were ever on my mind, there were books on the subject all over our house, and we talked about politics all the time. But she may well be right: Chandler and I took the burdens of the past on ourselves when the children were young, and wanted them to see other possibilities in the future.

DC: However, you've said it, there were letters from members of the family who remained in Eastern Europe... Did you ever find out what happened to them?

NZD: Of the letters my grandfather Zemon received, only one came into our hands and that one only much later, in the 1970s. It was written by his niece in 1916, in response to the postcards sent to his mother, brother, and sisters during World War I trying to find out where they were. His brother, Moses Ziman, went to Palestine in the 1920s; but these sisters and their children, living then in Petrograd and Vilnius and Minsk, may have all been lost in the Holocaust if not before. Grandpa Zemon himself died in 1943, and our link to his European relatives was gone. His brother once wrote my father from Palestine and reproached him for not knowing Hebrew (now that I've learned that Moses was a founder of the Hebrew Lyceum in Białystok, I can see why he was so shocked by his American nephew).

These are not the only kinds of secrets kept from the young in my family. There was one Lamport who did not immigrate to Vermont with his various cousins, but stayed in Belarus in the late nineteenth century. His son Leo Lamport came to New York with his young wife sometime in the 1920s and then in 1934 decided to go back to the Soviet Union "to build socialism." He stayed there all through the Stalin years, living as a journalist and especially as a translator into English of Russian books on Marxist philosophy and socialism and equality and the like. His name was never mentioned in the Lamport family, never. To paraphrase my mother's exclamation, "We've never had Marxists in our family." [*laughter*] We learned of him only from an article that appeared in the *New York Times* in the 1980s: his son, who had been taken over to the Soviet Union when he was only four, appealed to Ronald Reagan to be readmitted into the United States. By then Leo was dead. I wish my family had told me about him: Chandler and I could have looked him up when I attended the International Congress of Historical Sciences in Moscow in 1970. Of course, he might have been fearful of meeting with us as foreigners.

These questions of family secrets are fascinating. Some families tell all, others keep secrets. This is a great subject for historians to look at in the past.

DC: Finally, you have unearthed several bits and pieces of this family memory that operated in secret. There again, we often have the feeling that, in your books, when you take on a subject and gradually lift the veil, however thick, that covers it, you avenge all these silences, all these things forgotten. Isn't history, for you, a form of compensation for the wordless history of this family that you so love, but with which you've never spoken, which remains mute, which can't respond to your desire to learn its story? Haven't you ever been inclined, as a result, to adopt a strategy that aims to make the people of the past speak despite themselves, even in spite of the mysteries found in the records they've left? Does your predilection for popular culture, for victims, the excluded and silent people, find its impulse in the unease created by this protective, reassuring culture of what's left unsaid, the culture of your parents and grandparents? For example, in your analysis of letters of pardon, there's speech on the one hand, in all its rawness, its repetitions, and then, on the other hand, beneath its simple literalness, you focus on the almost-hidden message of the speech, what's left unsaid and all that which recovers social and gestural codes.

NZD: Possibly there's a compensatory mechanism at work here, though I've never felt it in that way. My interest in working people, in people outside of the usually defined centers of power, was connected with my youthful politics, and that was certainly reinforced during the Red hunt. My experience of being part of what was then an out-group, of a Jewish immigrant family, may have played some role. Their stories, if they were to be told at all, would not be told by the standard political history, but only by a new social history. Perhaps, too, it's relevant that I no longer believed in a supernatural God by the time I was in university: these unmarked lives were not going to get their recognition in another world. Only history and memory were there to try to give them their due. I had the sense—and still have it very intensely—that these lives counted for something, that they made a difference. I had a very strong sense of the humanity of these people, and that they once existed as I do now, and I wanted to recapture that. I wouldn't want to draw on an exclusive maternal image here, because this is something men might and do feel as well—but at the time I started writing the way I did, it may have been professionally easier for a woman historian to embark upon some of these quests.

On the matter of family secrecy itself, I'd add one thing. When I began working on French family account-book/journals—what were called *livres de raison*—and memoirs, and later when I was concerned with the autobiographies of Glikl and Marie de l'Incarnation, I noticed that they contained omissions, that is, topics that you'd expect them to elaborate upon or events that I knew had happened from independent evidence, but were not treated in these texts. And these journals and memoirs were usually written first and foremost for children, to pass on the family's past or the parent's life and wisdom, whatever other audience they might have expected.

Reading these texts led me to thinking about the matter of secrecy, and I used it as an organizing concept in the essay I wrote about the autobiography of Leon of Modena, the rabbi of Venice, whom I mentioned earlier: "Fame and Secrecy" was my title. The "fame" part was connected with what he was happy to broadcast to the world, Jews and Gentiles alike: all the books he'd written, all the people who wanted to meet him or sought his opinion, the crowds that flocked to his sermons, including even Christians. The "secrecy" part was double: what he wanted to withhold from Christians and what he wanted to withhold from Jews, including those close to him. His Hebrew autobiography, written for his male descendants and his Jewish pupils in the ghetto of Venice, is full of lively quarrels, complaints, and troubles—including the dire economic predicaments brought on by his own gambling habits. When he came to describe the Jewish world to Christians in his Italian *Rites and Customs of the Jews,* this living world is cleaned up in favor of liturgy, orderly laws, and charitable practices.[12] Games of chance aren't mentioned even in connection with the few holidays, like Hanukkah, when they were licit and even part of the festivity. These were Jewish secrets. But there were also secrets that Leon did not want to pass on to progeny or pupils, especially one concerning his son who was in some kind of liaison, presumably homoerotic, with two different men. Here there is only an allusive reference and the exclamation, "miseries of my heart."

I've been using this idea of secrecy in examining other texts, including right now in connection with slave narratives—who says what to whom? I always thought that my notion of secrets in my own family came from applying my historian's insights into my family past, but maybe it was the other way around.

DC: The more I listen to you, the more I'm struck by the fact that we cannot detach—as becomes evident for many historians the moment they write their own biographies—this familial past from your work, or rather

the manner in which you've worked, your method in approaching the sources as well as your constant search for new characters, almost as if you're creating a parallel family. You didn't tell us whatever happened to your grandmother after the death of her husband.

NZD: I knew my Grandma Lamport rather little because after marrying off her three daughters—my mother's wedding in 1926 was the last—and after being assured that the family textile firm and its branches were well established, she left for Palestine. She had relatives there; indeed, her father-in-law, Tsvi Hirsh Lamport, had long before left Belarus for Jerusalem and was buried on the Mount of Olives. But according to what I learned many years later, her desire to move there had less to do with a form of political Zionism than with religious piety: she felt she could not live with full Jewish devotion in the United States. I've wondered whether that feeling didn't have something to do with the fact that two of her daughters, my mother and my aunt Esther, had stopped keeping kosher households, in both cases following the wishes of their Reformed husbands. Anyway, Ethel Lamport succeeded in her wish: my cousin Naftali Herzog told me that after her death, so pious had she been that her synagogue had a *bimah* cloth made from her apron.[13] I met her only when she came back to Detroit for a time to live when I was five or six years old. I have a photograph of the entire family, all her children and grandchildren, at a seder in Detroit. My brother and I and one cousin from New York are the youngest, and are looking at the camera with baffled expressions. I remember her apartment with bowls of pistachio nuts, Mediterranean style, on the table. I have a very strong impression of her physical person, but we really did not have a common language.

DC: To stay in this rather simplistic vein on memory and its relationship with historical problems, could your interest in women's history be rooted in these feminine figures from your youth: grandmothers, mother, aunts, and so on, even if this interest only became apparent much later? It was in thinking about the parallels with Glikl, incidentally, that this question occurred to me. For didn't your grandmother do what Glikl would have wished to do, namely, go to Palestine, to see Palestine, to live in the Promised Land?

NZD: Yes, Ethel Lamport did what Glikl Hamel only theorized about. After a time in Detroit, to visit with her family and also to be able to hold on to her American citizenship, she went back to Palestine and died in Tel Aviv a few years after the establishment of the State of Israel. As for the women in my family, my first efforts at shaping myself as a young woman were aimed at being different from them in my way of life and in the breadth of my political concerns. I did recognize that I had inherited the Lamport energy, and Chandler always noted after being at a large family gathering that he saw an affinity among these many Lamport women buzzing around, all about the same size. But my aunt Esther and my mother, Helen, had not gone on as active businesswomen like their mother and their sister Anna. For them, the successful American middle-class dream was to be able to withdraw from paid work. My mother was very attentive to her husband and her children, to her house and lovely garden, to her furniture and antiques (I now have some of these antiques on my shelves), to her golf—she played very well—to her friends and bridge parties. When I first told her I wanted to be a professor, she said it might be okay if I did it as a volunteer.

Notes

1. A Mons Pietatis is a Catholic charitable institution going back to medieval times that lends money at little or no interest at all.

2. George Lyman Kittredge (1860–1941) was an American scholar of English literature and an influential literary critic in the early twentieth century.

3. Richard Rodgers (1902–79) and Lorenz Hart (1895–1943) were prominent American songwriters who composed twenty-five stage musicals and over five hundred songs between 1919 and 1943.

4. Irving Berlin (1888–1989) was a prolific and popular American composer and lyricist who wrote an estimated 1,500 songs during his long career.

5. George Gershwin (1898–1937) was an American composer and pianist and Ira Gershwin (1896–1983), his brother, was a lyricist. Together they created music for dozens of Broadway shows and films, as well as for ensemble performance across the genres of jazz, classical, and popular music.

6. *Porgy and Bess* premiered on Broadway in New York in 1935. DuBose Heyward (1885–1940) wrote the libretto.

7. The Order of Knights of Pythias is an international, nonsectarian fraternal order established first in Washington, DC, in 1864.

8. Ashkenazic Jews are those Jews living in central and eastern Europe and Russia. Their language of communication was Yiddish, and they developed distinctive liturgical and festive customs.

9. Eero Saarinen (1910–61) was a Finnish-American architect and product designer who stressed the principles of simplicity and functionality.

10. James Joyce (1882–1941) was an influential Irish writer and poet known for his experimental works, particularly the landmark modernist novel *Ulysses* (1922). Banned in the United States as obscene, it could not be published there until 1933.

11. *Reader's Digest* is a monthly general-interest family magazine founded in 1922.

12. The book appeared in Paris in 1637 as *Historia de gli riti hebraici* and in Venice in 1638 as *Historia de' riti hebraici*.

13. The *bimah* is the platform from which the Torah is read and prayers are led during services.

Chapter 5

Women

DC: This image of your mother will serve for us, however brusquely but not altogether illogically, as a transition point. When did you begin to become interested in women's history?

NZD: Later in my career. Let me explain. When I was a student at Smith, I took marvelous courses in the Renaissance and Reformation and the English and French Revolutions. My professor, Leona Gabel, was a woman, like most of my Smith professors, but we did not talk about women in the courses. Maybe some of the Sforza women were mentioned when she lectured on the Italian Renaissance, but I have no memory of it.[1] Mary Ritter Beard's *Woman as a Force in History* was published while I was an undergraduate, a pioneering work, and if I had read it then (and I don't recall that I did), I would have thought "My, that's interesting."[2] But I would not have been disposed to follow up that subject ahead of my senior thesis on the radical Renaissance philosopher Pietro Pomponazzi.[3]

What was essential for me at that time was that I had a woman as a professor—not a scholarly topic or fancy methodology about women. I was at a women's college where women were taken seriously as students; I had exceptional women as teachers; I could see the possibility of being a historian, of having a career.

Then while I was doing my doctoral studies at the University of Michigan, I took a seminar with a professor, Palmer Throop, toward whom I feel considerable gratitude—indeed, I feel it more now than I did at the time.[4] Professor Throop had a sociological vision of history and he had us read Baldassar Castiglione's *Courtier* side by side with Theodore Newcomb's brand new text, *Experimental Social Psychology*.[5] It was very fruitful, very avant-garde for a Renaissance history seminar in 1951. Throop suggested that I do my seminar paper on the amazing poet Christine de Pizan, whom I had never heard of until then. Reading her was a revelation. In my paper, I especially concentrated on her 1405 *Cité des Dames* [*The Book of the City of Ladies*], and her attitude toward herself as a woman writer and her demands for respect for women. I tried to do for her what I had done a year or so earlier in a paper on Guillaume Budé, written for a Harvard graduate seminar: connect her own precarious status with her thoughts and ways of writing about women. I entitled the paper something like "Christine de Pizan as a Prototype of the Professional Literary Woman." But when Professor Throop suggested I write my doctoral dissertation on her, I bridled. I said to myself, "Not possible. He's just asking me to write on a woman because I'm a woman." By then I had discovered the printing workers of Lyon and the great questions of Karl Marx and Max Weber, and the life and writings of a woman in the world of kings and counts did not seem as important. I found her fascinating, but marginal to the big questions that interested me. I don't at all regret the choice I made at that time, but twenty years later I could understand the significance of Christine de Pizan in a new way.

DC: What later led you to ask the question anew? What inspired you to take up female subjects again?

NZD: There was a conjuncture of personal, political, and intellectual experiences. I had married when I was nineteen, and had to figure out how to be a married woman and have a career at the same time. My women teachers at Smith were historians, but they weren't married with families. And that was the case with most women with PhDs teaching in the 1950s in American universities: they lived with other women or perhaps had male lovers, but they were ordinarily not married; indeed, there was often prejudice against them if they were. Then, during the 1950s, while I was doing the research for my thesis, I had my three children. So now there was a huge organizational challenge, which my husband and I somehow met: Chandler gave me complete support from the start of my scholarly work and helped enormously with our children. Still, in the mostly male university world that I was trying to enter, I looked like a wife and a mother, while I considered myself a historian as well. In other words, I was in a situation that had some resemblance to that of the poet Christine de Pizan, who by the way had also been married and had a son; despite all the differences between the early fifteenth century and the mid-twentieth century, her question was becoming *my* question.

In the 1960s, I finally became an assistant professor at the University of Toronto, where very few women were then teaching, even in the humanities, and where women graduate students were relatively small in number. With a group of women graduate students (including Louise Tilly[6] and Germaine Warkentin[7] and Alison Prentice,[8] who went on to have spectacular careers), I organized a study of all the women we could locate who were combining doctoral study at UT with raising families. We asked them about their experiences as women at the University of Toronto and what suggestions they had for improving the situation. This may seem an obvious project now, but in 1965 to 1966, people thought it was daring. We mimeographed our report and gave it to some of the University of Toronto deans, who paid it no mind and dismissed the suggestion for a day-care center for the children of students as laughable. It took much turbulence at the University of Toronto before the center was finally set up. I tell this story as part of the background to the feminist movement that flowered on the University of Toronto campus at the end of the 1960s, as did the antiwar movement and the movement to restructure university life. I began to see the interconnection between issues concerning women and issues about other power structures. So much for my personal and political path to the study of women, but there was also an intellectual path.

DC: How were you gradually able to become involved in developing a form of history that, even though it didn't offer or dispose of any special methodological tools, came to acquire the same standing as social or economic history?

NZD: As is so often the case in life, the persons one meets play a catalyzing role. Jill Ker Conway had come to the University of Toronto and by the late 1960s, we had become fast friends. An extraordinary and striking woman, Jill had grown up in Australia, had spent some years in England, and had come to Canada after completing her doctorate at Harvard. Her dissertation was on the first generation of American women to obtain doctorates, their experiences and their mentalities in the late years of the nineteenth and early twentieth centuries. Like me, she had chosen a country different from her own birthplace on which to do her research and a topic that represented a break with the standard historiography in her field. Through many conversations over lunch with Jill, I began to see how the history of women was linked to major issues of culture, social structure, and historical change. In the next few years, I started writing essays in the history of women, and Jill and I decided to teach a course together.

The first essay I wrote was on the Protestant women of Lyon in the sixteenth century. I had already written on the attraction of Protestantism to men in Lyon, especially in the printing industry and other artisanal trades. I asked myself, "Why not do the same thing for women?" I already had information on the wives of the Protestant men in all occupations in Lyon and on some well-known women. I went back to the archives to find women's wills and other evidence—and rapidly made the same discovery that I had years before when people had claimed one couldn't find anything about the lives of working people in the archives: that wasn't true at all, there was loads of material on women if you looked widely. In fact, I loved the challenge of finding sources and I loved seeing where the women's story paralleled or differed from that of the men.

The other essay I wrote in those first years concerned women as historical writers in late medieval and early modern Europe. Hardly anything was then known on this subject; scholars thought of women as poets and writers of romances and novels, but as unlikely producers of history books. And women faced many obstacles: they were not thought to have an appropriate voice for the grand themes of history, they couldn't get ready access to the kinds of documents available to men of the law or diplomats who wrote historical accounts, and so on. So how did the women manage to write history, I wondered. It turned out that Christine de Pizan herself had been commissioned in 1404 to write a history of the life of King Charles V, whom her father had known from his days at court and whose former servants she could still interview. She scoured chronicles about his deeds just as she did for women for her *City of Ladies,* which she wrote not long after. Then in the sixteenth and seventeenth centuries, you find examples of women writing histories of their husbands and families—a seemly topic for a good wife—but because they were married to major political actors, the histories widen out readily into histories of the events of their own time. The Protestant Charlotte Arbaleste[9] accomplished this in her life of her husband Philippe du Plessis-Mornay,[10] one of the most important figures of the French religious wars and a close associate of Henri IV.[11] And Margaret Lucas did the same in the *Life* of her husband William Cavendish, Duke of Newcastle, who was a Royalist general in the English Civil War.[12] By the eighteenth century, Catharine Sawbridge

Macaulay, a staunch republican, felt quite entitled to write a full-fledged and influential *History of England* and included a portrait of herself as Clio as its frontispiece.[13] I collected information on many women historians on into the twentieth century, but decided to end the essay with Madame de Staël on the *French Revolution*.[14] When it was finally published, I entitled it "Gender and Genre: Women as Historical Writers."

DC: That's a play on words that's difficult to translate into French.

NZD: True—"gender" as the construction of sexual identity and "genre" as a literary typology are distinguished in English because we adopted your French *genre* into English. In concluding the essay, I commented on how different these women historical writers were—different in their politics, different in religion. But at some moment in their books, they all found a way to reflect on what it was to be a woman writing on a historical subject. And I, Natalie Davis, was doing the same thing in writing "Gender and Genre." I even said so in the last paragraph.

DC: According to you, was it the fact that you highlighted in these women their own introspective search that enabled them to question themselves both as women and historians, that convinced you to do the same? Or rather was it you who earlier underwent this experience that you then transferred to your subjects of study? Don't you believe that you sometimes allow yourself to become bewitched by your extraordinary, almost magical power as a historian thanks to this pleasure—which we've spoken about—in endowing persons from the past with your own role, your incredibly lively capacity to prompt self-searching?

NZD: No, I do not think I was projecting my own experience back on these women writers. For each case, I established the mental universe in which they wrote their historical texts, including what male readers expected from women writers. For each case, I found a text where the woman reflected on her status as a woman writing the kind of history she was writing. These women taught me, rather than the other way around.

Those years, the end of the 1960s and the early 1970s were a wonderful turning point for me, so many discoveries. I was doing social and literary history of women. It was also the moment when I was turning to anthropology; gender themes were part of my essays on charivari and the world-upside-down. That's when I wrote "Women on Top." And in 1971, Jill Conway and I gave our course at the University of Toronto on the history of women, one of the earliest in North America: I did the first half on early modern Europe and she continued with women in colonial America and the United States. We called the course Society and the Sexes and I kept the title in later years, when I taught the early modern section of the course on my own, first at Berkeley, then at Princeton.

DC: In your career as a teacher and researcher, weren't these years of extreme intensity also the most important years?

NZD: I don't know that they were *the* most important years—working on Martin Guerre, film and book, was another turning point for me—but it was an amazing time. Oh, the excitement around the history of women—at Toronto, at Berkeley, in New York, across North America. We were all rushing around to find primary sources. I fished out all my notes on Christine de Pizan and opened my course with the *City of Ladies*. There was not a paperback of the book then, so I made copies for my students from the Renaissance English translation. I haunted rare book rooms, including medical rare book libraries, legal collections, and collections of religious books and sermons. I developed a bibliography of primary and secondary sources on women in western Europe—especially in France and England—mimeographed it, and sent it by mail to anyone who asked for it. We also circulated our course syllabus for Society and the Sexes. I was able to assign Glikl's *Autobiography* from the beginning, because it did exist in English translation, and I helped get word of her to many others beyond the Yiddish specialists to whom she was then known.[15] Other people were doing similar searching for their fields and were spreading word of their discoveries. I'll never forget the meeting of the second Berkshire Conference on the History of Women held at Radcliffe in 1974: a few hundred people were expected, well over a thousand attended, women and men as well.[16]

DC: Female students must have certainly been quite attracted to your course at Berkeley, but what about male students?

NZD: There were always some men who took the courses, but they were a minority—although a very smart and imaginative minority. Still we always regretted that there weren't more men, because from the beginning, Jill and I and younger colleagues like Joan Scott[17] and Louise Tilly saw the history of women as a history of *relations* between men and women and the social and economic significance of these relations; a history of what it was to be a man as well as of what it was to be a women—these can't be separated, they're bound together in the same story.

Let me elaborate. The first task was simply "to put women into history"—facts about their activities, their roles, their attitudes in all features of life at a given period: family, sexuality, economy, religion, political life... For me, it was expanding the kind of work I'd done for workers and artisans. The second associated task was to think about this evidence in a relational way, to see women in relation to other women and in relation to men, to sort women out by class and religious status and education—by ethnicity and color and country, when these were part of the picture. The third associated task was the most challenging: what was the *gender system* at a given period? What was its significance for other systems of power and exchange at the time? What consequences did it have for historical change? By "gender system," I'm thinking not only of the patterns of social and political relations in which men and women were involved with each other, as expected by their gender, but also of the symbolic systems defining the "masculine" and the "feminine" at a given period. These symbolic systems had meanings of their own in cultural life, quite apart from what role they played in shaping the activities and relations of men and women.

Such were the questions we were working on in the 1970s and afterward. It was very lively and there was much fruitful debate. Some scholars wanted to stress the history of *women,* and tended to see "women" as the grouping of importance in a given society; other scholars—and I was one of them—preferred the history of *gender* as the central concept, since it stressed the relationality of the idea of "men" and "women," the changing historical definitions of the categories "man" and "woman," and allowed a wider range of possibilities for description. We usually ended up, as in our program at Princeton and at many other places, with putting both "women" and "gender" in the title. Another debate was about which kind of social system "was good for the women": did women have more power in aristocratic regimes or were they in a better position in republican contractual regimes? This debate ended up with important insights into the gender features of both regimes, of limits and possibilities for women in both settings, and into the gendered elements in eighteenth and nineteenth-century notions of citizenship. The same thing is true of Catholic and Protestant societies, as I mentioned earlier: you look at the possibilities and limits in both settings and how they work out in practice.

DC: It's a very empirical domain, as I can gather from listening to you.

NZD: Empirical certainly, but important also for advancing our understanding of historical structures and historical change. For example, nowadays it is no longer possible to understand the establishment of sovereign power during the early modern period in Europe without taking into consideration royal policy toward families and the attitude of families toward the state; without noting the diverse roles of women in the political sphere, from grain rioters to queens; and without examining the implications of gender symbolism and prescriptions in the law, political writings, and public festivities. It is no longer possible to analyze economic transformations in the early modern period without looking at the different positions women had in the production, distribution, and consumption of objects and services, and the ways in which women were represented in the debates and policies concerning luxury and poverty. As for the religious transformations of the early modern period, including the religious aspects of European expansion, the role of women and the importance of the issues of sexuality, gender definitions, and marriage have been demonstrated in many studies.

DC: If we were to characterize your position, could we say that the history of women definitely has its own dialectic, its own particular way to ask questions, its own claims to disciplinary autonomy, even though at the same time it shouldn't be seen in isolation, that it should instead be fully considered a way to understand the whole of history better, an analytical tool just as useful as labor history or cultural history? That doesn't mean we need to declare that gender history has a political aspect that pits moderates against radicals. But, to put it more concisely, haven't you conceived of it, beyond its obvious ties with personal experiences and family memories, as a tool that always opens up more room to pursue this pleasure or this feeling about the mysteries of the past that we touched upon at the beginning of our conversation? Perhaps it's even a means of conducting a form of self-analysis that otherwise you wouldn't dare to broach?

NZD: "Disciplinary autonomy" would be too strong a term for me. I don't think of the history of women and gender as a separate discipline any more than I do the history of the Jews or the history of Christianity or peasant history or urban history. These subjects are all part of the historian's inquiry (which, to me, can draw on several disciplines). But yes, there are a distinctive set of questions, perspectives, and modes of analysis that one draws upon while concentrating on women and gender. And yes, these must always be linked to other features of the historical landscape and period, both to describe them better—and I've just given you some examples of that—and to be enriched and renewed by them. It's a two-way process: the history of women contributes to history more generally, and questions generated elsewhere should modify the formulations regarding sameness and difference that overdetermine too much of women's history.

As for your second question, I don't see my inquiries about women and gender relations in the past as a form of self-analysis. Insights from the past can always turn out to have relevance to our own persons, but I experience this study as an expansion beyond myself, sometimes having a familiar ring, but often going beyond anything I've ever known or suspected. And I've found the study of gender a great enhancement of pleasure, as you suggest: the persons I've learned about, the books I've been led to, the conversations with students—just fascinating over the years. Right now I'm on the trail of two slave women in eighteenth-century Suriname, trying desperately to understand them, to find a way to catch their voices and hopes...

DC: The women you've studied are women who have found a certain measure of happiness in their lives, even if they knew, like Maria Sibylla Merian, that catastrophes lay on the horizon. But they created a relative kind of happiness in what might be called symbolic strategies—strategies involved in their writings, in their work, in their religious activism, in their collections of insect drawings, and so on. A sense of happiness or rather equilibrium that differs from men's and accepted social mores. It's a very optimistic history, which suits you well, I believe, because a woman sees you recognize in her a capacity to circumvent the selfish world of politically dominant men, to cast off their supposed fragility. In that way, history as you write it is never taken in a single sense or as immediately obvious. But don't you believe that this optimism can lead you astray?

NZD: I'd much prefer to use the word "fulfillment" or "satisfaction" for the women I write about rather than "happiness," and for myself "a history of hope" rather than "optimistic history." I have always shied away from constructing women as mere victims or as remarkable heroines—though sometimes a life is marked by intense suffering or admirable courage. The people I research and write about, women and men both, more often follow a middle path of trying to cope, of trying to manage somehow in difficult situations that come along. I'm struck by their ingenuity, the craft by which they respond to challenges, obstacles, hardships—by their talent for improvising, their resourcefulness. I am struck by human *resilience* and want to understand its sources. With Maria Sibylla Merian, you have unusual gifts—she was a fine artist and naturalist—but she also used housewifely ingenuity to observe the metamorphoses of insects in her kitchen when she was cut off from the universities and academies of men. With Bertrande de Rols, the wife of Martin Guerre, you have an ordinary peasant woman, who, abandoned by her husband, used all the craft she had to fashion a marriage with a substitute, Arnaud du Tilh, and then to try to hold on to her honor and still save Arnaud when he was attacked as an impostor. Her situation was unusual, but her resourcefulness was nourished by the forms of behavior she learned from village women. Olwen Hufton described the improvisation of rural women in eighteenth-century France, their skillful patching together of ways to survive—I really loved that book.[18] I found the same pattern in writing on women in the crafts in sixteenth-century Lyon, and now I'm noting how the slave women in Suriname have diverse strategies to make life tolerable for themselves and their children.

Memoirs from the Holocaust or the Gulag are filled with the same varieties of craft, improvisation, and resourcefulness, some of it put to horrendous and murderous ends, some of it for personal survival at the expense of or indifferent to others, some of it carrying the best of human qualities. Primo Levi's *Survival in Auschwitz* has it all—the book is an exploration of what it is to be human—but etched on my memory is the moment when Primo Levi recites the canto of Ulysses from Dante's *Divine Comedy* to a young Alsatian student, translating it into French for him as they carry their hundred-pound water buckets on poles.[19] He wants him to understand it now, for tomorrow they may be dead.

Historians have different goals in regard to the past, but my wish is to save or preserve people—women and men—from obscurity, from the hidden, and give some dignity or sense to their lives, even when they end tragically. This is part of what you might call a "mission" [*laughter*] to write a history of hope.

DC: The term "mission" leads us to the idea of history as a wondrous world made to seem real by virtue of the historian's magical powers, but also as a form of engagement, of duty. I would like to ask you if, especially in the history of women, you haven't had the feeling you've crossed a threshold, certainly already latent in your earlier work, by which you conceive of

history as a way to fulfill an ethical duty. I don't want to allude to a "moral" problem in the trivial sense of the term, but in an ethical sense where, through several characters chosen from amongst those offered up by history, you again endow with life a society of women who could not speak or write except within limits, who might have been unhappy, oppressed, and to whom you give an identity... An ethical duty to the extent that, for you, these reconstructed lives of women, sometimes difficult, cramped, suffocating, overly active, or intensely devoted to service or other persons, become worthy indicators of a hope that never dies. If we wanted to sum up your thoughts, it would be that, in human history, nothing is completely blocked or foreclosed, that there exist cracks in every system, even the most coercive ones, through which freedom can find its own expressions.

NZD: Yes, I do think there are cracks or possibilities in systems, but I'd add that it's human cleverness that sees them and human resourcefulness that finds a way to take advantage of them. And of course, some systems have considerable flexibility.

I'd like to give an example of how I experience that "mission" that I spoke of. When I write of Marguerite de Navarre, I always enjoy it: her *Heptameron* has taught me much, and I've used stories from it to advance important arguments in my books on pardon tales and on gifts.[20] She's one of the sixteenth-century observers I run things by, as I said earlier. But Marguerite de Navarre does not need me; many other fine historians and literary scholars have written about her and will continue to do so.

In contrast, I felt a woman like Glikl Hamel "needed" me, especially in 1970, when I started reading her. By now, other people have written splendidly on her—Chava Turniansky[21] and Gabriele Jancke[22]—but thirty years ago the one edition of her Yiddish autobiography was inaccessible to most people, and it was known primarily through a 1913 German translation by a male scholar, Alfred Feilchenfeld, who had mutilated Glikl's memoirs.[23] In fact, an acceptable German translation already existed, made by the remarkable social worker Bertha Pappenheim,[24] but it had been circulated in a limited edition and was dismissed by the learned Feilchenfeld, who could win the interest of publishers for his translation. He showed little respect for Glikl and the intricate literary ordering of the text she had worked over so many years. He changed the order of her life all around to suit himself and omitted the folktales that she had carefully inserted at critical points in her narrative. For him, the stories interrupted the text, and were an embarrassing expression of backward Yiddishkeit; he thought the book useful simply as an antecedent of the prosperous German-Jewish bourgeoisie. What an idea! What a way to treat Glikl and her book. (I should add that the main English edition circulating over the years I taught Glikl was drawn from this Feilchenfeld mutilation; fortunately, a woman translator had salvaged the text somewhat in another edition I could have my students read. We still need a good critical edition in English.)

DC: Everything for you seems to go back to a feeling of injustice and the desire to redress it in terms of historical memory...

NZD: I wanted to give Glikl her due, to give her back to herself. And it was a fascinating project from an intellectual point of view. I enjoyed the search for the origin of all the stories she told, and figuring out where she could have found them. It was a way to understand her mental universe and the world of print and books around a seventeenth-century Jewish woman. And I enjoyed trying to figure out why she placed the stories where she did in the course of recounting her life: they were a way of commenting on her experience and posing moral questions to her children and herself—I called it "arguing with God," an old Jewish tradition.

I also felt complicity or solidarity with Glikl's first translator, Bertha Pappenheim, who lived on to the early years of the Hitler regime. She had been one of the first patients of Josef Breuer and Sigmund Freud, who had treated her for hysteria. There are three faces to Bertha Pappenheim. There's the clinical, hysterical Bertha Pappenheim, known as Anna O in the early Breuer-Freud writings. There's Bertha Pappenheim the social worker, reformer, and feminist in Frankfurt, especially attentive to issues concerning Jewish women. And there's Bertha Pappenheim the writer and storyteller, who had begun with a translation into German of Mary Wollstonecraft's *Vindication of the Rights of Woman,* had gone on to translate Yiddish tales into German, and then turned to Glikl's book.[25] She herself was descended from one of Glikl's in-laws, but that wasn't the important thing. She saw in Glikl's active life and stories a model and a message to transmit to the Jewish women of her day.

DC: Don't you believe that, in this context, we should replace this idea of history as devoted to "human science" [*science humaine*] with an approach informed by this ethical regard you have for other people, an approach that would be the story about or study of *human differences*? Don't the

various methods of studying humanity, as opposed to the social sciences with all their assumptions, still remain sterile because of the underlying modernist premise that people, in all their anthropological diversity, are still basically the same when it comes to the ways they act and think, albeit in anonymity? When reading or listening to you, we sense that you're seeking out the Other, with the aim to recognize and restore what makes every individual unique, less perhaps for them personally than for all the other men and women like them who have lived in the world.

NZD: I like your formulation about seeking the difference and distinctiveness of people in the past, and your comment about finding a link among them that's more meaningful than an abstract anonymous universality. We tend to say "humanities" rather than "human sciences" in English, and I don't want to get bogged down in a discussion of whether history is a science. But I do want to hold on to the knowledge and distance suggested by the word "science," which must always be in tension with the interpretive and imaginative movements of the historian's self.

DC: We return at our peril to the question of subjectivity. I would be more radical than you in asserting that I understand mutual sympathy not as some kind of process of emotional osmosis but rather as a tension in the very formation of an identity, however incomplete, through exchange with written documents. This doesn't mean we need to buy into the personal mythos of the self, but rather to be open to a kind of inverse introspection in which messages inherited from the past become realized by the self. This doesn't signify negating the irreducible distance between the past, with all its own words and signs, and the present, but that rather this distance conceals in its depths and by necessity the strange otherness of the subject of research. In other words, our encounter with the past goes in both directions because the past is nothing but a shared memory. After all, we only know the past by what's remembered or written by someone connected to the past. Indeed, a portion of the past actually lies dormant in the recesses of the historian's mind, ready to be awakened through the rigors of research.

Let's all admit there's no pure history, but instead it only arises through personal experience. It thus becomes a form of self-delusion, conscious or not, on the historian's part. Consequently, once we've identified and designated the relevant "real" sources, it's mistaken to oppose objectivity to subjectivity, history to historicizing, rationality to fantasy, and fiction

to truth. Can't the historian dream, if only for a brief while, of intermixing, reintroducing, and reshaping some part of this strangeness of the past and those who live in it? Isn't the past always prologue to the future, with infinite possibilities that all virtually coexist until one of them finally takes shape in the historian's mind, giving us at least the illusion that the historian can penetrate individual as well as collective imaginations from the past?

NZD: Yes and no. The historian seeks to find and communicate the strangeness and the familiar in the past. In doing so, she may end up with a new understanding of the strange and the familiar both. For me, "subjectivity" isn't just a philosophical question—though the history of that term, currently being explored by Lorraine Daston[26] and Peter Galison,[27] is very interesting—subjectivity is also a daily practice. I want to push my research as far as I can in order to discover and understand the mental and affective worlds of persons and communities of the past. In approaching the traces and texts that they've left me, I'm simultaneously helped and constrained by my own subjectivity and abilities. I want to hold on to that tension. The historian's work finally goes on in her head, but I want to always remember the existence outside of me of those traces from people of the past. I want to be a storyteller, not a cannibal.

DC: If you were to define present prospects for the history of women, which would you consider the most important?

NZD: Thinking now of the United States and Canada, I would want to distinguish between undergraduate programs and advanced research and graduate teaching. On the undergraduate level, there is a continuing need for the classic introductory history-of-women courses, enriched by comparative material drawn from non-Western countries and other new materials. In our big cities, many of our students have been born into immigrant families or have themselves been born abroad. Most of them have attended high schools where themes on the history of women have a scant place in the curriculum. For women undergraduates, these courses are really important. The students attend them in large numbers; they enjoy them and get perspectives helpful for other courses and their own lives.

For advanced research and graduate teaching, I think it's important to prevent ghettoization. When we started programs or departments in the history of women and gender, the idea always was that they would have porous boundaries and be in close dialogue with different disciplines. When that's not present, there's the danger of recycling the same set of questions and theories, and getting predictable answers. The study of gender groups routinely opens with locating the women and locating the men and asking about likeness and difference. Superb books have emerged from this approach, some of them models for the comparative study of other groups (like ethnicities) as well. But new directions are opened when the gender axis, the axis male/female, is not the central issue at the beginning: you start with an important issue of another kind and gender can show up in a fresh way, along with other findings.

I urge my own students interested in women in history to vary their themes, sometimes focusing around a gender question, other times on something quite different—but keeping their eyes open for places where male/female matters enter into the story. And I've certainly found this in my own work. I centered *Women on the Margins* around gender, and hoped it would also be useful in thinking about margins more generally. With *Pardon Tales* and *The Gift*, I started with another theme, and was delighted by the moments when contrasts between the practices or sensibilities of sixteenth-century men and women suddenly emerged.

DC: **But hasn't there been a movement among historians of women, especially in North America, to ask new kinds of questions?**

NZD: Of the first generation of historians of women in North America, some of them have redirected their interest toward the history of the colonies, postcolonial studies, the history of ethnicities and immigration. The more classic histories of women have been sustained, both by younger scholars and by some of the pioneers as well. But some of the most interesting insights into questions of power and difference have emerged from postcolonial studies.

DC: **And slavery?**

NZD: Slavery has been one of the most important areas of scholarship in the last twenty years, and matters of gender and sexuality have been cast in a new light in that context. And while we're talking of the recentering of historical inquiry, we should not forget all the writing on the history of sexuality, especially gay and lesbian sexuality—by now, I should say the history of sexualities. In North America, one talks of "queer theory." Is this discussed in France?

DC: Yes, but they haven't met with the same startling enthusiasm that greeted them in the United States, or at least not yet. Whether that's a good or a bad thing, I won't say.

NZD: Queer theory takes French post-structuralism and deconstruction as important ancestors, so it should have French echoes! Queer theory goes well beyond earlier approaches to the history of sexuality, in which sexual practices and identities were thought of as partly constructed over time and related to different historical milieux. The main debates in the 1970s and 1980s concerned the amount of construction: how much input was there from biology? Was there an identifiable current of, say, homoerotic culture in the West from antiquity on? But whatever the fluidity in sexual practices and identities, the binary of heterosexuality/homosexuality was the main frame.

Queer theory effaces that binary. It argues for no "natural" or biologically determined sexuality. One's DNA has no necessary consequences for one's identity or one's sexual preference or practices. I'm not sure how psychoanalytic theory plays into queer theory, but you can see that it argues for particularity and particular choices. To me, it seems a reaction in gay studies to the kind of routine repeating of questions and approaches that I mentioned as a danger in the history of women and gender. In that sense, queer theory has cleared the air and challenged historiographical categories, and it has prompted some interesting writing in philosophical and literary criticism. But it's hard to see how its radical and individualist particularity can be a practical guide to historians, who really do need to look at the play of culture and social experience in defining possibilities in a particular period. And some recent work by geneticists and specialists on infant physiology is showing a whole new way to think of the nature/nurture binary—much more porousness and interchange between genetic codes and life experience than believed before.

DC: I would like to ask you the following question: In France, despite the big projects to which you've contributed, such as the *Histoire des femmes,* directed by Georges Duby and Michelle Perrot, there doesn't exist as strong a commitment to the history of women, perhaps because of certain methodological shortcomings.[28] Take, for example, the awkward translation of "gender" as *genre*. There have been noteworthy works for sure, but—perhaps because French university life has been and remains more or less secretly misogynistic—there still hasn't been a truly original

work, properly speaking, for the early modern period. We could cite Éliane Viennot's book, but it remains very much a classic in the sense you spoke of earlier, because it treated Queen Margot...

NZD: A very good book!

DC: Certainly, but it's worth pointing out that it's a work of a historian of literature. Tell me precisely what you see it contributes, if anything, in terms of methodology.

NZD: Methodological shortcomings of the history of women? I don't think that's the issue in France, for there are, as I've just tried to suggest, several ways in which the history of women and gender can be practiced. I think it has more to do with the different settings in the two countries. In France, the first wave of feminist criticism after World War II was dominated by literary and philosophical thinkers—Simone de Beauvoir[29] first, then Luce Irigary[30] and Hélène Cixous[31] (Julia Kristeva[32] in the next generation). Beauvoir had a historical chapter in her *Second Sex*, but it was just one long refrain of women's subordination. In the United States, the first wave was less infused with high literary/philosophical theory. (The contrast between Betty Friedan's *Feminine Mystique* of 1963[33] and Beauvoir's *Second Sex* of 1949 is fascinating, and is not just a matter of generation.) Important though the French school was, there was more space open in the U.S. for pioneering critical thought in other fields. A second difference was the greater commitment in France to the primacy of social class as the exclusive category of analysis, and the sense that categories like "women" and "men" were just a diversion. I felt that this was the issue in the reluctant and tardy interest of some of my *Annales* friends in the study of gender. Resistance to the history of women and gender in the United States existed, but it was less likely to hinge on that, partly because "class" had fallen into disrepute as a mainstream term during the cold war ("social stratification" was preferred). The main quarrels I recall on that subject were among us on the left: there was a famous debate in Paris, where Joan Scott, Louise Tilly, and I took on Edward P. Thompson—we wanted gender to be part of the story along with class, and we felt we won the day.[34]

Another contrast is in the more decentralized structure of American universities compared to France. In France, decisions about curriculum and examination subjects were made by central bodies. In the United States, it was easier to get courses and research projects going in universities, and skeptical colleagues had the chance to see what the possibilities were for gender history.

In any case, one of the most exciting places intellectually in France that I knew during the 1970s was the seminar—we might even call it the "salon"—that Michelle Perrot organized at Jussieu for historians and other scholars to talk about research methods and topics concerning women.[35] I used to attend whenever I was in Paris, and marvel at Michelle's role of leadership, great historian as she was of the working class in the nineteenth century. Out of this ferment was born a whole network of historians of women and gender. Michelle Perrot and Georges Duby drew together the team that did the collective volumes of *A History of Women in the West,* published in several languages. A periodical was founded, *Clio: Histoire, femmes et sociétés,* now in its fourteenth year, which includes outstanding historians such as Christiane Klapisch-Zuber and Gabrielle Houbre[36] on its board of editors. And as for innovative writings and methodologies in the late medieval and early modern period, you can hardly do better than Klapisch-Zuber's books and essays on family, kinship, and wives in late medieval Florence and Arlette Farge's studies of women as part of the world of protest, public expression, and criminality in eighteenth-century Paris.[37] Éliane Viennot is in some ways the Michelle Perrot of her generation, as she's been the leading figure in founding the new International Society for the Study of Women of the Old Regime (SIEFAR in French), which has an enthusiastic following. Every week my email brings news from SIEFAR of activities and publications.[38] And what's interesting about Éliane Viennot's study of Queen Margot is not just the queen's life and career within the political universe of the late sixteenth and early seventeenth century, it's her long study of the myth of the Queen Margot.

DC: France, whatever else it might be, has never succeeded in becoming fully attuned to American research approaches to the history of women. There don't exist, as far as I know, in the great Parisian universities any professorial chairs in the history of women.

NZD: American research approaches are not the relevant criterion. It would be helpful to have a chair or two in France focused on the study of women and gender, and maybe that will come in the not-too-distant future. But the more important thing is that the history of gender became part of the teaching of history more generally. And that's happening. Catherine Coquéry-Vidrovitch,[39] celebrated Africanist in France and worldwide, has published on *les Africaines,* African women in the nineteenth and twentieth centuries, and her work has been snapped up for use by others. At the Collège de France[40] itself, there are scholars working on themes central to the study of women and gender: the anthropologist Françoise Héritier[41] in her explications of kinship and Mireille Delmas-Marty[42] in her reflections on gender relations in her courses on law. And long since, Georges Duby was teaching there on medieval marriage (I wrote the introduction to his wonderful book on the subject, when it appeared in English),[43] and Michel Foucault on the history of sexuality, while more recently Daniel Roche[44] included women in his fascinating research on the history of clothing. So themes on women have penetrated the august halls of the Collège de France. Much more could be done on masculinity, the other part of the story, but maybe that requires more daring.

Notes

1. Leona C. Gabel (1895–1980) was a scholar of the later Middle Ages and Italian Renaissance and published an important edition of the *Commentaries of Pius II* (1957). The Sforza family ruled Milan in the fifteenth century, and Caterina Sforza (1463–1509), the natural daughter of the duke, played a role in contemporary politics.

2. Mary Ritter Beard (1876–1958) was a historian who played a major role in the women's suffrage and labor movements. In addition to assisting her husband, the historian Charles Beard, she published pioneering books on women's role in history, including *On Understanding Women* (1931), *America Through Women's Eyes* (1933), and *Woman as a Force in History: A Study in Traditions and Realities* (1946).

3. Pietro Pomponazzi (1462–1525) was a major Aristotelian philosopher of the sixteenth century and known for his controversial *Tractatus de immortalitate animae* (*Treatise on the Immortality of the Soul*). There, following the two-truth theory of Averroës, he argued that one could believe in the immortality of the soul by faith, but by reason, one must follow Aristotle's argument that the soul was mortal.

4. Palmer Throop (1900–1986) was a specialist of the Crusades and medieval papacy, and published *Criticism of the Crusade: A Study of Public Opinion and Crusade Propaganda* (1940).

5. Baldassar Castiglione (1478–1529) was a churchman, diplomat, and author of the influential manual of courtly etiquette, *Il cortigiano* (*The Courtier*), published in 1528. Theodore M. Newcomb (1903–84) was an American social psychologist interested in the area of interpersonal attraction. His book referenced here first appeared in 1937.

6. Louise Tilly (1930–) is a pioneer in using sociological and statistical methods in the historical study of women, labor, and family life in modern Europe. Her works include *Women, Work and Family* (with Joan W. Scott; 1978) and *Politics and Class in Milan, 1884–1901* (1992). She was elected president of the American Historical Association in 1993.

7. Germaine Warkentin (1933–) is a specialist of Renaissance English literature, Canadian literature of exploration, and the history of the book. She served as director of the Centre for Reformation and Renissance Studies at the University of Toronto from 1985 to 1990.

8. Alison Prentice (1934–) is an expert on the history of nineteenth-century education and, more recently, gender and the teaching profession and the history of women and higher education in Canada. She was a professor at the Ontario Institute for Studies in Education and founder of the Ontario Women's History Network.

9. Charlotte Arbaleste de la Borde (1548–1606) began composing the memoir of her husband's

life in 1595 as her son was leaving home for the first time. It was not published until 1624, the year after her husband died, as *Mémoires de Messire Philippe de Mornay, Seigneur du Plessis.*

10. Philippe du Plessis-Mornay (1549–1623) was a noted French Protestant leader and writer best known for his works on political theory and theology.

11. Henri IV (1553–1610) was the first ruler of the Bourbon dynasty. On his life, see Vincent Pitts, *Henry IV* (2008), and Michael Wolfe, *The Conversion of Henri IV: Politics, Power, and Religious Belief in Early Modern France* (1993).

12. Margaret Lucas (1623–73), Duchess of Newcastle-on-Tyne, was a prolific English author of poetry and plays, and also composed an early form of science fiction. Her biography of her husband was published in 1667 as *The Life of the Thrice noble, high and puissant Prince, William Cavendish.*

13. Catharine Sawbridge Macaulay (1731–91) was an English historian and political pamphleteer, supporting freedom of the press and wider suffrage, among other causes. Her *History of England* was published in eight volumes between 1763 and 1783.

14. Anne Louise Germaine de Staël (1766–1817) was a prolific writer, literary critic, and commentator on public affairs during the revolutionary era. The book referenced here first appeared in 1818 and can be found in English translation as *Considerations on the Principal Events of the French Revolution* (2008).

15. *The Life of Glückel of Hameln 1646–1724* was translated by Beth-Zion Abrahams and published in 1963. See above on pp. 118–19 for the history of this translation.

16. The Berkshire Conference of Women Historians began in the 1930s, while the Berkshire Conference on the History of Women began meeting in the early 1970s. The papers presented at the conferences can be found in the Arthur and Elizabeth Schlesinger Library on the History of Women in America, Radcliffe Institute for Advanced Study, Harvard University.

17. Joan Wallach Scott (1941–) is a historian of France and a major innovator in the cultural and political study of gender. Her works include *Gender and the Politics of History* (1998), *Only Paradoxes to Offer: French Feminists and the Rights of Man* (1996), and *The Politics of the Veil* (2007).

18. Olwen Hufton (1938–) is a historian of early modern Europe and a pioneer in social history and the history of women. The book referenced here is *The Poor of Eighteenth-Century France* (1974).

19. Primo Levi (1919–87) was a Jewish-Italian chemist, Holocaust survivor, and author of memoirs, short stories, poems, essays, and novels. His *Survival at Auschwitz* first appeared in Italian in 1947 as *Se questo è uno uomo* (If This Be a Man) and was subsequently translated into English in 1958 by Stuart Woolf. The passage referenced here appears in chapter 11.

20. Marguerite de Navarre (1492–1549) was a noted patron of humanists and religious reformers, and sister of King François I and queen consort to King Henri II of Navarre. Along with her works of spiritual poetry and theatre, she composed novellas modeled after Boccaccio's *Decameron*. These stories were collected together and edited by Claude Gruget for a posthumous 1559 publication entitled the *Heptameron*.

21. Chava Turniansky (1937–) is an Israeli scholar of Old Yiddish. The work referenced here is her essay, "Literary Sources in the Memoirs of Glikl Hamel" [in Hebrew], in *Studies in Jewish Culture in Honour of Chone Shmeruk,* edited by Israel Bartal, Ezra Mendelsohn, and Chava Turniansky (1993). In 2006, Turniansky published a critical edition of Glikl's memoirs in Hebrew.

22. Gabriele Jancke (1958–) is a German historian specializing in the cultural study of gender and autobiography in the early modern era. The essay referenced is "Die Sichronot (Memoiren) der jüdischen Kauffrau Glückel von Hameln zwischen Autobiographie, Geschichtsschreibung und religiösem Lehrtext. Geschlecht, Religion und Ich in der Frühen Neuzeit," in *Autobiographien von Frauen: Beiträge zu ihrer Geschichte,* edited by Magdalene Heuser (1996).

23. Alfred Feilchenfeld (1860–1923) was a German schoolteacher and author of several books on Jewish history. His abridged edition of the memoir translated into German appeared as *Denkwürdigkeiten der Glückel von Hameln* (1913).

24. Bertha Pappenheim (1859–1936) was an Austrian-Jewish feminist, a social pioneer, and the founder of the Jüdischer Frauenbund (League of Jewish Women). Her translation is entitled *Die Memoiren der Glückel von Hameln* (1910).

25. The German translation was entitled *Mary Wollstonecraft—Eine Verteidigung der Rechte der*

Frau (1899). Mary Wollstonecraft (1759–97) was an eighteenth-century British writer, philosopher, and major feminist thinker. Pappenheim translated into German the *Maase-Buch,* a well-known medieval collection of Yiddish tales, drawn from the Talmud and folk traditions, much reprinted in the early modern period and especially directed to women readers, as *Allerei Geschichten, Maase-Buch* (1929).

26. Lorraine Daston (1951–) is an American historian of science, currently director of the Max Planck Institute for the History of Science in Berlin. Her books include *Classical Probability and the Enlightenment* (1988) and, together with Peter Galison, *Objectivity* (2007).

27. Peter Galison (1955–) is an American historian of science and physics. In addition to *Objectivy* (2007) coauthored with Lorraine Daston, his books include *How Experiments End* (1987) and *Einstein's Clocks, Poincaré's Maps: Empires of Time* (2003).

28. Georges Duby (1919–96) was a French medieval historian and prominent public intellectual in France. The full reference of the books cited is *Histoire des femmes en Occident,* 5 volumes (1991–92). Among his many books is *The Three Orders: Feudal Society Imagined* (1980; French edition, 1978).

29. Simone de Beauvoir (1908–86) was a French writer, existentialist philosopher, feminist, and social theorist best known for the work mentioned above. Her celebrated book *Le deuxième sexe* (1949) first appeared in English translation in 1952.

30. Luce Irigary (1932–) is a Belgian feminist philosopher and cultural theorist best known for her works *Speculum of the Other Woman* (1974) and *This Sex Which Is Not One* (1977).

31. Hélène Cixous (1937–) is a French feminist writer, literary critic, and academician. Among her major works is *Laugh of the Medusa* (1975).

32. Julia Kristeva (1941–) is a Bulgarian-French philosopher, critic, and feminist. She is a prolific writer across many fields, beginning with her first book, *Desire in Language: A Semiotic Approach to Literature and Art* (1969).

33. Betty Friedan (1921–2006) was an American feminist writer and activist who cofounded and was first president of the National Organization of Women (NOW) in 1966. Her *Feminine Mystique* of 1963 first appeared in French translation in 1964.

34. Edward P. Thompson (1924–93) was a British historian and public intellectual, who took Marxist historical writing in new directions after World War II. His 1963 *The Making of the English Working Class* had great impact on the writing of social history and the concept of class.

35. Jussieu refers to the campus in Paris where the Université de Paris 6 and 7 are located. Michelle Perrot was for many years professor of history at Université de Paris 7.

36. Gabrielle Houbre (1962–) is a French historian who specializes in the history of gender, sexuality, the body, and education, especially in regard to gender issues. She has published *La discipline de l'amour: L'éducation sentimentale des filles et des garçons à l'âge du romanticisme* (1997).

37. Arlette Farge (1941–) is a French social and cultural historian of the eighteenth century. Among her many works is the one referenced here, *Subversive Words: Public Opinion in Eighteenth-Century France* (1995). Together with Natalie Zemon Davis, she coedited *Renaissance and Enlightenment Paradoxes* (1993), volume 3 of *A History of Women in the West.*

38. See www.siefar.org/?lang=fr.

39. Catherine Coquéry-Vidrovitch (1935–) is a French historian of modern Africa from precolonial to modern times. Among her major works are *The History of African Cities South of the Sahara* (2005) and the one mentioned here, *African Women: A Modern History* (1997).

40. The Collège de France was founded in the sixteenth century and remains one of France's premier institutions of higher learning.

41. Françoise Héritier (1933–) is a French anthropologist of African societies and author of *Masculin/feminine: La pensée de différence* (1996) and *Two Sisters and Their Mother: The Anthropology of Incest* (1999).

42. Mireille Delmas-Marty (1941–) is a French professor of legal studies and international law.

43. The book is *The Knight, the Lady, and the Priest: The Making of Modern Marriage* (1994).

44. Daniel Roche (1935–) is French social and cultural historian of eighteenth-century France. The book referred to is *The Culture of Clothing: Dress and Fashion in the Ancien Régime* (1994).

Chapter 6

Commitments

DC: Let's now return to your life story. Let's go beyond your involvement in investigating the history of women in relation to the whole of history to the larger question of your commitments. Your family, in terms of its politics, was for the Democrats, no?

NZD: Yes. Except for the 1936 election, when he bizarrely voted for the Republican Alfred Landon, my father was a firm Democrat.[1] I don't know my mother's political views; I don't remember her ever talking to me about them.

DC: But as for you, during your youth, which political camp did you identify with?

NZD: In 1940, my father subscribed to *PM,* a new liberal-left periodical, which I read faithfully the minute I got home from school.[2] I especially followed Max Lerner[3] and I. F. Stone.[4] But even earlier in my grade-school years, I recall being concerned about questions of justice. This was linked with my being a Jew in a neighborhood with few Jewish families and in a world where anti-Semitic expressions were common, from the virulent sermons of Father Coughlin in nearby Dearborn to Hitler's hysterical harangues that we'd hear about on the radio.[5] I reacted in two ways. At Christmastime, when all the houses around our dark one were decked with lights, I hoped that the true messiah would come soon and tell the neighbors of their mistake, and also save us all from Hitler. As I grew a bit older, I began to have the sentiment—more enduring and important—that Jews, as a minority people, had a special mission to struggle for justice. If you wish, this was a social version of the idea of the chosen people, but one born from my personal experience rather than from formal teaching.

Then at Kingswood, my high school, a Jew among the *goyim,* I was president of the student council: I took my role very seriously indeed and wrote in the student newspaper about "an alert, enlightened student body" and about how "there can be no barrier between the [student] groups, for each of us finds her place in the scheme of things." My politics were more liberal than those of my classmates from Detroit's elite families: one of my best friends and I were the two Democrats in a sea of Republicans. Then during my last year at Kingswood, we had a mock election at the time of the U.S. presidential election and I voted for Norman Thomas, the Socialist candidate.[6] At that date, I assure you, I knew virtually nothing about socialism. In our current events class, we talked of the concentration camps as they came into the news, but never of socialism! I guess I must have wanted to appear as a rebel.

Two experiences of my high school years also influenced my moral and political sensibilities. One was the excessive competition I saw around me, which seemed so characteristic of American life: competition for grades among students, or competition for boyfriends or for popularity, competition for the best material goods—clothes or cars or houses—and the highest income among the middle-class families, and the inequalities all this resulted in. I found this very troubling, and it bothered me when that spirit hooked into me, say, in regard to grades, and set me at odds with my classmates, with whom I wanted to have friendship. I struggled for moral perspective on this—I can see now that an earnest phrase of mine from the school newspaper, "for each of us finds her place in the scheme of things," was an early effort to get an alternate view.

The other big experience was the race riots in Detroit in 1943, the uprising of the blacks who had come to Detroit from the South to work during the war and the fights between them and the whites.[7] The only black people whom I actually met up close during those years were the women who came to our house to cook or iron—the *Schwartzer,* my mother called them in Yiddish. But I knew of the discrimination against the black families in Detroit, and the riots and the reaction to them made it very evident. I felt solidarity with black people, a solidarity against discrimination. And in those days, there were political alliances between some Jewish groups and groups fighting for the rights of blacks—in fact there still are such alliances, despite the emergence in the last decades of right-wing Jews close to the Republican leadership.

Anyway, I had all these ideas and feelings in my head and heart when I arrived at Smith College in 1945. The political life there was very active in those years right after the war, with all the shades of opinion. I had friends of all different views, but I directed myself toward the little group on the left, of socialists and Marxists.

DC: Did you discover Marxism because you shared the intellectual affinities of your friends or by directly reading Marx?

NZD: A bit of both. I still remember how enthralled I was when I first read *The Communist Manifesto* in a history class.[8] I could see how the forms of competition that I had found so troubling were embedded in a whole capitalistic system with its profit motive. The idea of a world of equality, where everyone could have access to what they needed to live, where learning and the arts would be open to everyone captivated me. This utopian world charmed me.

DC: Wasn't this a sort of symbolic transfer of the image of the new Jerusalem or the overdue reclaiming of a Jewish hope that enabled Marxism to give history a purpose for you?

NZD: In a way, but not via the channel of Zionism. My knowledge of that movement did not come from my aunt Anna, who, though a devoted Zionist, did not discuss it with me, and in any case her brand of Zionism had no connection with socialist or left Zionism. A boyfriend from my high-school days told me about the Zionist founder Theodor Herzl.[9] I read some of his writings and about his life; I was interested, but not persuaded. My turning to the socialist ideal was rather a secularization of the messianic hopes of my girlhood, nourished by my reading and my history studies and my conversations with Smith friends.

DC: What kind of reading did you do?

NZD: I read some of the Marxist classics—parts of *Capital*; Plekhanov's essay on the materialist concept of history,[10] which did not impress me; Lenin's *State and Revolution*,[11] which was fun to read while I was studying revolutions; Engels's *Origin of the Family*.[12] These Marxist perspectives were always seasoned by other reading, for at the same time I was deep into Vico's *New Science* and Max Weber's works. Thinking back, I especially enjoyed the cultural criticism of British and European Marxist intellectuals: Christopher Caudwell's *Illusion and Reality*[13] and Georg Lukács's writings on the novel.[14] They suggested ways to fit literary creations together with social life.

DC: Didn't the time at which you were reading these authors coincide with a certain hardening of your own political commitments?

NZD: Hardening? I don't know that "hardening" is the word I'd use. *Acquiring* political commitments might be more like it. We were busy handing out pamphlets against racism, including in everyday matters. Any time we got onto a bus, we would always try to find a seat next to a black person. (By "we," I'm speaking here of the white progressives at Smith, though we did have one woman of color among us.) We campaigned against the atom bomb and for the international control of atomic energy. We spoke out against the Marshall Plan—that will seem to you really strange today, since the plan worked to rebuild Europe and was also so much more benign than America's other foreign adventures over the years. We were not at all hostile to foreign aid to help Europe, but *at the time,* the cold war was beginning, and we campaigned for the granting of such aid through the United Nations. Now I see that period with a more realistic eye, more cognizant of both Soviet and U.S. hidden agendas. A few years ago, when I was working on my book on *The Gift,* I was very struck by how your French Georges Bataille[15] interpreted the "gifts" of the U.S. Marshall plan when it was first being developed: he was glad of the cold-war opposition of the Soviet Union because it would keep the American gifts coming, but at the same time prevent them from being overly "warped in the direction of American interest." A very shrewd point. But as for us in those days, we wanted the world to be united to reconstruct Europe.

DC: Did these militant groups attract a lot of students or only a small number?

NZD: We were only a handful on the Marxist or "progressive left," as it was called then. There were one or two Trotskyists in our class. The liberal or social democratic group was larger—I had friends in all these camps.[16] As for me, I was doing my usual number of being active in two arenas: at the center, serving on some of the student government councils, and on the margins in leftist activities. I also wrote the words for a number of college songs while I was there.

DC: Much like the so-called Lutherans between 1530 and 1550, with their "spiritual songs" that denounced the pope as a corrupt man who offended God, Satan's agent to pervert the faith, and that sang about the glory of God by appropriating secular melodies. The Calvinists did the same thing in

the 1550s when they poked fun at the Roman Church in their satires. Isn't it curious to note that you lived through comparable experiences before you took up the study of these militant decades of the French Reformation?

NZD: The songs we lefties sang in those days were from the time of the Spanish Civil War, such as "Los cuatro generales," and from the 1930s U.S. labor movement, "Joe Hill" and "Solidarity Forever," and the "Peat-bog Soldiers Song" from the refugees from the Nazis.[17] And I surely did remember this when I came upon the printing workers of Lyon in the 1550s brazenly singing the Psalms in French in the streets so that all the priests could hear.

But the songs I myself wrote were of a different kind—class songs, college songs. One that I wrote for our annual Rally Day became something of a college favorite over the years, despite its problematic words for the later feminist movement. I wrote it to the music of "You Can't Get a Man with a Gun," a well-known song from the Broadway musical *Annie Get Your Gun*.[18] Mine was a takeoff: "You Can't Get a Man with Your Brains." It was really quite funny, and I even snuck in some of my political ideas in one of the verses: "You know the futility / Of marginal utility / That our enterprise is free / But that's all irrespective / For love's a thing collective, / Oh you can't get a man with your brains." I really have to laugh that I wrote that song not too long before I met my husband. And to think of me, the feminist, writing this song sung by generations of Smith students. [*laughter*] And yet the song was ironic about the relations between men and women, and I think there was something true about the line "you can't cram for a man / as you can an exam." Bookish relations are quite different from human relations.

DC: You introduce us here to one of the key dates in your biography, when you met Chandler Davis, an encounter that seems well to symbolize, yet again, this mix of rigor and romanticism, of the serious and the joyful that so characterizes both you and your work. Did you meet at Harvard?

NZD: Yes. At the end of my third year at Smith, I went to Harvard summer school to take a course in the history of science, a topic not then covered at Smith. It was the summer of 1948, the summer before the presidential elections. I had been active at Smith in support of the new third party, the Progressive Party, which put up Henry Wallace, the former vice president, as its candidate.[19] Of course, I attended the Students for Wallace meetings at

Harvard, and there I saw Chandler Davis, good-looking, intelligent, interesting—and he had a Ping-Pong paddle under his arm. Now I come from a sporting family, as I mentioned, and I always liked sports, especially tennis and Ping-Pong. I said to myself, "There's a young man on the left, who is handsome, intelligent, and he likes sports." By which I meant he's more "normal" than other young men I often saw at such gatherings. So I asked him if he'd like to play Ping-Pong with me. He said "Yes." Six weeks later, we eloped.

DC: A sudden elopement just like in the sixteenth century, only this time without abduction! But why so hush-hush, especially since, as you've already told me, this kind of furtiveness had made you so wary when seeing it in your own relatives? Was it because you feared your family's reactions?

NZD: Oh, yes! The major problem was that Chandler was not Jewish. I think if he had been Jewish, we would perhaps not have thought of eloping. He did not consider himself a Christian in any sense and was not even a believer in the supernatural, but he came from an old American family: some of his ancestors had arrived on *The Mayflower*. The family traditions were a mixture of liberal Protestantism. There were the Quaker Hallowells—pacifists, abolitionists, and even some early feminists among them.[20] Other ancestors were Unitarians; his great-great-great-grandfather Aaron Bancroft had been one of the founders of American Unitarianism.[21] His maternal grandmother had worked at Hull House.[22] Chandler's parents were on the left, and Jews were among their closest friends, especially refugees from Nazi Germany. Chan himself had had a Jewish girlfriend before he met me. So for him, there was no issue in marrying a Jew. If anything, he was favorable to Jews. He was a graduate student in mathematics and many of his fellow students were Jewish. And he and I shared our political ideals. I must say that if Chandler had been a *believing* Christian, there's no way I would have married him. As it was, he was completely at home with Jewish people, and such a marriage was not shocking for his parents.

As for a secret marriage, remember this was 1948. Today many young people might just move in together. But that was unthinkable for us. We had our ideals for a life together, married equality, and we thought that my parents would gradually accept us as a couple.

DC: Did you each give your parents any forewarning?

NZD: Not that we were planning to marry. One of Chan's cousins and her husband were our witnesses. Chan's parents took the news in stride. They had lived in Greenwich Village for a time when they were young and had somewhat bohemian friends in their circle of acquaintances. They were very warm and welcoming.

But it was quite otherwise with my parents, especially with my mother. I may not even have been the first member of her family to marry a *goy*; I think there was another family secret hidden away here. My mother was beside herself when she learned of our marriage; my father was upset, but less so, and he got over it fairly soon. In retrospect, I've wondered whether the strength of my mother's reaction may not have been partly fueled by her guilt toward her own mother for having stopped keeping a kosher household. It was my father's initiative, but she did it. And then I went farther yet...

DC: What happened with your mother? Did she refuse to see you? Could you tell me a bit more about your relationship with her?

NZD: My mother did not want to see me or even talk to me on the phone for several years. My marriage was so sudden for her. I was only nineteen, Chandler had just turned twenty-two. She didn't like the idea of my being married to a future professor—she wished for a businessman or a lawyer or a physician. She did not approve of my having a professional career: had her family come to America so that women would have to work? But the most serious thing was a marriage with a non-Jew, a profound rupture and act of disobedience. All this was very difficult for me—and most assuredly for her as well. My father and my brother, who was then a college student, continued to see us, as did my aunt Gertrude, my father's sister, who was preparing her doctorate, and even one of my cousins on the Lamport side. My mother finally came to visit me some weeks before the birth of our first child. During the next few years, she became involved in trying to market a silverware caddy that she'd designed—so she entered the business world after all. And she was pleased, I think, when my first book was published, but we never came to understand each other very well. Later when I came to write about clandestine marriages in sixteenth-century France and the family quarrels and state intervention that they aroused, I thought back to my own experience. Later still, I was able to tell my aunt Anna that I was writing about Jewish Glikl Hamel. "Such a pious lady," she commented.

DC: **Didn't socialism at that time enable people to transcend religious differences, to go beyond the habits of thoughts passed down through families? Wasn't this an ideal occasion to go beyond them?**

NZD: Chandler and I were united by common values, though this never effaced my Jewish identity, which I held onto. We were in agreement on our political values and our life project: we would be equals, we would both work, we would have children, and we'd organize our life around these goals. We didn't think we were going to save the world by mathematics and history—we sorted out our intellectual commitments from our politics. I thought our marriage could succeed despite our differences, and the social ones loomed much larger than the religious. That is, Chandler was from a family with an old American lineage, his father had a doctorate, his mother almost had one. They were college professors, albeit with modest posts. Chandler was marrying a young woman from a prosperous bourgeois family. We thought we could simply erase these differences, that they'd have no consequence for how we lived. We managed to do it, but we were naïve, I have to say...

DC: **Do you still consider yourself Jewish or do you affirm a kind of mixed creed, one in which this dream of overcoming all such differences is finally realized?**

NZD: Certainly I consider myself Jewish, and I never for a moment stopped having that as a part of my identity. What it means to me to be Jewish has been deepened by my personal and political experiences and by my later plunging into Jewish history. But no matter what, I've always held to the belief I had since my girlhood: being Jewish meant being distanced from worldly idols and being obliged to speak against injustice, suffering, and wrongdoing.

As for Chandler, I wouldn't talk so much about a "mixed creed" as an expansion of our family culture—expansion for both of us. I was glad to acquire through him and his relatives and their memories a link with American traditions, especially those of the American Revolution, abolitionism, the pacifist Quakers, and the movement for women's suffrage. Through my marriage, I was connected to another past. And Chandler felt the same way. When asked whether he's Jewish, he answers, "I married into a Jewish family" or "None of my ancestors are Jewish, but all my descendants are Jewish."

DC: And your children?

NZD: We have three children, a son and two daughters. We tried to suggest the mixture in their backgrounds by the names we gave them. So our son is Aaron Bancroft. Aaron is a Jewish name, but also an old New England name: Aaron Bancroft was one of the early Unitarians I mentioned, Chandler's ancestor. Our older daughter was Hannah Penrose, Hannah a clearly Jewish name, but also New England Quaker: Hannah Penrose was the mother of Chandler's abolitionist great-grandfather. Our younger daughter is Simone Weil. I wanted a name that could link the Jewish and French parts of my life. "Simone" is a version of my maiden name, Zemon, itself a version of Simon. Simone Weil came from a Jewish family, and Chandler and I much admired her courage, her empathy with suffering, and her moral vision during the 1930s and World War II. I must say, now that I think of it, that it was a heavy name to lay on a child. [*laughter*] Our Simone said to us one day when she was fourteen, "Couldn't you have named me Simone de Beauvoir?" Later, though, she became interested in Simone Weil's life and writings. On the whole, I think these names were more important for us than for our children.

DC: Did you give them a religious upbringing or did you allow them to make their own choices?

NZD: As we were not believers in a supernatural deity, the main link with our religious identities was through holidays, and we entwined the traditions. We celebrated the Jewish Passover and Hanukkah, and Christian holidays like Christmas, but with no reference to a divine Jesus or to God, as Chandler always insisted firmly that he was not Christian. He was not a religious believer, he was a man of science. Over the years, with all he heard from me about the history and anthropology of religion, he softened his attitude toward religious performance and he presided very nicely over our Passover seders. We actually composed our own Haggadah,[23] which linked the themes of Passover to our own ideals.

In retrospect, I wish we'd had more contact with other families like ourselves, left-wing or liberal Jews or mixed families, with whom we could have shared these holidays. We were rather isolated when our children were little because of the Red hunt—I can tell you about this later—and when we moved to Toronto, our time was very taken up with our intellectual work and our own household. So though Chandler and I had friends, we didn't belong to a network of families; we somehow didn't hear about the Winchevsky Centre, an old-time secular Jewish center in Toronto;[24] the various egalitarian synagogues of today may not have even existed in the 1960s, or if so, we knew nothing about them. And by accident, we had ended up in a Toronto neighborhood with few Jews. Hannah got the impression when she was a little girl that a seder was a special ceremony of the Davis family!

Now they're all grown up and with families of their own. They all three think of themselves as Jewish and welcome their mixed ancestry. Hannah's husband is from an ancient Jewish family of Tunisia, so there the mixture is spread in another direction. One of our Toronto grandsons has already had a humanist bar mitzvah at the Winchevsky Centre; the other is studying Hebrew for a more traditional rite of passage. All three of our children have done much better than we in creating family networks with people of different origins.

I must say that the whole question of creating families where different backgrounds and values are given their due is fascinating and challenging. I hope we did a good job. In any case, I'm thinking a lot about culture crossings in my current work on al-Wazzān.

DC: After your elopement, you followed your husband as he pursued his career while at the same time you also began your doctorate, right?

NZD: First I finished up my last year at Smith, and then moved to Harvard, where Chandler was writing his doctoral thesis in mathematics. There I took seminars with Myron Gilmore[25] on humanism—that's when I did the essay on Guillaume Budé—and got my first real introduction to social history in studying with W. K. Jordan.[26] In his seminar I wrote papers on artisanal movements in sixteenth-century Norwich and Ket's Rebellion in Norfolk in 1549.[27] Many archival sources were available in printed form in the Harvard library: Chandler helped me lug them home from Widener. What a discovery this was for me! Chandler finished his thesis that year and got his first job at the University of Michigan. So I switched to the University of Michigan graduate program. That's where I studied with Professor Throop and wrote on Christine de Pizan, and that's where I found in the library Henri Hauser's book on the workers of Lyon and his essays on the Reformation there. I now had the perfect case I could use to examine the question of the social sources of the Reformation. But at the very same moment, we were confronted with the cold war and Red hunt—

and they had unexpected consequences for the direction of my research.

DC: But weren't you able to go to France before?

NZD: I went in the midst of all this troubling excitement. Let me go back a bit. The first postwar meetings of the House Committee on Un-American Activities (HUAC)[28] took place before I met my husband. I was distributing pamphlets at Smith in the fall of 1947 protesting HUAC's attack on the Hollywood Ten, the screenwriters and filmmakers accused of communism. Little did I know that I'd one day be in a similar predicament! [*laughter*] Chandler and I were married just as the Red hunt was beginning. By the beginning of 1952, HUAC announced it was planning to have hearings in Michigan, with all the attendant publicity in the newspapers and on the radio that they whipped up. So I did research and drafted a pamphlet on the actual operation and goals of the committee; a wonderful friend of mine, Elizabeth Douvan,[29] a graduate student in social psychology, reviewed it with me for the final version. We called it *Operation Mind.*[30] We had it duplicated in photo-offset and it was distributed by two campus organizations, one of them a progressive faculty group, the Council of the Arts, Sciences and Professions. Nonetheless, Chandler and I both got our passports. The pamphlet appeared not long before our departures for France...

DC: You thus left for France in 1952, where you began your archival research in Lyon for six months before returning to the U.S. Did these troubles begin then?

NZD: In September 1952, I returned from Lyon pregnant. That was another benefit that I received from France. We had always planned to have a family, but didn't know when we'd start. Then at Lyon I saw for the first time in my life students who were mothers, women who were biking around the university and the student residences with babies on the back of their bicycles. So I said to Chan, "Okay, why don't we start now?'" I was twenty-three, and we figured we could begin our family while I was continuing the work on my doctoral thesis.

But a surprise awaited us upon our return to Ann Arbor: two agents from the State Department, prompted by the Federal Bureau of Investigation, came to withdraw our passports, with the accusation of communism, but especially because of *Operation Mind.*

DC: A pamphlet dated six months earlier... Tell me, what do you now think about this imputation of communism? What did you and Chandler feel at the time? What was so disturbing or radical about *Operation Mind*?

NZD: In fact, I was not a Communist, but we felt a solidarity with the men and women who were being attacked—Communists and non-Communists—in the witch hunt, and we were very troubled by the mood in the universities and across America: fear, suspicion, self-censorship, the shrinking of vision and thought. *Operation Mind* showed that the questions being posed by HUAC to the subpoenaed witnesses had nothing to do with the supposed charge of the committee, which was to uncover a plot to overthrow the government of the United States by force and violence. In the sessions with the Hollywood filmmakers and screenwriters, the questions put to them concerned the themes of their movies, the representation of the rich and the poor, for example, and had nothing to do with any illegal act they'd committed. The pamphlet pointed out the range of the people accused: many distinguished professors, including recipients of the Nobel Prize, rabbis, pastors—that is, people of diverse political views, ordinarily on the left but not necessarily Communists. We talked of the consequences for the employment and the lives of the people attacked—their pictures plastered all over the newspapers, fired from their jobs, and so on. And we insisted on the importance for teaching of an open atmosphere, as we put it in the pamphlet: "There is no area of human endeavor which needs more the assurance of freedom from fear and intimidation than the instruction of young people in the pursuit of knowledge." A very troublesome idea for the members of HUAC!

DC: I imagine this was the beginning of a very upsetting time for you.

NZD: I felt very sad about the loss of my passport. I was without it for eight years. I finally got it back in 1960—I might have retrieved it if I'd tried the year before. What a frustration for a historian so oriented toward the French archives! I'd collected quite a lot in Lyon, but I'd been there only six months. I had been counting on a second research trip and now I had to give it up. The positive side to all this was that I turned toward the riches of the American rare book collections.

DC: All printed documents?

NZD: Yes, sixteenth-century books printed at Lyon. Publications from

Lyon are found in abundance in the American rare book libraries.

DC: **Did your interest in the book start at this time, not only for its textual content as a historical or literary expression, but also as a source of information on the networks and the modes of distribution and expansion of ideologies, on the implications or sociocultural determinants of working in print shops?**

NZD: Yes, it helped me enormously in understanding what it meant to be a printer in sixteenth-century Lyon to have *the actual books they'd made in my hands.* In regard to the journeymen printers, I could understand so much better what it meant to create a book. I could have a stronger sense of the pride in the products of their labor that they expressed in their strike pamphlets, that dignity, that claim to be as much printers as their masters. Having the objects they had made in my hands gave me many new ideas.

DC: **Can we rediscover the socioreligious or sociopolitical experience even in the production of an object, in its very form, in its distinguishing characteristics, its typographical organization, its diverse modes of expressions, as in a poster, a science book, or a religious polemic?**

NZD: Both the content and the form were important. I came across popular religious literature and tracts not known before. And I discovered all kinds of things by examining dedications, images, accompanying material, author portraits, and the like. In 1956 I published a paper on the "Catholic" and the "Protestant" editions of Holbein's *Pictures of Death;* the same pictures and verses were given a different frame by the religious tracts that different printers placed in the edition. The Sorbonne doctors of theology noticed it, and put the "heretical" editions on their list of prohibited books. But I could never have observed this without having the actual books before my eyes.

And I took time out from my doctoral dissertation to work on the history of mathematics. I had taken a minor field in the history of science at the University of Michigan and, of course, my husband was a mathematician! Columbia University possessed very great collections of books in the history of mathematics and accounting, and there I came upon commercial arithmetics published in sixteenth-century Lyon and elsewhere. The dedications and introductory poems of some of them presented commercial arithmetic as if it were a noble and distinguished activity. I said to myself, "That's strange. I always thought commerce was looked down upon as demeaning [*dérogeant*] in early modern France, and here so much fuss is being made about it." I followed this path in several directions and ended up publishing an essay on "Sixteenth-Century French Arithmetics on the Business Life." I never would have done this if I hadn't had the books as objects, a compensation...

DC: Compensation for the fact that you couldn't go to France!

NZD: Exactly. But those were also challenging years in other ways because my husband got subpoenaed by HUAC.

DC: Didn't he cover up for you, especially because even he in the end didn't know about the editing of this loose-leaf pamphlet, *Operation Mind*?

NZD: Actually, Chandler's political engagement had been much more important and longer standing than mine. The FBI knew only a little bit about him. Some of their agents had visited a historian who had been a Communist during his student days at Harvard. They had shown him a list of persons who they said had been Communist students there and asked for his confirmation. Chan's name was on the list, and he confirmed Chan had been a Communist. We learned of this only thirty years later from a third person to whom the historian told the story, assuring her that he confirmed Chan's name only because it was already there, that he would never have volunteered it, and that he was sorry. Chan had no memory of ever meeting him at any political event, though perhaps their paths had in fact crossed. But I knew the historian. He was afraid. I pardoned him for that reason, when I heard the story, and because he expressed his regrets. I never saw him again, but I pardoned him totally in my mind.

As for HUAC, it was woefully ill informed about Chan's political actions; he was almost insulted. Its main recent evidence concerned the pamphlet *Operation Mind*. He had been treasurer of the University of Michigan Council of the Arts, Sciences, and Professions, which had distributed the pamphlet, and had signed the check for the printing. When the FBI came to the printer to inquire, he obliged with Chandler's name and this information was given to HUAC. (It's amusing to think that all this was going on while I was following clandestine printing and repression in sixteenth-century Lyon!) Then HUAC sent its agents to the president of the University of Michigan and presented him with a rather long list of alleged Communists whom it was planning to subpoena.

DC: Whatever might be said, there was cowardice on the part of your colleagues, and it's very important to see here that the university world can very quickly become divided, lose all sense of unity because academics, while apparently always very proud of their training, are often more easily frightened and cowed than others.

NZD: Let me describe in more detail what happened. The HUAC agents met privately with the president of the university, Harlan Hatcher,[31] and presented him with a list of fifteen persons they planned to subpoena, most of them professors. Hatcher himself decided which ones he wanted to protect and which ones he would get rid of—because they were young or otherwise dispensable. Chan was the youngest of the professors; he was then twenty-seven and without tenure; he was very brilliant and had publications, but he was early in his career. Hatcher selected four professors who he was sure would not cooperate with HUAC and whom he promised to fire after their testimony. Chan was one, the other three were older: a distinguished mathematician and two brilliant physiologists. For the others, special arrangements were made, testimony *in camera* where they may have been "friendly witnesses" or some other accommodation.

I tell this story because even though Chandler got a warning ahead of time from President Hatcher or the vice president that he would be fired, I didn't assimilate that at the time. I didn't want to think of our fate, of the outcome of our difficulties, as predetermined at a private meeting of three or four individuals. I wanted to think about it the way I thought about historical events, as the product of social movements and with diverse causes. I was waiting for the resistance from our colleagues and the students. I wanted to see us as in a situation that had not been determined, subject to the contingent, the possible.

DC: You thus don't separate your experience even from history, the small incident of Chan's appearance before a congressional committee, from the way in which you then conducted your close analysis of history? You have this sense of certainty, shared among historians, that an event is not reducible to the individual actions of particular people, but to a congeries of structural factors, long-term and medium range, that intervene more or less clearly.

NZD: I think that the individual actions of particular people have consequence, but always in conjunction with other movements and variables. That's the way I've viewed the past in my decades of pursuing the historian's craft.

For example, I've never accepted the explanation of the Saint Bartholomew's Day Massacre as simply the result of the decision of Catherine de Médicis, Charles IX, and their counselors. Their decision had a role, but more interesting to me were all the variables, all the feelings, beliefs, sensibilities, rituals of violence (to go back to my own essay), which came together in Paris in the events of the night of August 24, 1572, and in other towns in the next days. The Holocaust has aroused the same debate. Was it simply Hitler's project? Did it take place following exactly his plan? Were there other real possibilities—expulsion rather than mass murder? Was improvisation part of the story? How essential was the initiative of local people? And so on. My preference in interpretation would be for complexity. There was Hitler, but also more than Hitler.

I want to make a chronological jump for a moment here in my own story. In 1989, a group of undergraduates at the University of Michigan decided to make a film about the professors who were fired in 1954 after the HUAC hearings.[32] In fact, only two of the four were finally fired, Chan and Mark Nickerson,[33] one of the physiologists; the older mathematician[34] was so very ill that he was able to avoid the HUAC hearings, the other physiologist was kept on partly because of faculty and student resistance—so we had a victory of a kind. The former president, Harlan Hatcher, was still alive in 1989—ninety years old or more; so was the vice president. The students interviewed the actors on all sides. Watching the film, I was shocked in listening to Harlan Hatcher, still very righteous about his actions: *he had decided that we would be excluded. He* had made a decision about *us,* a decision that affected us deeply. I was very unsettled, but I laughed and made fun of myself: "Natalie Davis, you've always been dismissive or at least suspicious of conspiracy theories in history as inadequate. You've always thought of history as complex. And now it turns out that the fix was in—you and especially Chandler were simply living out a decision already made by a few people behind closed doors."

This experience has not profoundly modified my practice as a historian, but I've chuckled over the irony—that a single person could seem to have such an impact on our lives. As I thought about it, I realized how impersonal it was for Hatcher. He hardly knew Chandler; Chandler was just available for being disposed of. And Hatcher did not get everything his way. He was finally prevented from firing one of the professors. And as for us, he didn't ruin us as scholars. Chan got huge support from his mathematical colleagues at the time and in later decades was invited back to Ann Arbor to give math colloquia. There's now an annual Academic Freedom lecture at the University of Michigan, sponsored by the Faculty Senate, to mark the wrongful firings of 1954.

DC: Doesn't this lead us back to history's mutually contradictory nature as simple and complex at the same time? That's because not only sources can be convoluted and slanted, but because the agents behind an event rendered them both simple and complex through the very systems of representation they used? If there's a self-fashioning of the individual due to the nexus of contingencies of a specific moment, it's the same for a historical event. Indeed, historical events go through a kind of self-fashioning before which the historian must avoid succumbing to positivist understanding.

If we consider the Saint Bartholomew's Day Massacre, it's striking to note that, contrary to theories about its premeditation or of Catherine de Médicis's Machiavellianism, contrary to the idea of a Guisard *putsch,* we can instead accept the notion that everything occurred as a kind of fevered frenzy, all very rapidly, during all the different meetings with the king during the evening and night of August 23 and 24. Several counselors, the Queen Mother, and no doubt the king readied a plan to kill the main Huguenot leaders in Paris to celebrate the royal marriage. The event, beyond the less immediate and long-term factors involved in it, was a human event, a decision that, even if it's a complex one only further complicated by other related incidents, even if there were attempts to cover it up, still in the end depended on a handful of individuals acting under pressure. Pressures such as the anger felt by Huguenot captains following the attempt on Admiral Coligny's life on August 22 and their desire to transform a recent political setback—the failure to gain royal support for the war in the Low Countries—into an accusation against the Guises. Pressures of the Catholic faction that did not accept the mixed marriage between the Protestant Henry of Navarre and the Catholic Marguerite of Valois and that hoped for some spectacular eradication of God's enemies, the Huguenots. Pressures in which, from one side to the other, politics and religion became intermingled in such a way as to undermine the viability of the monarchy's efforts to maintain political order and render the elimination of the Huguenot leadership—some sixty men in all—as the lesser evil to solve an otherwise impossible dilemma and thus escape a political crisis that targeted the monarchy. We can then think that the crime, even if Charles IX and his mother tried thereafter to cover it up, sprang from their initiative, from an action they took only under extreme duress. The entire problem arose from the loss of control around seven or eight o'clock in the morning when the massacre escalated into a huge orgy of sacral violence that killed at least two or three thousand Huguenots and pushed the crown, in order not to lose total control of the panic-stricken capital, to cast about for justification. But the original crime began in effect as a conspiracy, a "ploy" [*pratique*] to use contemporary parlance, cunningly improvised by a small group of counselors who set it in motion... Men who were probably then responsible for the sudden disjointed explanation that left open any number of possible histories, that better rendered history ever malleable and subject to change due to the unstable course of destiny...

What I'd like to say here about events from the sixteenth century is that we must always be careful and modest in our claims. When history eludes our ability to analyze it with any assurance or sense of control, it isn't by chance. It rather reflects a political culture that fashioned the present—in a world marked by transience, the uncertainty of individuals, dissimulation or duplicity, or both—as a moment open to any number of possibilities. In this way, history can ceaselessly be shaped and reshaped. If we don't truly know what happened on the night of August 23 to 24, it's also because the idea and practice of history by the groups involved wanted a level of uncertainty to persist, or rather these uncertainties persisted even beyond the words that were spoken.

But I stray from our conversation. I only went off on this tangent when hearing you describe the insight that came to you that actual life and the theory of history don't necessarily coincide, that what we can personally realize from history becomes revealed as a result of other possibilities or scenarios than the ones we plan for the past lives of other people.

After Chan was expelled, how did you live since he was without work? Did it take you long to find alternative solutions?

NZD: There was more at stake than his firing from the University of Michigan. Chandler had decided in his testimony before HUAC to plead the First Amendment in the Bill of Rights, and not the Fifth. The Fifth Amendment allows silence only because you fear a criminal charge might ensue. The First Amendment forbids Congress to interfere with freedom of expression. So by pleading it, as had the Hollywood Ten years before, Chandler was inviting once again a test case of HUAC. He was then duly indicted by the Department of Justice for contempt of Congress, but don't feel sorry for us because of that—he had sought the test case and we were in agreement on it. But the case dragged on for years...

DC: **You must have had the impression that it would never finish, didn't you?**

NZD: Yes, he was subpoenaed in 1953, testified before HUAC, and was fired in 1954, and then his First-Amendment case was in the courts till the end of 1959. It went up to the Supreme Court. After Chan's appearance before HUAC, a friend of ours—a professor of psychology at Vassar—read his testimony and decided to take the same position when he was subpoenaed, and his test case happened to get to the Supreme Court before Chan's.[35] The Court denied his appeal in a split decision. When Chan's similar appeal came up not long afterward in late 1959, the Court declined to hear it—though even then two judges, Justices Black[36] and Douglas,[37] would have liked to hear argument. So in January 1960, Chandler went off to prison to serve his sentence for a misdemeanor.

DC: **How long did he spend in prison?**

NZD: Five months. He was sentenced to six months, but given one month off for good behavior.

DC: **Which prison was it?**

NZD: Danbury Federal Correctional Institution—a relatively "privileged" prison. Men who have been incarcerated elsewhere, but have been good prisoners, get transferred there for the last years of their sentence. U.S. Senators and wealthy people convicted of corruption serve their time there. An amusing irony—J. Parnell Thomas,[38] the head of HUAC during the days of Hollywood Ten,[39] was convicted of corruption and was imprisoned at Danbury a few years before Chan walked through its gates. [*laughter*] Chan was a fellow-con with businessmen who had cheated on their business accounts... If the Enron directors are ever convicted, no doubt they'll go to a prison like Danbury.[40]

DC: **But Chan was a bit of an odd duck among this set of distinguished prisoners!**

NZD: The prison population at Danbury was much more varied than that. Two other First-Amendments challengers were there, our friend from Vassar and another professor, and also one or two men who had passed secrets to the Soviet Union. Apart from the white businessmen and small-scale traders, there were many black people and Hispanics who had been involved, say, in stealing government checks. They were impressed when Chan said he was in for contempt of Congress, which sounded like a big deal, and also congratulated him on exercising with the weights after all those years of exercising his brain. One Saturday toward the end of his time, he was listening to the allowed jazz program from New York on the prison radio when it was suddenly preempted by live coverage of the huge demonstration against HUAC in San Francisco. He knew it was the beginning of the end for HUAC—and he was right!

As for the six years in the 1950s while his case was in the courts, Chan's situation was unstable. To keep our heads above water financially, he worked for about two years for an advertising agency in New York, which for its own reasons wanted to have a mathematician with a doctorate on its staff. He kept doing mathematics and publishing, but he couldn't get a regular university post: each time a mathematics department recommended his being hired, the FBI and/or someone in the administration would intervene and the offer would be dropped. He did give courses at the School of General Studies at Columbia and also at the New School, which had received so many refugees from Germany and France in the 1930s—and they deserve credit for being willing to give him something. Then the American Mathematical Society came to his aid, and invited him to be one of the editors for its reviewing journal in Providence, Rhode Island.

DC: How did you put up with all this?

NZD: Let me say first of all that there were wonderful things in those years: our three children. Our son Aaron was born in 1953, several months after our passports were lifted, and Chan was subpoenaed later that year. Then in 1954 and 1957 we had our daughters, Hannah and Simone. The children were a total joy, completely overshadowing the challenges with Chan's case. And then I was working on my dissertation, using the marvelous libraries in New York, especially the New York Public Library and Columbia, and doing the other research I mentioned. I even taught a night course one term at Columbia's School of General Studies. So we survived, though we didn't have much of a social life.

DC: Was this the time when people you knew stopped wanting to see you due to these same political reasons?

NZD: Yes, there were some who did not want to see us. We were a little bit pariahs. But, you know, I was already somewhat hardened to this because of the conflict with my mother over our marriage. And my father and brother continued to visit us and some other dear friends. I went to history conferences to try to stay in touch. I especially remember one of the early meetings of the new Society for French Historical Studies. Two people whom I had known and cared about brushed by and would scarcely greet me. I was sitting by myself in dismay, when Father Moody—Monsignor Joseph Moody, a stalwart of the society—came up and started chatting with me.[41] I never forgot his kindness, and have taken him as a model when I go to professional meetings.

So there were times when I did feel alone. But I had the presence of the people from the past, whose history I was studying. And one or two friends: Rosalie Colie, then teaching literature at Barnard, would give me supper before I taught my night school classes. My friendship and correspondence about French history with Nancy Roelker was precious. And Chandler and I had the children and each other. I said to myself after those years that if we'd had a more normal path, we might have had other kinds of anxieties: "Am I going to get tenure at my university? Am I as important as the other assistant professors? Have I published enough? Am I doing the kind of scholarship that will get me promoted?" I would have been submitted to the pressure and the competitive system that I had found disagreeable since my girlhood. I might have been worried about what people would say if I went in new directions with my work, I might have been less willing to take risks. As it was, I was somewhat isolated, but at least I was not in the "success" struggle.

DC: How do you feel today? You have, despite everything, managed to overcome these difficulties, but don't you still feel some indignation about it all?

NZD: I decided long ago that it wasn't worth the trouble to be bitter about what happened. I won't say I pardoned everyone—I certainly felt angry at Harlan Hatcher when I heard him telling his story with such pride in the students' film—but on the whole I look back at that period without resentment. It's not as though Chandler were in a Nazi or Soviet prison or as if we had been dragged off to a concentration camp in Germany or to the Gulag.

DC: Was the decision to leave the United States to go live in Canada a political act, a kind of temporary rejection of the United States that arose from a sense of injustice?

NZD: No, not at all.

DC: Was it fate yet again? Was it against your will?

NZD: Colleagues at the University of Toronto were very ready to hire Chan. We would not have thought of turning to Canada while his case was still in the U.S. courts. The initiative to bring him to Toronto was taken by a very great mathematician, Donald Coxeter,[42] a remarkable man, who has just passed away at ninety-five years of age. Chandler went to the University of Toronto in 1962, and that's been the base for his professional life ever since. There have been times when he's disagreed strongly with some university policy, but it's always been within the limits of a "loyal opposition." The University of Toronto is *his* university–it welcomed him when he could not get a university post in the United States; he cares a great deal about it. But he was not rejecting the United States as such and has been very active in both the professional and political life there over the decades.

DC: When did you receive your PhD? Was it before you left for Canada?

NZD: I finished my dissertation on "Protestantism and the Printing Workers of Lyon" in 1959, and mailed it to the University of Michigan from Providence, Rhode Island, where we were then living. My daughter Simone was two years old. Several months later Chan got a leave from his job as mathematical editor and went off to Danbury federal prison to serve his sentence. As for me, I taught for three years at Brown University, where I had students I much enjoyed. I'm still in touch with some of them. I gave courses on the Reformation and participated in the introductory history courses, one of them organized around primary texts and quite experimental and interesting. Barbara Lewalski,[43] just beginning the career that was to make her one of our greatest Miltonists, was a very special friend, as was her husband, the historian Kenneth Lewalski.[44] They were staunch friends, as were others in Providence as well, when my husband was in prison. And there was the John Carter Brown Library, one of the great libraries of the world for travel and geographical literature; that's where I first came upon the beautiful 1556 French edition of Leo Africanus's *Description de l'Afrique*.

So the social and cultural resources of the place one happens to live can turn one in new directions.

In 1962, I followed Chandler to Toronto. There were some years where I had difficulty in getting a regular post in a history department. For a year I taught in a Great Books course in humanities at the recently founded York University, and finally became part of the Political Economy Department at the University of Toronto. This was a very interesting department, which put together politics, economics, and economic history—really in the grand tradition of the early twentieth century. For several years I taught economic history, rather like your great-grandfather Henri Hauser. I'm glad I had this chance. My publications from that period on "A Trade Union in Sixteenth-Century France" and on welfare reform in Lyon didn't just grow out of my doctoral dissertation, they were nourished by this milieu. And in my undergraduate lectures I was able to introduce material on women's work and early trade unions into the traditional narrative of the Industrial Revolution. But the field of economic history was starting to become very mathematical. That was not my direction—I was moving toward the anthropological and the cultural—and I knew I'd never have graduate students in economics wanting to work with me.

DC: What happened then and who decided upon this new course?

NZD: I was invited to Berkeley to be a visiting professor of history in 1968. When the Department of History at the University of Toronto learned that Berkeley was interested in me and took seriously my publications, they decided to offer me a post. After my months in California, I taught three years in the UT history department. I had some very exciting graduate students—we read Foucault's *Madness and Civilization* together and Ariès's *Centuries of Childhood* and various *Annales* historians and lots of sixteenth-century sources—and Jill Conway and I started our course in Society and the Sexes. Then Berkeley invited me to join the Department of History as a tenured professor. Chan and I talked it over for quite some time: his job was in Toronto and, if Aaron and Hannah were already in their midteens, Simone still had high school ahead of her. In January 1972, I started teaching at Berkeley...

DC: Did you actually participate in the great sit-ins in Berkeley, in the demonstrations, and did all this give you some sense of what the seditions and religious upheavals of the sixteenth century must have been like?

NZD: The great Free Speech sit-ins at Berkeley were back in 1964, but the anti-Vietnam War movement was going strong when I visited there in 1968.[45] I took part in a number of demonstrations; at one point I felt my graduate seminar was meeting on antiwar marches. [*laughter*] One of my sharpest memories is of witnessing David Harris,[46] then the husband of Joan Baez,[47] burn his draft card in front of the Oakland Army Induction Center. We had all gathered very early in the morning, before sunrise. I immediately thought of the Protestant artisan in Lyon, imprisoned in 1534 for having distributed heretical works and who from his prison cell had mocked the great cathedral of Saint Jean: "It's only a piece of stone. Heaven is our church." Though I know history never repeats itself exactly, I had this sense of connection: our little band of demonstrators, this man with his draft card burst into flames, and the severe stone military building.

DC: Wasn't your commitment to opposing the Vietnam War linked to your long-standing pacifism, to your long-standing hostility to American interventionism?

NZD: I considered the Vietnam War an unjust war. I have never been an absolute pacifist. My strong preferences have always been for diplomatic solutions, solutions through negotiation, arbitration, compromise when possible. But despite the war crimes committed by all parties along the way (the Germans, the Japanese, the Soviets, the British bombing of Hamburg and Dresden, the U.S. atomic bombing of Hiroshima and Nagasaki), despite that, World War II was a just war to stop the Nazi murders, the German conquest of Europe, and Japanese aggression. In Vietnam, no, the U.S. invasion of Vietnam was not a just war.

DC: You rediscover here the rhetoric of the sixteenth century and the debates over just and unjust war, for war could not be just for a number of Erasmian humanists, for example, unless it was a war of self-defense against a foreign invader.

NZD: True. And, of course, this reflection has surfaced once again in debate over the invasion of Afghanistan in 2001 and now the invasion of Iraq.

Notes

1. Alf Landon (1897–1987) was the Republican governor of Kansas from 1933 to 1937 who lost the 1936 presidential election to Franklin D. Roosevelt.

2. *PM* ran from 1940 to 1948 and was a pioneer in photojournalism as well as an early venue for cartoons by Dr. Seuss. See Paul Milkman, *PM: A New Deal in Journalism, 1940–1948* (1997).

3. Max Lerner (1902–92) was an American journalist who wrote for *The Nation* in the 1930s and then had a syndicated column the *New York Post* after the closing of *PM*.

4. I[sidor] F[einstein] Stone (1909–87) was an American investigative journalist known for his outspoken and independent left-wing views. He wrote for many newspapers and magazines, and then, blacklisted during the McCarthyism of the 1950s, founded his own *I. F. Stone Weekly Reader,* which kept his critical voice alive for decades.

5. Father Charles Coughlin (1891–1979) was a Roman Catholic priest who early on used the radio to reach a mass audience. After initially supporting the New Deal in 1932, he turned to views sympathetic to the social policies and violent anti-Semitism of the Nazis. See Donald Warren, *Radio Priest: Charles Coughlin, The Father of Hate Radio* (1996).

6. Norman Thomas (1884–1968) was a leading American socialist, pacifist, and six-time candidate for president of the United States. See Ralph F. Gregory, *Norman Thomas: The Great Dissenter* (2008).

7. The Detroit Race Riot broke out in June 1943 and lasted three days. Thirty-four people were killed before federal troops restored order.

8. *The Communist Manifesto* by Karl Marx and Friedrich Engels first appeared in 1848.

9. Theodor Herzl (1860–1904) was an Austro-Hungarian journalist and founder of modern political Zionism. In 1896, he published *The Jewish State,* calling for a state in "a portion of the globe" (Palestine or elsewhere) to which European Jews who wished to would move; in 1902, he published a utopian novel, *Old-New Land,* in which he imagined a multilingual, open Jewish polity in Palestine, without an army.

10. Georgi Plekhanov (1857–1918) was a Russian revolutionary and Marxian theoretician. His book *The Materialist Conception of History* appeared in 1891.

11. Vladimir Ilyich Lenin (1870–1924) was born Vladimir Ilyich Ulyanov and became leader of the Bolshevik Revolution in Russia in 1917 and the first head of the new U.S.S.R. *The State and Revolution* came out in 1917 and presented his views on the role of the state in society and the necessity of a proletarian revolution.

12. The full title of this work is *The Origin of the Family, Private Property, and the State* (1884).

13. Christopher Caudwell is the pseudonym of Christopher St. John Sprigg (1907–37). He was a British Marxist writer, thinker, and poet whose works appeared posthumously, beginning with *Illusion and Reality* (1937).

14. Georg Lukács (1885–1971) was a Hungarian Marxist philosopher and literary critic. Among his many books were *Theory of the Novel* (1920), *History and Class Consciousness* (1923), and *The Historical Novel* (1937).

15. Georges Bataille (1897–1962) was an avant-garde French novelist, cultural critic, and philosopher who, influenced by the writing of Marcel Mauss on the gift and sacrifice, developed a theory of a general economy in the universe: all energy, erotic and economic, was somehow expressed or exchanged. His reference to the Marshall Plan in this regard appeared in the last chapter of volume 1 of *The Accursed Share* (1947).

16. Trotskyists were followers of Leon Trotsky's teachings that socialism in one country, as practiced by the Soviet Communist party, was impossible and that the Stalinist regime was a deformation of communism. One of the Trotskyist youth groups in the 1940s was YPSL, the Young People's Socialist League. The social democrats were various groups of European socialists who opposed the Communist notion of a vanguard party. The social democratic student group at Smith College in the late 1940s was SDA, Students for Democratic Action. The progressive student groups at Smith College at that time were AYD, American Youth for Democracy, and the Marxist Discussion Group.

17. "Los Cuatro Generales" is a song from the Spanish Civil War that uses the Andalusian tune "Los Quatro Muleros." The four generals are Francisco Franco, Emilio Mola, José Varela, and Gonzalo Queipo de Llano. Joe Hill (1879–1915) was a songwriter and labor activist or "Wobbly" in the Industrial Workers of the World (IWW). His execution in Utah stirred great controversy and inspired "Solidarity Forever," written by fellow Wobbly Ralph Chaplin in 1916, and the song "Joe Hill," originally composed as a poem by Alfred Hayes around 1930 and set to music by Earl

Robinson in 1936. The "Peatbog Soldiers Song" was composed by German prisoners in an early concentration camp in 1933 and written down by Hanns Eisler in 1935.

18. *Annie Get Your Gun* is a musical with lyrics and music written by Irving Berlin that premiered on Broadway in 1946.

19. The United States Progressive Party of 1948 was a loose coalition of leftist parties formed after World War II. Henry A. Wallace (1888-1965) was the thirty-third vice president of the United States (1941-45). The student group formed at Smith College in 1948 was entitled Students for Wallace.

20. The Hallowell ancestors of Chandler Davis settled in Pennsylvania, where the Quaker merchant Morris Longstreth Hallowell and his wife, Hannah Penrose, were parents of Norwood Penrose Hallowell (1839-1910). Norwood Penrose Hallowell and his two brothers were staunch abolitionists and served as colonels of Massachusetts black infantry troops during the Civil War. John T. Galvin, "The Hallowells: Fighting Quakers," *Proceeding of the Massachusetts Historical Society* 104 (1992): 42-54. Reference courtesy of Hannah Davis Taïeb.

21. Aaron Bancroft (1779-1839) was educated at Harvard University and came to reject the Calvinist theology of his forebears in favor of Unitarian teachings and spiritual liberty. Jesus Christ was perceived as a morally perfect human, and God's nature was unitary rather than trinitarian, a view that won him much opprobrium for a time from other Christian ministers. In 1786, with like-minded believers, he founded the Second Congregational Church in Worcester, Massachusetts, and in 1825 became president of the newly formed American Unitarian Association. He was married to Lucretia Chandler, and their daughter Eliza became the wife of Governor John Davis of Massachusetts.

22. Hull House was a community center or settlement house established by Jane Addams (1860-1935) in 1889 in Chicago, Illinois, in which active women provided social and cultural service to working families. Addams was the second woman to receive the Nobel Peace Prize, in 1931.

23. The Haggadah is the Jewish religious text that sets out the order of the Passover seder.

24. Winchevsky Centre and the Morris Winchevsky School were established in 1928 and are affiliated with the United Jewish People's Order of Canada, a progressive group founded in 1926. Its mission is to strengthen ties to Jewish culture and heritage within a secular humanist framework.

25. Myron Gilmore (1910-78) was a Renaissance specialist and the author of *The World of Renaissance Humanism, 1453–1517* (1952) and *Humanists and Jurists* (1963), among other works.

26. W[ilber] K[itchner] Jordan (1902-80) was a historian of early modern Britain best known for his four-volume *The Development of Religious Toleration in England* (1932-40) and his *Philanthropy in England 1480–1660: A Study of the Changing Pattern of English Social Aspirations* (1959). He was president of Radcliffe College from 1943 to 1960.

27. On the Norfolk Rising, see Anthony Fletcher and Diarmaid MacCullough, *Tudor Rebellions* (5th ed., 2008).

28. The House Un-American Activities Committee existed from 1938 to 1975. It was originally created to investigate German-American involvement in Ku Klux Klan and Nazi activity. It soon added and then largely focused on suspected Communist subversive and propaganda activities, especially during the Red Scare of the 1950s associated with Senator Joseph McCarthy.

29. Elizabeth Douvan (1926-2002) went on to become a distinguished professor of psychology at the University of Michigan, where she also helped to found the program in women's studies. Her 1966 *The Adolescent Experience* became a classic.

30. The full title is *Operation Mind: A Brief Documentary Account of the House Committee on Un-American Activities,* Ann Arbor, University of Michigan Council of the Arts, Sciences, and Professions and Civil Liberties Committee of the University of Michigan (1952). For a firsthand account of these events, see Chandler Davis, "The Purge," in *A Century of Mathematics in America,* edited by Peter Duren, part 1, pp. 413-28 (1989).

31. Harlan Hatcher (1899-1998) was a professor of American literature at the University of Michigan, specializing in the novel and in the history of the Great Lakes, and served as president of the University of Michigan between 1951 and 1967.

32. *Keeping in Mind: The McCarthy Era at the University of Michigan* was produced by Adam Kulakow

and debuted on campus on April 9, 1989. In November 1990, the University of Michigan also instituted the Chandler Davis, Clement Markert, and Mark Nickerson Lecture Series on Academic and Intellectual Freedom. Clement Markert (1917–99) was a professor of zoology. Though he continued to teach at the University of Michigan, his promotion to associate professor, previously approved, was delayed for a year or two; after it came through, he left for Yale University. He later served as president of the American Institute of Biological Sciences.

33. Mark Nickerson (1916–98) was a prominent pharmacologist who, after his dismissal from Michigan, joined the faculties at the University of Manitoba and McGill University in Canada. He later became president of both the Pharmacological Society of Canada and the American Society of Pharmacology.

34. Nathaniel Coburn (1910–71) was an applied mathematician who made important contributions to fluid mechanics, and an associate professor at the University of Michigan. When he was called to testify by HUAC, he stayed away on his physician's orders as he was suffering from serious multiple sclerosis. Though the committee read his name publicly, the United States Congress did not cite him for contempt and the university did not move against him.

35. This was Lloyd Barenblatt. The case was *Barenblatt v. United States,* 360 U.S. 109 (1959), in which the Supreme Court upheld the lower court's ruling that HUAC's action to force Barenblatt to testify did not violate the First Amendment and thus upheld his conviction for contempt to Congress.

36. Justice Hugo Black (1886–1971) was a Democratic senator from Alabama before joining the Supreme Court in 1937, where he served until his death. He dissented in the *Barenblatt v. United States* decision.

37. Justice William O. Douglas (1898–1980) was a law professor at Yale who joined the Supreme Court in 1939 where he served until his resignation in 1976. He concurred with Justice Black's dissent, as did Chief Justice Earl Warren.

38. J. Parnell Thomas (1895–1970) was a Republican congressman from New Jersey. He chaired the HUAC from 1947 until his conviction for fraud in 1950. He spent eighteen months in prison.

39. The Hollywood Ten was a group of screenwriters, producers, and directors from among many entertainment professionals summoned in 1947 to testify before HUAC about their real or suspected political beliefs and associations. The ten who refused on the grounds of the First Amendment were convicted for contempt to Congress and imprisoned. Two of them, Lester Cole and Ring Lardner Jr., were actually at the Danbury correctional facility when Thomas served his term.

40. The Enron scandal began in October 2001 and resulted in the bankruptcy of Enron, an energy company, and its auditing agency and consultancy partner, Arthur Andersen. Convictions for obstruction of justice and defrauding investors were eventually handed down for a number of Enron's top officials, most of whom now are serving sentences in federal penitentiaries in Colorado and Texas. Chandler Davis described his experience at Danbury Correctional Institution in "So You're Going to Prison!" *The Nation* (December 3, 1960): 435–37.

41. Monsignor Joseph N. Moody (1905–94) was a specialist of Catholicism in modern France and taught at the Catholic University of America for most of his career. His books include *Church and State: Catholic Social and Political Movements, 1789–1950* (1953), *The Church as Enemy: Anticlericalism in Nineteenth-Century French Literature* (1968), and *French Education since Napoleon* (1978).

42. Harold Scott MacDonald "Donald" Coxeter (1907-2003) was a major geometer of the twentieth century and professor of mathematics at the University of Toronto.

43. Barbara K. Lewalski (1931-) is a professor of English literature and history at Harvard University. Her books include *Protestant Poetics and the Seventeenth-Century Religious Lyric* (1985) and *The Life of John Milton: A Critical Biography* (2002).

44. Kenneth Lewalski (1926–2007) was a professor of history at Rhode Island College and a specialist in French and Polish history and culture in the late eighteenth and nineteenth centuries.

45. The Free Speech Movement occurred at Berkeley in 1964 to 1965 as students protested university restrictions on their political activities and speech. It marked a pivotal moment in the civil rights movement as well as rising student activism against the Vietnam War. See Robert Cohen and Reginald Zelnik, eds., *The Free Speech Movement: Reflections on Berkeley in the 1960s* (2002).

46. David Harris (1946–) is an American journalist and writer. His books include *Our War: What We Did in Vietnam and What It Did to Us* (1996). He was married to Joan Baez from 1968 to 1973.

47. Joan Baez (1941–) is a renowned folk singer and songwriter known for her commitment to nonviolence and civil rights. She was an important figure in the protest against the Vietnam War.

Chapter 7

Hopes

DC: Let's go further into your involvement in the events of this tumultuous era. Your appointment at Berkeley brought you an ever-growing number of students, right?

NZD: The idea of becoming a professor at Berkeley attracted me not only to train more graduate students, but especially because it was then a larger intellectual world than what I had at Toronto and more open to the new directions in which I was moving. Right away I got to know anthropologists working on peasant studies and folklorists. I had contacts in the literature departments, and especially with the young Stephen Greenblatt: over lunch we would talk of ideas from my essays in *Society and Culture* and approaches he would take in his *Renaissance Self-Fashioning*. With Svetlana Alpers,[1] historian of art, I began our lifelong friendship of discussion, gossip, and argument; she was then writing her pathbreaking book *The Art of Describing*. And in the history department I had spectacular colleagues in the early modern period: William Bouwsma,[2] Randolph Starn,[3] and Gene Brucker.[4] What conversations we had about our courses and our scholarly projects! There was only one other woman teaching in the large department when I arrived, but with the help of some male colleagues, we finally brought in terrific young women, Lynn Hunt[5] in eighteenth-century French history and the U.S. historian Paula Fass.[6] The political ambiance of the 1970s was exciting in Berkeley; there were coffeehouses for discussion all around the campus. It was a time of intellectual exuberance, an adventure.

DC: Why then move again, as if after a certain moment you needed a change of scene to avoid the routine of the same faces and conversations, as if you wanted a new life, you who set for yourself a mission to restore

past memories, the itinerant treks of preachers in the early Reformation, always in search of new people to meet?

NZD: I'm not simply a missionary! Personal elements played their part, too. When Chan and I first agreed that I'd take the Berkeley post, there were not many academic couples teaching in different cities, and especially not women who initiated the separation, Today you see commuting academic couples more often in North America, but in 1971 it was unusual, and I had never imagined Chandler and I would live that way. We decided to look at it as an experiment, and we used a special formula that I sometimes quote today in advising young people facing what Chan calls "the two-city problem": "Let's try it for five years, and then we'll see. If after five years, things are not working, we'll try something else."

So that's what we did, starting off with our usual naïve optimism that we'd work out all problems. Chan took leaves from UT and taught as a visitor at Berkeley, but it became clear that he was not going to get a good permanent post in California, despite all he had been publishing and the esteem in which he was held for his mathematics. He needed to spend time with his own UT graduate students. And commuting between Berkeley and Toronto took six hours on the plane alone and crossed three time zones...

DC: You thus chose to try something else. When did Princeton recruit you?

NZD: Princeton had already expressed its interest in my joining the history department, and after one complicated weekend in the spring of 1977, when Chan and I both had professional trips to the Midwest and met in St. Louis, I phoned Lawrence Stone[7] and said, "Next time you make me an offer, I'll accept." Berkeley and Toronto were just too far away from each other. And then Simone, our youngest child, had finished high school and had gone off to the next stage in her life, and I was alone in our big redwood house. I was very sorry to leave my friends in Berkeley and my graduate students. The students got back at me in a delicious way. They interrupted a lovely but very traditional good-bye party with an uproarious costumed charivari, with masks, drums, processions, and shouts. I was required by the rules of charivari (I should say the rules of misrule here) to pay a forfeit. My son, Aaron, was there and he proposed I sing "You Can't Get a Man with Your Brains." Red-faced in front of my feminist students, I belted it out, to much laughter. Ruth Rosen,[8] one of my students who went on to write terrific books in U.S. women's history, gave me a hug of forgiveness.

So I went to Princeton in 1978, stayed there for eighteen years till my retirement, and never regretted my decision. Chan and I worked out the commute quite well, taking turns to fly to one of our two homes almost every weekend, and spending long summers, holidays, and sabbatical years together in one place; we worked out Davis's Rules for Commuting Couples and stuck to them. And once again I had changed my intellectual community, a very different universe, or so it seemed when I first arrived. California was very open, expansive, outdoorsy—we all did lots of sports and mountain climbing—brilliant sun once the fog dissipated. Princeton was very pretty as well, but small, intense, civilized, a culture of conversation around dining room tables. I rejoiced in my colleagues. Lawrence Stone was directing the Shelby Cullom Davis Center,[9] with its weekly seminars full of debate and new ideas. Bob Darnton[10] and I compared notes on the history of the book. The young Tony Grafton[11] was already enlivening every conversation with the sparks of his wondrous erudition. Carl Schorske[12] had founded a program in European Cultural Studies, which offered a broad model for teaching to the department. Bob Darnton and Clifford Geertz started their course on history and anthropology within this ECS frame, and once or twice I taught the course with them. When, in the wake of my Martin Guerre adventures, I wanted to start a seminar on History and Film, it was welcomed by ECS. Though I first had the idea of trying to turn the Martin Guerre story into a film while I was at Berkeley, I think I would never have followed through on it if I had not come to Princeton.

Meanwhile there was our "woman question." Princeton had become coed in the fall of 1969, and when I arrived in 1978, I think we had only about eight tenured women on the entire faculty. But we were a very determined group, we met and met, agitated and coaxed, and finally things began to change.

DC: You thus feel you've taken part, certainly within limits but with no lack of will, in a history that saw women begin a long journey to promote their rights. You've lived this history with exuberance, joy, and a total commitment similar to the ones we see in your own historical work, haven't you?

I believe, at this point in our conversation, we should shift to consider the historian's conscience as you confront history; no longer the history that motivated you in your essays to reclaim past experiences or even lives, but henceforth the history that you've actually witnessed and to which you often seek to attest in your books through a kind of appeal to dialogue between past and present: an appeal that quietly grows in the framework of your analyses, which isn't apparent but which the reader must suspect is there. How would you describe this relationship to an immediate moment, more or less proximate, that certainly serves as an anchor point from which you strive to develop or modify your outlook and questions?

NZD: Let me begin with a remark about my general state of mind in regard to current politics. If there were any vestiges of my youthful utopianism still left in my spirit, they have been erased by events of the past years. Bitter war and cruel rape in so many places. Ethnic cleansing in the Balkans and parts of Africa.[13] The United States with its triumphal and aggressive military power in Afghanistan and now Iraq, Islamicist merciless violence put to such wrongful ends. Think of the protest mounted in so many parts of the world this past spring against Bush's invasion of Iraq. Huge marches in so many cities, an avalanche of protest, and yet no effect. So many situations proving so difficult to resolve or to change.

DC: Did you become disenchanted or rather, more specifically, did you gradually become more realistic after a long and growing series of disillusionments and disappointments that in the end just wore you out?

NZD: More realistic, yes, but not worn out. My realism is still accompanied by hope. There are moments in recent times infused with hope: 1989, when the Berlin Wall came down; 1990, when apartheid laws were repealed in South Africa and Mandela[14] was released from prison. The unexpected can still happen. I think back to 1949, when I had just graduated from Smith. What Chandler and I most feared as a possibility at that time was nuclear war. Now that didn't happen—or at least it hasn't happened yet—but we didn't dream of the possibility of a new worldwide plague of AIDS or the resurgence of such extreme ethnic hatred and violent religious fundamentalism as we have seen. What we might have hoped for as discovery was the exploration of outer space—Chan had even published science fiction stories about that—but we would not have imagined the electronic revolution of our time. So hope is nourished by the element of surprise, even though often the surprise is very bad news.

And hope can be nourished by a chastened realism. I long ago gave up on full-scale state socialism as a panacea, not only because of the atrocities of the Soviet regime, but because of the absurdities and failures of command economies. But one can take heart from the varieties of mixed economies, as in Scandinavian lands or as recommended by Karl Polanyi[15] or Amartya Sen,[16] where the family interest and competitive enterprise are always in relation with belief in sharing and the public good.

Especially painful for me has been my sorrow and my shock at the unjust violence associated with the establishment of the State of Israel and continuing there, as well as at the emergence of a group of Jewish political thinkers in America of the extreme right, allied to centers of power and admirers of brute force. Now I know well, both from my own experience and from my historical studies, that there are all kinds of Jews. But the rabbis who excommunicated Baruch Spinoza[17] in 1656 from the Portuguese Jewish congregation of Amsterdam did not have "the power of the sword"; that is, they could excommunicate Spinoza, but not execute him. The court Jews of the seventeenth and eighteenth centuries, including in the circle of Glikl, served as bankers for and provisioners to emperors, princes, and dukes and accepted absolute rule for strategic reasons, but they didn't *believe* in the divine right of kings or embrace the mystique of absolutism; their loyalty was elsewhere.

As for Israel, I had never been a partisan of the nationalist elements of Zionism, as I've mentioned, and always took to heart the vocation or special challenge of the Diaspora. But I considered Palestine as a necessary place of refuge for the Jews fleeing Europe after the horrors of the Holocaust and unable to go elsewhere. And I initially hoped the diverse forms of Jewish culture and different Jewish peoples could develop in a society together with Arabs and Muslims. (Too bad I couldn't have been there with my great-uncle Ziman and my Grandma Lamport under the British Mandate,[18] when there was still a chance for that.) My Smith College history teacher Hans Kohn[19] had been a cultural Zionist in Palestine in the 1920s, like Martin Buber[20] seeking spiritual and cultural renewal, but he was very opposed to political-nationalist Zionism and its response to Arabs there, and finally left the movement. I don't recall that we talked about Zionism when we studied his famous book on *The Idea of Nationalism,* where he distinguished between civic liberal forms of nationalism and ethnic illiberal ones. But he wrote about it in the 1950s, saying that Zionism had gone the way of an ethnic territorial nationalism that was betraying the Jewish prophetic tradition. I wish I had discussed these matters with him while I was at Smith.

During my first visit to Israel in 1976, I was filled with ambivalence. I marveled at the old quarter of Jerusalem, with its historical juxtaposition of religious cultures and the contiguity of the sacred and the profane. I was impressed by the diversity among the Jews, people from so many different places, by the literary success of the Hebrew language, and by the flourishing university and research institutions. But I was constantly uneasy at the traces of displaced Palestinian Arabs. The houses of my friends were often the former homes of Arabs, involuntary exiles. One of my dear historian friends felt guilty about this, but my cousin Naftali Herzog, a warm supporter of the violence of the Irgun,[21] crowed to us about his role in the seizure of Safed from the Palestinians and was delighted to be living in one of their houses. Then in the 1980s the Israeli New Historians[22] gave documentary proof of the expulsion of Arabs, of the confiscation of their lands, and the destruction of their villages in 1947 to 1948. Meanwhile since 1967 Israel had illegally occupied and sent settlers into the Territories and East Jerusalem; Israel invaded Lebanon in 1982, the butcheries of Sharon, and so on: none of these could help bring peace to the region in any way and were unjust.

DC: I would see things somewhat differently, but that's not the question. I would like to know how your thinking about Israel has evolved. In listening to you, it seems Israel is as much a threat to herself as she faces from her adversaries, no?

NZD: Let me answer by saying how reflecting on Israel—and here I'm referring to its governments, its army, its settlers, and their supporters—has changed the way I define the Jewish condition in the world and my own relation to it. For quite a while I kept in my heart the naïve idealism of a Jewish girl in a *goyishe* neighborhood who thought the Jews had a special calling to defend justice and unmask false idols. But for some time now, I've understood, not just as a historian, but as a moral person, how diverse are the interpretations of a religious tradition or of any grouping where deep identity issues are at stake. You could almost say that a defining mark of religion is serious quarrels about the right way to worship God. The Bible is full of such arguments. Early Christianity exactly the same. The first generations of Islam. Early Protestantism and onward. Arguing about the right way to be Jewish or Muslim and about who's a heretic is the name of the game. And the same is true of intense political movements. Maybe arguing within a tradition about how to relate to the sacred has more going for it than we have understood. Anyway, the call to the defense of justice against wrongful power and to the unmasking of false idols, including those of land and blood, is *one* of the Jewish traditions, and that's the one I identify with. At Toronto, I support a group, organized initially by Jewish women, that draws together Jews and others, too, each Friday for a vigil before the Israeli Consulate, with signs saying "End the Occupation," "We Refuse to Be Enemies." The vigil has gone on for some years, always in the hope of a change for the better and of getting passersby to think about the question.

But in Israel itself, I see this tradition sustained through the actions and courage of those who resist the politics of exclusion, expansion, theocracy, and cruelty. I think of my friend and political ally at Smith College, Judith Blanc,[23] who already fifty years ago was circulating mimeographed news about "the other Israel" and has worked for decades with Palestinian women toward a viable solution. I think of Gadi Algazi,[24] a superb historian of medieval and early modern cultural history, who did prison time for refusing military service in the Territories and was one of the founders of Ta'ayush,[25] an organization of Jewish and Arab citizens of Israel who bring help to besieged Palestinian communities. I think of the insightful writings of Sidra Ezrahi[26] on the Israeli poets and novelists, who hold on to a sense of exile and distance even while living in the land of Israel—a distance that leaves room for moral questioning. I think of the Israelis and Palestinians who—in opposition to both their authorities—have just negotiated the Geneva Accord[27] for two neighboring states; I think of a few other voices there who have proposed the establishment of a binational secular state (an idea already bruited about by some cultural Zionists in the 1920s). These are positions difficult to reconcile, but they open the way to fruitful communication and negotiation, in contrast with the repetitious and belligerent arguments you usually hear.

So that's my current stance, using the Israel-Palestine case as an example. I try to have a realistic understanding of the comedies and tragedies of history and the present-day world; but it's a realism informed by a passionate interest in human activities and by hope—I'd like to say a belief—that there will always be some persons who will speak against injustice, indifference, cruelty, and oppression.

DC: You say you've recently experienced this displacement, or at least you've in some way theorized or assimilated it for yourself. But haven't the

vicissitudes of your historical research proceeded from this realization? Because when we study your works in succession, we note that you've always roamed broadly and chosen subjects one more different than the next, covering expanses ever larger and farther away... How do you interpret this desire to constantly renew your research by leading it elsewhere? Does this tendency provide some compensation because, for you, the present has slowly lost its ability to offer hope, even though the search for hope remains? Doesn't it seem that you've tried to go back into the past to show that even in a character stricken with the saddest fate there survives a radiance and sense of confidence? In reality, almost all your heroes and heroines are unhappy, but they always manage to salvage some hope, striving to transform the worst into something better, even just a little bit better. Didn't your own writing, in its choices, in the ways it assigns value to these fragments of a past person, precede this realization? Hasn't it entailed a kind of intimate conversion that would have required you to surrender some of your dreams? Isn't it because you wanted to enter into the dreams of your historical characters that you ended up deciding to abandon some of your own dreams, your own personal truths?

NZD: Perhaps it worked in the order you describe, but I hadn't thought about it that way. It seemed to me that my assessments of lives in the past and lives in the present were just going in tandem with each other, except that in assessing the past I have always had to define "dreams" and "disappointments" in *their* terms, not ours. If anything, I learned from thinking about them. In any case, as I finish my book now about al-Wazzān, I'm once again balancing off disappointments and unfulfilled dreams with legacies and compensations. He seems never to have done all the writing he'd hoped to after he returned to North Africa, but during his Italian years, he did find a *peaceful* way to think about the world—a world around him that was saturated by war and violence: wars between Christians, wars between Muslims, wars between Christians and Muslims, slaughters, massacres, expulsions, the sacking of towns, rapes...

In our present-day world, torn between imperialist, nationalist, and religious movements with their unshakeable certitudes and convictions, it is a relief to be able to write about al-Wazzān, because he was situated "in between." He was not a saint: he used ruses, shrewdness, and craft to survive in between and to prevent himself from falling into despair. The legacy of his life is modest, but I see in it a hope: the possibility to find a voice and to live in between, at a distance from exclusive claims. I think we can see in him not a betrayal of Islam, but an art of living.

DC: But aren't there other ways to pose questions that don't require this constant give and take between past and present, between your life and the lives of the people from the past you've chosen and fashioned, after all, for yourself and by yourself?

NZD: I can answer only with another example of a perspective from the past that has given me insight into some features of the present and ways to live in the present. I'm thinking of the concept of "the sect," developed by Ernst Troeltsch[28] and elaborated as an ideal type by Max Weber, and of the eschatological spirit, which you have used so remarkably in your book on the Wars of Religion in France. In quietist sects, like the Mennonites[29] or the Labadists,[30] whom my Maria Sibylla Merian joined for a time, families lived a perfect life, without private property and without bearing the sword, in communities separated from the world; they would serve simply as an example for others, "a mirror for the wicked world." The militant sects wanted to impose their perfect way of life on others through war, a violence anticipating the millennium from which would follow the end of the world. And then there were the sects in between, like the Society of Friends or Quakers,[31] where families lived among themselves in a spirit of charity, but also intermingled in the world in a peaceable fashion, that is, without bearing the sword. For me, the people of Ta'ayush in Israel/Palestine resemble this last form, for these young Jews and Arabs put aside their differences to speak and live their truth, a truth of cooperation, respect, and nonviolence. They bring help to Palestinian villages deprived of food and water, isolated by the wall being built.[32] There's the mirror aspect here as well. For they hold up to a world riven with strife around them the *possibility* of another life.

It is fascinating to watch the emergence right now of militant eschatological movements of the right, in America, in Israel, and in the Islamic world. Look at the government of the United States and the enthusiasm of its American supporters for the policies of George W. Bush, this utopian fervor to remake Iraq after the fall of Saddam Hussein. Some commentators claim that only the desire for oil is behind the American policy. But there's more to the story. We are at an extraordinary moment in U.S. history: the richest country in the world, the most powerful military country in the world dreams of ever greater power, ever greater wealth, desires to have even more oil and to change the rest of the world according to its own image.

DC: Messianically?

NZD: Absolutely, a sort of messianism of the Right.

DC: But then why do you think that right now there's this equally strong resurgence of providential beliefs allied with a sense of universalism that runs to the highest levels of power in the White House? Why does this resurgence show up now, at the moment when we notice that other cultural or religious systems are similarly affected, from Islam to Hinduism and Judaism? Who can explain this shift towards exclusivity among the great world religions, a shift that bears an obvious resemblance to confessional trends in the sixteenth century?

In Christian Europe from 1500 to 1650, we can argue there came into play, along with the hope to return to a faith purified of abuses and pollutants, a faith similar to that preached at the time of the early church, an anguish toward death heightened by the foreboding that the Last Judgment was at hand, an anguish sustained since the last decades of the fifteenth century by the assurance that the world was more rife with sin than ever before, that it was old and near its end, and that it was going to be subjected to the awesome justice of a jealous God. The emergence of alternative beliefs, then the process of building rival confessions within which the Roman Church reached its own sense of completion, can all be understood as related modes of response to eschatological distress. Be it a response by means of interiorizing this apocalyptical eschatology and then by imagining the redemptive involvement in the battle during the end times against evil. It's the response of German spiritual radicalism, with Karlstadt[33] or Müntzer,[34] the Anabaptists in Frisia or Westphalia,[35] or the Catholic faithful in France during the Wars of Religion. The certainty to participate in the last battle against Satan's minions, the assurance to realize or advance one's salvation through violence and exclusion made it possible to quiet the conscience, to overcome distress or to sublimate it. Be it the response that came with the shift toward an imagination not haunted by such fears of salvation, with for example Calvin's ideas that overcame the dread of the Last Judgment and that instead enabled Christians to rediscover, by breaking with the papacy, a serenity in the conviction to live one's daily life to advance the triumph of the Reformed religion on earth, by obeying the Ten Commandments and struggling against the corruption of God's majesty, to live for the greater glory of God. In one way or another, the forceful rise of rival systems of belief stabilized or hid from view the power of this unsettling anguish of the imminent encounter between a creature fashioned by God in his image but who knows more than ever he's tainted by worldly sin, more than ever tainted and condemned by it.

But we find it difficult to see this anguish before death or the Last Judgment today. Or perhaps it's deeply buried inside us... Who today could thus determine this drive in the world toward exclusion in which each religion aims to affirm, in varying degrees of intensity, its messianic character or its views on humanity's ultimate destiny? Why has there been a return of the sacred and why has it become so colored by these feelings about the end of the world?

NZD: That's a very difficult question, a mysterious one. Eschatological movements have developed in many parts of the world in the last thirty years. There must be several causes, different explanations for this depending on the place. As for America, the first arrivals from Europe, the seventeenth-century pilgrims, brought to the lands and indigenous peoples the idea that God's providence was guiding them. Far from corrupt old Europe, they would create a holy society. Much later, the belief in Manifest Destiny inspired and justified American expansion on the continent and elsewhere.[36] As for sects and utopian communities, there have been many of them in the United States, but they have been removed from centers of governmental power. President Woodrow Wilson wanted to create "a world safe for democracy," but good Calvinist that he was, he did not expect a millenarian era in the near future.[37] And now, with the fall of the Soviet Union and the appearance of Islamicist movements, the Apocalypse is in the White House. But what a contrast between the millenarianism of Bush and that of the sects of the sixteenth and seventeenth century. The latter renounced private property and preached a simple life, the pure Gospel, necessary for the period of waiting for the thousand years of the reign of Christ. Much current American evangelism and the particular sect that forms the sensibility of George W. Bush and his entourage preach the total acceptance of material life and a glorification of riches as the ways of accomplishing God's will in the world. Here there's no longer any tension between religion and the worldly life of riches.

DC: A tension that's long since disappeared. We are both very far from but also still close to Max Weber who, faced with a world that he considered disenchanted as a result of the shift from the spiritual to a mechanistic or cold objectivity, faced with modern societies devoted to the cult of materialism and the search to control knowledge, reintroduced eschatology as a possibility in the future, after the time of the *Entzauberung* [demystification]. But in a dramatic sense of dread. It seemed possible to him that rationalization, once it had purged all "final and sublime values," could one day bring about its own critical fate in the time of the "iron cage." It was as if Max Weber were haunted by the coming of a time marked by an unspoken, unapparent nihilism in which sense and points of reference became lost. He talked about, building upon Nietzsche,[38] the "depersonalization," the "loss of the soul," and the "dehumanization" of modern humanity. It seems that this collision between the cult of worldly things and the Bible that you've described to us comes from a calibrated accommodation in which rationality and irrationality, the preoccupation with plenty and the belief in a final end become dependent on each other, in which that which is the same becomes other, in which all borders disappear.

NZD: In the evangelical sects in the United States, there are still some walls between the self, religion, and the world, for example in the areas of alcohol and sexuality. George W. Bush had a serious drinking problem till he was forty; through religious conversion, he decided he was a sinner, broke with alcohol, and began to perceive himself as a Christian to whom God had entrusted a mission. Before 9/11 there were also "lesser demons" that the evangelical movement wanted to crush, like homosexuality, fornication, and abortion. After the destruction of the World Trade Center, there was the great anti-Christian Satan and the "axis of evil" against America. Now Bush could have the Christian certitude that he was in a position to remake the world.

DC: Does Judaism in this context reflect a resurgence and serve as a reminder of this belief in the end times?

NZD: With the Jews, the eschatological spirit has a different character in different places. The Jewish advisors, the Neocons[39] so influential in the circle around Bush, are not to my knowledge part of orthodox movements. Rather they are admirers of the philosophy of power known as "decisionism" [*Dezisionismus*], associated with the German philosopher

Carl Schmitt,[40] and of Machiavellian methods like preemptive war to accomplish their goals. Among the orthodox groups in Brooklyn, Paris, and Mea Sharim in Jerusalem,[41] there are those who expect the messiah in the near future. A few of them have even turned their back on the State of Israel, saying that such a political establishment must await the coming of the messiah.

Today the eschatological spirit in Israel is most often associated with the expansion of the settlers into the Palestinian Territories and the violent actions carried on by them and by the Israeli army against the villagers and their lands. The terrifying memory of the Holocaust, the absolute and sweeping affirmation of "Never Again" that elevates even little boys throwing stones into the start of a new Holocaust, the understandable fear of suicide bombers—all this gets confounded with the belief that God gave the Jews the extended land of Israel and that their cause must prevail. So against menacing forces, any action is justified to fulfill the glorious promise.

The wall currently being constructed by the State of Israel across the lands of the Palestinians makes me think of Sura 18 of the Qur'an, in which Dhu-l-Qarnayn (often associated with Alexander the Great) constructs a wall to protect humans against the wicked and dangerous forces of Gog and Magog until the last days.[42]

DC: How would you characterize the actual type of eschatology that's become so strong in Islam?

NZD: As the wall against Gog and Magog suggests, Islam has an important eschatological current. At the end of time will arrive the Mahdi, a just man, descended from the Prophet and guided by God, who will destroy false religions, restore virtue and justice, and establish Islam throughout the world. In certain eschatological prophecies, the Mahdi will be accompanied by Jesus. From time to time in history, a Mahdi has been identified, the charismatic leader of a purificatory movement, which defends Islam against corrupt Muslims and infidels who have not accepted God and his Prophet Muhammad. In the sixteenth century, the Ottoman sultan Suleyman the Magnificent[43] was named by some of his followers as both Mahdi and World Conqueror in a great war against the Christians. This happened at the same time that some European preachers were naming Emperor Charles V as a world conqueror, who was defeating Islam and would bring Muslims, Jews, and the American Indians to Christianity.

Now you can see the possibilities in this eschatological tradition for inspiring the Muslim holy warriors of our own day—and in particular Osama bin Laden and his disciples. It's interesting that the eschatology of Osama bin Laden, like the right-wing eschatology of George W. Bush and company, accepts and uses the world capitalist economy and private or family property, even while fulminating against the materialism of the West.

DC: If I follow you, there would be both similarity and a distance in the rapid expansion of these worldviews today.

NZD: These various holy warriors on the different sides draw examples from the past to support their aspirations for the seizure of power and the wealth of the golden age. Along with the eschatological metaphors, they choose the model eras that they'd like to restore. For example, there were the many articles in the American press citing Condoleezza Rice,[44] security advisor to George W. Bush, before the invasion of Iraq. In her view, the U.S. must relive in Iraq the inspiring events after World War II, when the polities of Germany and Japan were restructured under the aegis of the United States. But historians specializing in the study of international relations and of the Middle East have pointed out—including in the popular press—how different these situations and periods are, and have recalled the failures of British policies in Iraq after the First World War. But to no avail. And even the historians are not in accord: one or two of them, dazzled by proximity to power, have given Bush their approbation.

DC: It's therefore the myth that history repeats itself that, for you, appears to pose another risk in our contemporary world. But doesn't it seem here that there would be a basic problem of discrepancy between the historical awareness of historians and the type of awareness of those engaged in political action?

NZD: Of course there's a difference, but this doesn't mean the historian has nothing of use to say. Since the nineteenth century, no historian would advance the thesis that there are exact repetitions in history: even if Condoleezza Rice had found a good analogy between the past and the present, unexpected events, contingencies, and surprises would end up complicating matters. When a historian responds to projects and declarations of public figures and political leaders—which can be a very good idea—he or she must do so in the spirit of a responsible scholar with public commitment, not in the spirit of an astrologer who flatters a prince or sultan.

DC: I remain attached to the principle that historical research need not be connected to contemporary affairs. Shouldn't this principle shape the past that the historian studies as a discrete period in time so it becomes but an artificial world, a virtual reality certainly based on the sources, but one virtual reality among many, whose claim to uniqueness rests on a combination of historical logic, documents, and the lack of any internal contradictions? Even if, as you said earlier, it's possible to offer the reader mirrors that can aid understanding present-day facts through historical ones, wouldn't the one lesson to learn from the past be distrust of all appeals to logic? Wouldn't it rather be a sense of historical irony that always comes undone whenever anyone has tried to think of it as a total world that can be articulated so it becomes consciously immediate? Wouldn't the one lesson to learn from history be that history is haphazard, uncontrollable, indeterminable, wanton, and pointless—even maddening—such as it was understood after Boethius[45] by people in the Middle Ages and the Renaissance in the image of Fortuna turning her wheel in ways absurd rather than comprehensible? To such a point as to render the historian's work a matter of chance, hypothetical, or inwardly self-critical!

It seems to me that historical writing must be built around structures and conditions that suggest facts; that it's a kind of mind game that works in terms of possibilities and variables, a game of artificial constructs meant to lead to a predetermined image. For me, it's all a game. If we concede that research into the past ends up as some kind of game, it's a game in which the historian tries to travel back to a time not his or her own. It's time indelibly inscribed by a "gap," in the linguistic sense of the term, that obviously forces us to accept that history can't help us understand the present or the future. Historical analysis also relies on proof that can't but be dependent on suggestive influences from the present, even as it condemns using the past to advance an agenda. This doesn't imply that we pursue history simply for its own sake, for when it's all said and done, making history is a way to affirm freedom. It affirms and models a way of life that questions the status quo and the very modalities of understanding or reading the past. It's a kind of history that becomes a stylistic exercise that artfully couches its appeal as a call for freedom of thought based upon a critical consideration of the sources. But all of this must recognize that a particular historical analysis is just one possibility among many others... Thus beyond any didactic purpose...

NZD: I think your doubts are leading you too far. One of the lessons of history is, in a celebrated phrase of Max Weber as reworked by the wonderful late Robert Merton,[46] "the unintended consequences of purposive social action." [*laughter*] This notion leaves a place for the contingent and the planned, for chance and coherence, for the mysterious and the explicable in history. The links between the past and the present are inevitable in our work as historians, and in the best of cases—when one is conscious of and conscientious in regard to this back and forth—desirable, as Marc Bloch maintained long ago. The past can deepen our understanding of the present—our own personal present and our public and political life—by its differences and by its approximate similarities. History offers us no well-defined or precise projects for improvement, but offers us many *possibilities*—fascinating for the play of our intellect, offering us irony, delight, indignation, but also helpful for our look at our own society.

DC: Doesn't historical analysis, to the extent it detects or recognizes the possibilities of history, which it studies, recounts, and even accepts, come close to becoming a work of literature? History is a close cousin of poetry, where a sudden passage always begins anew because of the nature of words and the imagination; it's a form of repetitious self-learning of a freedom rooted in language and various related intellectual pursuits; it's what a number of works on rationalist and positivist epistemology ignore, clearing away from the field of analysis all possible heuristic exercises in language and instead building its case on the basis of a tentative move towards a final, fixed kind of knowledge. But don't you share this mistrust with respect to any rhetoric of certainty?

NZD: To be sure I blur the boundary between poetry and history as Aristotle established it so rigidly centuries ago: "the historian relates what happened, the poet what might happen..."[47] Historians, including Thucydides,[48] often consider the plausible and the possible—explicitly or implicitly—in evaluating documents, texts, and reports, especially when there are conflicts and differences among them. I'm drawing on "the possible" right now in trying to draw meaning from the silences around al-Hasan al-Wazzān, the silences in contemporary sources about him (where I might have expected observations), and omissions in his own writings. As I said before, I'm trying to turn these silences into a plus, a silence that signifies, that says something about the place of the man in the society around him and about his own personal practices. To speak of what is *possible* here, I must use my imagination—but it must be nourished by and tightly guided by the sources from and around al-Wazzān.

The poet has more choice. He or she can stay close to the historical sources or leave them freely. I'm thinking here of a beautiful poem by Amy Clampitt, "Matoaka," on the Indian woman known as Pocahontas.[49] One learns much in reading it, Clampitt enlarges both our human and our historical vision, but she goes in very different directions from those I took when I imagined the responses of the Huron Theresa Khionrea[50] to the Ursuline Marie de l'Incarnation. And the poet does not have the responsibility to indicate at each moment the truth status of what has been said, while the historian is obliged to signal it through either "perhaps" or "it's certain that..." and other markers. I'm not complaining. I accept completely these conditions of my craft like those of an ever-present companion, familiar and supportive.

DC: **Have you encountered in your books, in the reactions to some of your books, this kind of obstacle blocking your idea of history as you write it?**

NZD: Yes. I'm thinking especially of the reaction of some people to *The Return of Martin Guerre*. This book has just appeared in Estonian, the twentieth translation as I recall, so from the point of view of readers, the reception has been positive. But some historians did not like the approach of the book, especially the way I depicted the peasants acting with some improvisation and creativity in regard to the events in their lives. They were also critical of my handling of the judge's book about the legal case. I used it not only as source for information about the case, but also as a literary text, as a story whose structure and ambivalences I could use to help me understand the judge's state of mind. These critics weren't numerous, but they were vociferous.

DC: **How have you felt about this criticism?**

NZD: Oh, but it makes no difference. [*laughter*] We write our books, we give them to readers, they circulate in the world, arousing reactions, for the most part unknown to us. For *The Return of Martin Guerre,* I was glad to have participated in a fruitful methodological debate in the *American Historical Review*.[51] Our books, once they leave our hands, have a life of their own.

DC: If you had to end our conversation with a few words that sum up all of your research, what would you say?

NZD: Historical research has been for me an arena of joy and intellectual passion. I always feel a shiver of anticipation when I enter an archive or a rare book collection: what am I going to find? Is the slave woman I'm looking for finally going to show up on the registers of a plantation? Might I even find her signature, left by her for some special reason and precious to me as a sign that she existed and really could write, as her lover claimed she could? What luck I've had to read so many interesting accounts, some moving me to laughter, others curdling my blood, some surprising, others familiar. This thirst for history and the struggle to understand the ways of living and thinking in the past have led me toward several methodologies—social analysis, anthropological questioning, literary techniques—and toward several settings, France always, but places very far from France. Over the years I've enlarged my categories of analysis, and not only in adding the category of gender. To start off, I was more centered on dualities and polarities, like domination/resistance, Catholic/Protestant. By now I stress equally the diverse forms of exchange, mixing, and crossing. My book on *The Gift in Sixteenth-Century France,* which has meant a great deal to me, was a culmination of this double approach.

Actually, I sometimes feel that my historical research has come to me as a gift, a gift from people of the past and from other historians, dead and living. The gift imposes on me the obligation to recount their lives and their worlds with responsibility—not recount them exactly as they would have done, but in being ever attentive to their statements and their claims. For me this responsibility involves the writing of a history that offers no direct lessons—a dead end—but that is a *critical* history, which displaces the historian herself and her readers. This history requires both closeness and difference, and it makes affirmations about the past with the certainty that they can be questioned and modified. This history reveals the possibilities of the past—admirable, troubling, irritating, astonishing—and as such, they encourage us to think of the possibilities in the present and future. For me, the possibilities of the past invite a commitment to humanity and offer a ray of hope for the future.

Paris/Toronto
September 2003

Notes

1. Svetlana Alpers (1936–) is a major innovator in conceptualizing artistic practice, the viewer's experience, and the history of art. *The Art of Describing: Dutch Art in the Seventeenth Century* appeared in 1983, and among her subsequent works is *Rembrandt's Enterprise* (1988), *Tiepolo and the Pictorial Intelligence* (with Michael Baxandall) (1994), and *The Vexations of Art: Velasquez and Others* (2007).

2. William Bouwsma (1923–2004) was an eminent scholar of Renaissance European culture and past president of the American Historical Association. His major books include *Venice and the Defense of Republican Liberty: Renaissance Values in the Age of the Counter-Reformation* (1968), and *The Waning of the Renaissance (1550–1640)* (2000).

3. Randolph Starn (1939–) is a historian and cultural critic who specializes in late medieval and Renaissance Italian history. He has written, among other studies, *Contrary Commonwealth: The Theme of Exile in Medieval and Renaissance Italy* (1982) and *Arts of Power: Three Halls of State in Italy, 1300–1600* (with Lauren Partridge; 1992). He served as director of the Townsend Center for the Humanities at the University of California.

4. Gene A. Brucker (1924–) is a leading scholar of the history of Renaissance Florence. His books include *Renaissance Florence* (1983) and *The Civic World of Early Renaissance Florence* (2008).

5. Lynn Hunt (1945–) is an eminent historian of the French Revolution, as well as cultural and gender history. A past president of the American Historical Association, she teaches at UCLA and has written a number of major studies, including *Politics, Culture, Class in the French Revolution* (1984) and, more recently, *Inventing Human Rights* (2007).

6. Paula Fass (1947–) is an expert on the history of the family and childhood. A professor at Berkeley, she has written *The Damned and the Beautiful: American Youth in the 1920s* (1977) and, more recently, *Children of a New World: Society, Culture, and Globalization* (2006). She served as general editor of the *Encyclopedia of Children and Childhood* (2003).

7. Lawrence Stone (1919–99) was an English historian of early modern Britain best known for *The Crisis of the Aristocracy, 1558–1641* (1965) and *The Family, Sex, and Marriage in England, 1500–1800* (1977).

8. Ruth Rosen (1945–) is a historian of American women and a journalist, who was for many years professor of history at the University of California at Davis. The books referenced are *The Lost Sisterhood: Prostitution in America, 1900–1918* (1983) and *The World Split Open: How the Modern Women's Movement Changed America* (2000).

9. The Shelby Cullom Davis Center for Historical Studies was established in 1968 to promote excellence in scholarship and the teaching of history at Princeton University.

10. Robert Darnton (1939–) is a leading scholar of eighteenth-century French cultural history and the history of the book. Among his many books are *The Great Cat Massacre and Other Episodes in French Cultural History* (1984) and *The Forbidden Best-Sellers of Prerevolutionary France* (1995).

11. Anthony Grafton (1950–) is a prolific scholar of the classical tradition from the Renaissance to the eighteenth century. His books include *Defenders of the Text: The Traditions of Scholarship in the Age of Science, 1450–1800* (1991) and, more recently, *Worlds Made by Words* (2009).

12. Carl Schorske (1915–) is a historian of modern European cultural and political history. His *Fin-de-Siècle Vienna: Politics and Culture* (1980) won the Pulitzer Prize. He was among the initial recipients of the MacArthur Fellowship in 1981.

13. The Yugoslav Wars were a series of violent conflicts between ethnic groups in the former Socialist Federal Republic of Yugoslavia during the 1990s and 2001. The conflicts in Africa include the Rwandan genocide of 1994 and the civil war and massacres in Sudan from the late 1990s to the present.

14. Nelson Mandela (1918–) is an antiapartheid activist and for many years leader of the African National Congress. Long imprisoned by the apartheid government of South Africa, he became South Africa's first democratically elected president in 1994.

15. Karl Polanyi (1886–1964) was an Austro-Hungarian intellectual and social thinker, who in 1933 immigrated to London and then to North America. His new vision of economic history, in which gift economies were the major form of exchange for centuries, was put forth in his influential

book *The Great Transformation* (1944).

16. Amartya Sen (1933–) is a professor of economics and philosophy at Harvard University, best known for his work on welfare economics and poverty, as illustrated in his 1987 book *On Ethics and Economics*. He received the Nobel Prize in Economics in 1998.

17. Baruch Spinoza (1632–77) was one of the most important philosophers of rationalism in the Western tradition. He was born in Amsterdam into a Portuguese Jewish family; after his excommunication for his "heresies" in 1656, he lived in the Netherlands until his death. His writings on ethics, theology, politics, and epistemology were widely read and, though condemned as atheistic, had a great impact on later thought.

18. The British Mandate was approved by the League of Nations in June 1922 and formalized British rule in Palestine from 1917 to 1948.

19. Hans Kohn (1891–1971) was born in Prague and lived in Russia for several years as a prisoner of war during World War I. After his years in Palestine in the 1920s, he immigrated to the United States in 1934. In 1930, Kohn brought out a study of the work and thought of Martin Buber. He described his own changing relation to Zionism in his autobiographical book, *Living in a World Revolution: My Encounters with History* (1964). The book referenced is *The Idea of Nationalism: A Study in Its Origins and Background* (1944).

20. Martin Buber (1878–1965) was an Austrian-born Jewish philosopher who taught in Germany until 1938, when he moved to Jerusalem. His philosophy of dialogic existentialism—existence as encounter—was articulated in his famous essay, *I and Thou* (1923). He became deeply interested in the study of Hasidism, a popular movement of Jewish mysticism, often expressed in folktales. From the 1920s on, he insisted on the peaceful relations between Jews and Arabs in Palestine and advocated a binational state there.

21. The Irgun was a militant Zionist group that operated in the British Mandate of Palestine between 1931 and 1948.

22. The New Historians are a group of Israeli scholars led by Benny Morris, Ilan Pappe, Avi Shlaim, and Tom Segev who, starting in the 1990s, challenged the prevailing nationalist picture of the foundation of the State of Israel and its relations with the Arabs. Their views continue to be a subject of lively debate in Israel.

23. Judith Mogil Blanc (1927–) was a 1949 graduate of Smith College, and since the late 1950s has lived as an advocate for peace and justice in Israel. Creator of the newsletter *Israleft,* she was among the founders of Women in Black and Bat Shalom and continues to this day to be in active collaboration with peace activists in Israel and the West Bank.

24. Gadi Algazi (1961–) is a professor of history at Tel Aviv University and editor of the periodical *History and Memory*. He is author of *Herrengewalt und Gewalt der Herren im später Mittelalter* (1996) [Seigneurial Power and Violence in the Late Middle Ages] and of numerous essays, including on the family life of late medieval and early modern scholars.

25. Ta'ayush (Arabic for "life in common"), or the Arab-Jewish Partnership, was created in 2000.

26. Sidra Ezrahi (1942–) is a professor of comparative Jewish literature at the Hebrew University of Jerusalem. Her books include the one referenced here, *Booking Passage: Exile and Homecoming in the Modern Jewish Imagination* (2000).

27. The Geneva Accord of 2003 was an unofficial, extragovernmental agreement between Israeli and Palestinian political figures, which provided for Israel and a new Palestinian state along lines close to those that existed before 1967, and removal of most of the Israeli settlements from Palestinian land. Palestinian representatives agreed to limit their "right of return" to a number of persons agreed upon by the government of Israel.

28. Ernst Troeltsch (1865–1923) was a German Protestant theologian and writer on the philosophy of religion and the philosophy of history best known for his *The Social Teaching of the Christian Churches* (1912).

29. Mennonites are a Christian Anabaptist denomination named after their founder, Menno Simons (1496–1561), and best known today for their commitment to pacifism.

30. Labadists were members of a radical Protestant sect founded by Jean de Labadie (1610–74),

who established a communal society of "saints" in Wieuwerd in the Netherlands. By the end of the seventeenth century, the Wieuwerd community had dissolved, though individual former members carried on the spirit of Labadie's teaching.

31. The Society of Friends, or Quakers, began as a Christian Dissenter movement in seventeenth-century England. They advocated pacifism and were among the first groups to call for the abolition of slavery.

32. In 1994, Israel began construction of a security wall around the West Bank.

33. Andreas Karlstadt (1486-1541) was a German theologian during the Protestant Reformation.

34. Thomas Müntzer (1488-1525) was a radical German theologian during the early Protestant Reformation, arguing against Luther's doctrine of the baptism of infants. He also supported the peasants during the uprising of the Peasants' War (1524-25), during which Müntzer lost his life.

35. Anabaptism began as a radical movement in the sixteenth-century Protestant Reformation; among their direct descendants today are the Amish, Hutterites, and Mennonites.

36. Manifest Destiny first appeared as a term in the 1830s and reflected the belief that the territorial expansion of the United States across the continent was inevitable and divinely ordained. The belief was sometimes expanded to include countries north and south of the United States.

37. Woodrow Wilson (1856-1924) was president of the United States between 1912 and 1920. In 1918, he articulated what came to be known as the Fourteen Points as a basis for a peace settlement on democratic principles following World War I. It was only partially realized in the Treaty of Versailles (1919).

38. Friedrich Nietzsche (1844-1900) was a major German philosopher and classical philologist who challenged the foundations of Christianity and traditional morality.

39. Neocons are exponents of neoconservatism, an American political philosophy that developed after the 1960s. It repudiates the tenets of modern liberalism and advocates the use of American military power to advance free-market capitalism and democracy.

40. Carl Schmitt (1888-1985) was a German political theorist and jurist known for his hard-boiled writings on the nature of the state, power, and political violence. He was professor of law at the University of Berlin from 1933 until Germany's defeat in World War II.

41. Mea Sharim is one of the oldest neighborhoods in West Jerusalem and today is populated mainly by Haredi Jews, the most conservative wing of Orthodox Judaism, also found in Brooklyn, Paris, and other places around the world.

42. Specifically verse 18:94, which reads "They said: 'O Zul-qarnain! the Gog and Magog [people] do great mischief on earth: shall we then render thee tribute in order that thou mightest erect a barrier between us and them?'" Yusuf Al English translation (1934).

43. Suleyman I (1494-1566) ruled the Ottoman Empire at the height of its power.

44. Condoleezza Rice (1954-) is a political scientist and specialist of the former Soviet Union who became national security advisor to President Bush between 2000 and 2004, after which she became secretary of state until 2009.

45. Ancius Manlius Severinus Boethius (480-524 or 525) was a Christian philosopher best known for his *The Consolation of Philosophy,* which he cast as a dialogue between himself and a beautiful woman representing philosophy. She teaches him not to put any trust in the vagaries of fortune but instead to place his faith in God.

46. Robert K. Merton (1910-2003) was a prominent American sociologist at Columbia University. The quote comes from his influential article by the same name that appeared in the *American Sociological Review* 1/6 (1936): 894-904.

47. Aristotle (384-322 BCE), the Greek philosopher, discussed this point in part 9 of his *Poetics.*

48. Thucydides (460-395 BCE), the Greek historian, considered these problems in his *History of the Peloponnesian War.*

49. Amy Clampitt (1920-94) was an American poet and author. The poem appeared in *A Silence Opens* (1994).

50. Khionrea the Huron was brought by her parents to the Ursuline convent for instruction in French and Algonquian, and in writing. She received the name Thérèse upon her conversion to Catholicism around 1640.

51. Robert Finlay, "The Refashioning of Martin Guerre"; and Natalie Zemon Davis, "On the Lame," in "AHR Forum: The Return of Martin Guerre," *American Historical Review* 93, no. 3 (June 1988): 572–603.

Epilogue

Six years have elapsed since Denis Crouzet and I concluded these conversations. The political landscape has changed in both our lands. We have both published works whose themes are anticipated in our exchange: Denis his brilliant study of Christopher Columbus, whom he portrayed as "a herald of the apocalypse"; I, my *Trickster Travels,* where I placed al-Hasan al-Wazzān between the worlds of Islam and Christianity. I turned eighty a year ago and chat with students about their doctoral dissertations on my parlor couch; Denis in his mid-fifties is busy training a new generation of young historians at the Sorbonne. Despite the decades that separate us, I feel a kinship in our ethical and scholarly goals, a complicity deepened by our discussions.

A year ago, too, Barack Obama was elected the president of the United States, an event totally unpredictable during the time of our conversations and, indeed, still chancy until the votes were finally counted and we knew that the election had not been stolen again and that Obama had won. So was ushered in one of those "moments of hope" in history, about which I spoke with Denis, here a very great moment, felt around the world. Now a year later, we are enmeshed in the old order of things—Iraq, Afghanistan, Israel/Palestine, the recession dropped on us by the bankers, the American health-care crisis, climate change, and more. Much of this was inherited by Obama and is part of the tough structure of institutions of power, infused as they are by greed and aggression. But the president's own decisions must bear part of the blame: some could be expected from his campaign speeches (though he had opposed the invasion of Iraq, he always said he wanted to intensify the war in Afghanistan); others come as more of a surprise (concessions he has made in perpetuating the unconstitutional treatment of Guantánamo Bay prisoners).

Yet the moment of hope is not an illusion: it stems from events and observations that can shape the possibilities and difficulties ahead. Barack Obama's life and family—his graduate-student anthropologist, socially engaged white mother, his Kenyan father, his Indonesian stepfather, his African-American lawyer wife (she was an undergraduate at Princeton!)—still confirm for us the multiple sites and sources of world leadership in the early twenty-first century. From the pages of *Dreams from My Father* still emerges the community organizer deeply committed to the black residents of Chicago's South Side: we can urge upon the president the strong needs of the poor and unemployed so that their voices, which he once headed, will not be drowned out by the Wall Street advisors he has selected. In fact, it seemed to me that I was hearing that young activist on the radio today as the president defended the current health-care bill, with its public option, and warned us not to believe what the insurance companies were saying against it.

Obama's great speeches still offer a vision of what we might strive for: his truth-telling speech in March 2008 on the wounds of slavery and racism in America and the need for alliance between white and black; his Cairo speech in June 2009, where he recast the relation between America and the world of Islam, noting the overlap between the two worlds, since there were many Muslims living in the United States, and calling for common endeavor toward shared goals.

And finally, there is the enduring fact that American voters chose an African-American to be president of the United States, an event many of us never thought we would see in our lifetime. That event reminds us that even in the face of situations fraught with violence and passionate and irreconcilable claims, we must keep our ears pricked for those still saying "Yes, we can," and trying to nudge the situation toward the better.

In my own life, too, there was a deeper relation with the world of Islam in these past six years, as I completed my study of al-Hasan al-Wazzān (Leo Africanus) and published it as *Trickster Travels: A Sixteenth-Century Muslim Between Worlds*. I had been struggling with the ending of the book during my conversations with Denis on two counts. One was the question of al-Wazzān's apparent failure to continue as an author after his return from Europe to North Africa and to Islam. In the end, I offered a cluster of possibilities: an enduring uprootedness drawn from the practices he developed to live between worlds during his Italian years; his failure to find patrons and listeners for a detailed travel account that would have conversion to Christianity as a necessary story line—and told by an apostate who had for a time been in the service of pope and cardinal. Right after *Trickster Travels* came off the press, I learned while lecturing in

Istanbul that there were a few captivity narratives written by Turkish Muslims in the late sixteenth and seventeenth century, but they never admitted to conversion to Christianity (I was able to add this reference to later editions and translations of my book!).

I compensated for al-Wazzān's silence in North Africa by stressing the balanced tone of the book he wrote in Europe, as he talked of Islam and wars between Muslims and Christians. He ridiculed some forms of popular piety as inefficacious and condemned harshly the Shia "heresy" in Persia, but his description of his Sunni religion was informative and often appreciative, yet not partisan—an unusual achievement for a writer on either side of the Mediterranean in those years. I left it to a seventeenth-century Spanish inquisitor to make the point for me in the last sentences of the main body of my book: on the title page of a copy of al-Wazzān's *Description of Africa* in the National Library in Madrid, the outraged cleric had written "Prohibited in full."

Denis and I had also discussed how I would shape the relation between François Rabelais and al-Wazzān, important to me as a final bridge-building across the Mediterranean. I decided to follow my outraged inquisitor with an epilogue on the two men. I showed how Rabelais, during his own visits to Italy, could easily have heard of the African "Giovanni Leone" and his manuscripts, and suggested possible faint echoes of the Africa book in Rabelais's great novel. But much more important were the parallels between the two men, parallels that Denis and I had talked about: the truth-telling role they gave to trickster figures; their distaste for world-conquerors of all religions; and their quest for grounds for common agreement. I had also wondered with Denis whether I might ever again resort to an imaginary dialogue with my subjects, as I did in the prologue to *Women on the Margins*. I didn't quite do that in the last pages of *Trickster Travels,* but I did imagine what might have happened if Rabelais and al-Wazzān had been able to meet—and while I was at it, I added al-Wazzān's Jewish collaborator, Jacob Mantino, to the party. Who knows whether I hit it right? But I wanted to end the book with a moment of peace and laughter.

Several times in my exchanges with Denis, I found myself saying that I wrote about historical figures or subjects that in some sense "needed" me, or to whom I felt a special responsibility. I felt this way about al-Hasan al-Wazzān and his books. This is *not* because Leo Africanus is ignored by other scholars; he is not—some splendid writing on him has been done and continues to be done. But as a scholar of Jewish background and an early modernist from the West, I wanted to take the time I needed to enter into the world of Islam in the fifteenth and sixteenth centuries, to discover the Muslim and Arab-speaking al-Wazzān behind the European construct of Leo Africanus, and to see Europe through his eyes. I hope to find—and indeed have found—common ground through the rules of my historian's craft with scholars from the Muslim world. Among my choicest experiences was meeting last year in Casablanca with young women and men in a graduate class in French literature (by then, my book had appeared in French) and being peppered with questions and comments about what it could mean to be "between worlds."

But now, as I turn eighty-one, there is less urgency to my calling. I look around me and see generations of scholars doing every kind of history I ever hoped for, reformulating older questions and asking new ones. I know that some among them carry in their breasts this sense of being needed by or of obligation to their subjects. As for me, I am deep in my current project on slavery, sociability, and crossings in colonial Suriname, following certain slave families and owners' families across the generations, and even running back to the archives and libraries in the Netherlands as though I were a youngster. And yet Seerie and Joanna, Sarah, Simcha, and Reuben don't "need" me the way Glikl did, for such wonderful studies of slavery are being done in every corner. Rather I can sit back and enjoy being a simple storyteller.

Toronto
November 2009

Works by Natalie Zemon Davis

Books

Society and Culture in Early Modern France: Eight Essays. Stanford, CA: Stanford University Press; London: Duckworth, 1975. Reprint, Cambridge: Polity, 1987, 1995.

Berkshire Conference Special Award for Historical Scholarship, 1976; Chicago Folklore Competition, second prize, 1976.

Translated into French by Marie-Noël Bourguet (Paris: Aubier, 1979). Translated into Italian by Sandro Lombardini (Turin: Giulio Einaudi, 1980). Translated into Japanese by Komao Naruse, Shiro Miyashita, and Yumiko Takahashi (Tokyo: Heibonsha, 1987). Translated into German by Nele Löw-Beer (Frankfurt-am-Main: Fischer Taschenbuch Verlag, 1987). Translated into Portuguese by Mariza Corrêa (São Paolo: Paz e Terra, 1990). Translated into Spanish by Jordi Beltran Ferrer (Barcelona: Crítica, 1993). Translated into Hungarian by István Csaba, Péter Erdõsi, and András Kappanyos (Budapest: Balassi Kiadó, 2001). Translated into Chinese by Zhong Zi (Beijing: Renmin University of China Press, 2010). ACLS Humanities E-Book, 2008.

Spanish translation of chapter 3, "City Women and Religions Change," and chapter 5, "Women on Top," in *Historia y Género: Las mujeres en la Europa Moderna y Contemporánea,* edited and translated by James Amelang and Mary Nash, 59–92, 127–160 (Valencia: Ediciones Alfons El Magnani, 1990). Chapter 3 excerpted in *The Other Side of Western Civilization: Readings in Everyday Life,* vol. 1, *The Ancient World and the Reformation,* 3rd ed., edited by Stanley Chodorow, 333–51 (New York: Harcourt Brace Jovanovich, 1984). Chapter 5 reprinted in *The Reversible World: Symbolic Inversion in Art and Society,* edited by Barbara Babcock, 147–90 (Ithaca, NY: Cornell University Press, 1978); and in *Feminism and Renaissance Studies,* edited by Lorna Hutson, 156–85 (Oxford: Oxford University Press, 1999). Serbo-Croatian translation of chapter 5 in *Gordogan* 22 (1986): 85–120. Chapter 6, "The Rites of Violence," reprinted in *Social History of Western Civilization,* vol. 1, *Readings from the Ancient World to the Seventeenth Century,* edited by Richard Golden, 287–301 (New York: St. Martin's Press, 1988); and in *The Protestant Reformation: Religious Change and the People of Sixteenth-Century Europe,* edited by C. Scott-Dixon and Mark Greenglass, electronic resource (Glascow: History Courseware Consortium, University of Glasgow, 1999). Polish translation of chapter 6 in *Odrodzeni I Reformacia W. Polsce* 30 (1985): 33–53. Russian translation of chapter 6 in *Istoriya i Antropologiya: Mezhdistsiplinarnye Issledovaniya na Rubezhe XX–XXI Vekov,* edited by Mikhail Krom et al., 111–62 (St. Petersburg: Aleteiya, 2006). Chapter 7, "Printing and the People," reprinted in *Literacy and Social Development in the West,* edited by Harvey J. Graff, 69–95 (Cambridge: Cambridge University Press, 1981). Chapter 7 excerpted and translated into Italian in *Letteratura e Cultura Popolare,* edited by Elide Casali, 116–25 (Bologna: Zanichelli, 1982). Chapter 7 excerpted in *Rethinking*

Popular Culture: Contemporary Perspectives in Cultural Studies, edited by Chandra Mukerji and Michael Schudson, 65-96 (Berkeley: University of California Press, 1991). Hebrew translation of chapter 7 by Yael Nadav-Manes in *Zmanim—A Historical Quarterly* 71 (Summer 2000): 20-35. German translation of chapter 8, "Proverbial Wisdom and Popular Errors," in *Volkskultur: Zur Wiederentdeckung des vergessen Alltags,* edited by Richard van Dülmen and Norbert Schindler, 78-116, 394-406 (Frankfurt am Main: Fischer Taschenbuch Verlag, 1984).

The Return of Martin Guerre. Cambridge, MA: Harvard University Press, 1983; Harmondsworth: Penguin, 1985.

Translated into French by Angélique Lévi in Natalie Zemon Davis, Jean-Claude Carrière, and Daniel Vigne, *Le Retour de Martin Guerre* (Paris: Editions Robert Laffont, 1982; Editions J'ai lu, 1982; France Loisirs, 1982). New French edition: Natalie Zemon Davis, sole author (Paris: Éditions Tallandier, 2009).

Translated into German by Ute and Wolf Heinrich Leube (Munich: R. Piper and Co. Verlag, 1984; Frankfurt-am-Main: Fischer Taschenbuch Verlag, 1989). Translated into Italian by Sandro Lombardini (Turin: Giulio Einaudi, 1984). Translated into Spanish by Helen Rotés (Barcelona: Antoni Bosch, 1984, 2005). Translated into Dutch by G. Groot (Amsterdam: Elsevier, 1985). Translated into Japanese by Komao Naruse (Tokyo: Heibonsha, 1985, 1993). Translated into Swedish by Ingemar G. Nilsson (Stockholm: Ordfronts förlag, 1985). Translated into Portuguese by Denise Bottmann (São Paulo: Paz e Terra, 1987), and by António Sabler and Helena Guimarães (Porto: Fio da Palavra Editores, 2009). Translated into Russian by A. L. Velichanskii (Moscow: Progress Publishers, 1990). Translated into Czech by Irena Janovcová and Vladimir Cadský (Prague: Rybka, 1998). Translated into Hungarian by Emese Lafferton and Marcell Sebök (Budapest: Osiris Kiadó, 1999). Translated into Greek by Paraskegas Matalas (Athens: Nefeli Publishing, 2000). Translated into Korean by Hee-Yeong Yang (Seoul: Vista Publishing, 2000). Translated into Danish by Ole Magnus Mølbak Andersen (Copenhagen: Akademisk, 2001). Translated into Hebrew by Miriam Eliav-Feldon (Tel Aviv: Hargol, 2001). Translated into Croatian by Andrea Feldman and Miloš Đrudević (Zagreb: Konzor, 2001). Translated into Finnish by Aulikki Vuola (Helsinki: Gaudeamus, 2001). Translated into Estonian by Ainiki Väljataga (Tallinn: Varrak Publishers, 2002). Translated into Catalan by Vicent Olmos and Joan Iborra (Valencia: Universitat de València, 2005). Translated into Chinese by Jiang Zhengkuan (Taiwan: Linking Publishing, 2000), and by Liu Yonghua (Beijing: Peking University Press, 2009). Translated into Slovenian by Polona Petek (Ljubljana: Studia Humanitatis, 2009). Translated into Polish by Przemyslaw Szulgit (Poznan: ZYSK i S-ka, 2010).

Frauen und Gesellschaft am Beginn der Neuzeit: Studien über Familie, Religion und die Wandlungsfähigkeit des sozialen Körpers, translated by Wolfgang Kaiser. Berlin: Klaus Wagenbach, 1986; Frankfurt am Main: Fischer Taschenbuch Verlag, 1989. Includes one essay, "Religion in the Neighborhood: The Stones of Ste. Croix Parish," published here for the first time.

Fiction in the Archives: Pardon Tales and Their Tellers in Sixteenth-Century France. Stanford, CA: Stanford University Press, 1987, 1995; Cambridge: Polity Press, 1988.

Translated into French by Christian Cler (Paris: Éditions du Seuil, 1988). Translated into German by Wolfgang Kaiser (Berlin: Klaus Wagenbach, 1988; Frankfurt am Main: Fischer Taschenbuch Verlag, 1991). Translated into Japanese by Komao Naruse and Shiro Miyashita (Tokyo: Heibonsha, 1990). Translated into Portuguese by José Rubens Siqueira (São Paulo: Companhia das Letras, 1991). Translated into Italian by Patricia Guarnieri (Turin: Giulio Einaudi, 1992). Translated into Chinese by Yang Yihong (Taibei Shi: Mai tian chu ban, 2001) and by Rao Jiarong and Chen Yao (Beijing: Peking University Press, 2010).

Women on the Margins: Three Seventeenth-Century Lives. Cambridge, MA: Harvard University Press, 1995, 1997.

History Book Club Selection; Book of the Month Club History Special Selection; shortlisted for the Fawcett Book Prize.

Translated into German by Wolfgang Kaiser (Berlin: Klaus Wagenbach, 1995, 1996, 2003). Translated into Italian by Maria Gregorio (Rome: Laterza, 1996). Translated into Portuguese by Hildegard Feist (São Paulo: Companhia das Letras, 1997). Translated into French by Angélique Lévi (Paris: Seuil, 1997). Translated into Finish by Jaana Iso-Markku (Helsinki: Otava, 1997). Translated into Swedish by Birgitta Schwartzman (Stockholm: Ordront, 1998). Translated into Russian by T. Dobronitskaya (Moscow: Novoe Literaturnoe Obozrenie, 1999). Translated into Spanish by Carmen Martínez Gimeno (Madrid: Ediciones Cátedra, 2001). Translated into Japanese by Mayuho Hasegawa (Tokyo: Heibonsha, 2001).

Lebensgänge: Glikl, Zwi Hirsch, Leone Modena, Martin Guerre, Ad me ipsum, translated by Wolfgang Kaiser. Berlin: Wagenbach, 1998.

Slaves on Screen: Film and Historical Vision. Barbara Frum Lectures. Toronto: Random House of Canada; Cambridge, MA: Harvard University Press, 2000; Canada: Vintage Canada, 2007.

Translated into Chinese by Chen Rongbin (Taiwan: La Gauche Publishing, 2002). Translated into Japanese by Ken Chujo (Tokyo: Iwanamishoten, 2007). Translated into Italian by Alessandro Portelli (Rome: Viella, 2007).

The Gift in Sixteenth-Century France. Madison: University of Wisconsin Press; Oxford: Oxford University Press, 2000.

Translated into German by Wolfgang Kaiser (Munich: Beck, 2002). Translated into Italian by Maria Gregorio (Milan: Feltrinelli, 2002). Translated into French by Denis Trierweiler (Paris: Seuil, 2002, 2003). Translated into Korean by Bok-Mi Kim (Seoul: Booksea Publishing, 2004). Translated into Japanese by Shiro Miyashita (Tokyo: Misuzushobo, 2007). Translated into Hebrew by Aya Breuer (Jerusalem: Historical Society of Israel, 2010).

L'histoire tout feu tout flamme, with Denis Crouzet. Paris: Albin Michel, 2004.

Translated into Catalan by Anacletons and Justo Serna (Valencia: Publicaciones de la Universitat de València; Granada: Editorial Universidad de Granada, 2006). Translated into Italian by Angiolina Arru and Sofia Boesch Gajano (Rome: Viella, 2007).

Trickster Travels: A Sixteenth-Century Muslim Between Worlds. New York: Hill and Wang, 2006; London: Faber, 2007, 2008.

History Book Club Selection. Wallace K. Ferguson Prize of Canadian Historical Association, 2007.

Translated into French by Dominique Peters (Paris: Payot, 2007). Translated into German by Gennaro Ghiradelli (Berlin: Wagenbach, 2008). Translated into Italian by Maria Gregorio (Rome: Laterza, 2008). Translated into Spanish by Aitana Guia (Valencia: Publicaciones de la Universitat de València, 2008). Translated into Korean by Cha-Seop Kwak (Seoul: Purnyoksa, 2010). Translated into Turkish by Ayşen Anatol (Istanbul: Kultur Yayinlari, 2010).

Coauthored and Edited Works

Founder and coeditor, *Renaissance and Reformation* (A Bulletin for Scholars in the Toronto Area) 1–5 (1964–69); continued as *Renaissance and Reformation. Renaissance et Réforme,* publication of the Canadian Society of Renaissance Studies.

Memory and Countermemory. Special issue of *Representations* (with Randolph Starn) 26 (Spring 1989). "Introduction," pp. 1–6.

Gender in the Academy: Women and Learning from Plato to Princeton; An Exhibition Celebrating the 20th Anniversary of Undergraduate Coeducation at Princeton University, with Stephen Ferguson, Anthony Grafton, Linda Lierheimer, Carol Quillen, and Patricia Schechter. Princeton, NJ: Princeton University Library, 1990. Introduction reprinted in *Princeton University Library Chronicle* 52, no. 1 (Autumn 1990): 126–29.

Dal Rinasciemento all'età Moderna, with Arlette Farge. Vol. 3 of *Storia delle Donne in Occidente,* edited by Georges Duby and Michelle Perrot. Rome: Laterza, 1991.

Translated into French by Anne Michel et al. (Paris: Plon, 1991). Translated into Dutch by Margreet Blok et al. (Amsterdam: Agon, 1992). Translated into English by Arthur Goldhammer as *Renaissance and Enlightenment Paradoxes,* with Arlette Farge, vol. 3 of *A History of Women in the West* (Cambridge, MA: Harvard University Press, 1993). Translated into Spanish by Marco Aurelio Galmarini and Cristina Garcia Ohlrich (Madrid: Taurus, 1992, 2001). Translated into Portuguese, edited by Maria Hela da Cruz Coelho et al. (Porto: Edições Afrontamento; São Paulo: Ebradil, 1994). Translated into German by Heide Wunder (Frankfurt am Main: Campus Verlag, 1993). Translated into Italian by Maria Gregorio (Rome: Laterza, 1995). Translated into Japanese (Tokyo: Fujiwara, 1995). Translated into Korean by Hyung-Jun Cho (Seoul: Seamulgyul, 1999).

Contributions to Books

"The Protestant Printing Workers of Lyons in 1514." In *Aspects de la propagande religieuse,* edited by Gabrielle Bethoud et al., 247–57. Geneva: E. Droz, 1957.

"The 1592 Edition of Estienne's 'Apologie pour Hérodote.'" In *Aspects de la propagande religieuse,* edited by Gabrielle Berthoud et al., 373–76. Geneva: E. Droz, 1957.

"Publisher Guillaume Rouillé, Businessman and Humanist." In *Editing Sixteenth-Century Texts,* edited by R. J. Schoeck, 72–112. Toronto: University of Toronto Press, 1966; reprint, New York: Garland Publishing, 1978.

"City Women and Religious Change in Sixteenth-Century France." In *A Sampler of Women's Studies,* edited by Dorothy McGuigan, 17–45. Ann Arbor: University of Michigan Center for Continuing Education of Women, 1973.

Reprinted in Davis, *Society and Culture in Early Modern France* (1975), chap. 3.

"Some Tasks and Themes in the Study of Popular Religion." In *The Pursuit of Holiness in Late Medieval and Renaissance Religion: Papers from the University of Michigan Conference*, edited by Charles Trinkaus and Heiko Oberman, 484–514. Leiden: E. J. Brill, 1974.

"The Historian and Popular Culture." In *The Wolf and the Lamb: Popular Culture in France from the Old Regime to the Twentieth Century*, edited by Jacques Beauroy, Marc Bertrand, and Edward T. Gargan, 9-16. Saratoga, CA: Anima Libri, 1977.

"Gender and Genre: Women as Historical Writers, 1400–1820." In *Beyond Their Sex: Learned Women of the European Past*, edited by Patricia H. Labalme, 153–82. New York: New York University Press, 1980.

Translated into French by Sylvie Deleris as "Genre féminin et genre littéraire: Les femmes et l'écriture historique, 1400–1820." In *Histoires d'historiennes*, edited by Nicole Pellegrin 21–43 (Saint-Etienne: Publications de l'Université de Saint-Etienne, 2006).

"Women in the Arts Mécaniques in Sixteenth-Century Lyon." In *Lyon et l'Europe: Hommes et sociétés; Mélanges d'histoire offerts à Richard Gascon*, edited by Françoise Bayard et al., 1:139–67. Lyon: Presses Universitaires de Lyon, 1980.

Expanded and revised as "Women in the Crafts in Sixteenth-Century Lyon," *Feminist Studies* 8, no. 1 (Spring 1982): 46–80. Revised and reprinted in *Women and Work in Preindustrial Europe*, edited by Barbara A. Hanawalt, 167–90 (Bloomington: Indiana University Press, 1986). Reprinted in *The Other Side of Western Civilization*, 4th edition, edited by Stanley Chodorow and Marci Sortor, 396–408 (New York: Harcourt Brace Jovanovich, 1992; 5th ed. 2000). German translation of revised version in *Arbeit, Frömmigkeit und Eigenstinn. Studien zur historischen Kultur forschung*, edited by Richard van Dülmen, 43–74, 304–10 (Frankfurt am Main: Fischer Taschenbuch Verlag, 1990).

"Charivari, honneur et communauté à Lyon et à Genève au XVIIe siècle." In *Le Charivari: Actes de la table ronde organisée par le CNRS et l'EHESS, Paris (25 avril 1977)*, edited by Jacques Le Goff and Jean-Claude Schmitt, 207–20. Paris: Mouton, 1981.

In English as "Charivari, Honor, and Community in Seventeenth-Century Lyon and Geneva." In *Rite, Drama, Festival, Spectacle: Rehearsals Toward a Theory of Cultural Performance*, edited by John A. MacAloon, 42–57 (Philadelphia: Ishe Press, 1984). Translated in Spanish edition of *Society and Culture* (1993), chap. 3. Translated into Japanese in *Shiso*.

"From 'Popular Religion' to Religious Cultures." In *Reformation Europe: A Guide to Research*, edited by Steven Ozment, 321–41. St. Louis, MO: Center for Reformation Research, 1982.

Translated into French in *Religion populaire, religion des clercs?* edited by B. Lacroix and J. Simard, 393–416 (Quebec: IQRC, 1984).

"Le monde de l'imprimerie humaniste: Lyon." In *Histoire de l'édition française*, vol. 1, *Le livre conquérant du Moyen Age au milieu du 17e siècle*, edited by Henri-Jean Martin and Roger Chartier, 255–78. Paris: Promodis, 1983.

"Introduction." In Georges Duby, *The Knight, the Lady and the Priest: The Making of Modern Marriage in Medieval France*, translated by Barbara Bray, vii–xv. New York: Pantheon, 1983.

"'The Sense of History': A Case Study." In *Historians and Filmmakers: Toward Collaboration,* edited by Barbara Abrash and Janet Sternburg, 28-39. New York: Institute for Research in History, 1983.

"Scandale à l'Hôtel Dieu (Lyon, 1537-1543)," translated by Alain Croix. In *La France d'Ancien Régime. Etudes réunies en l'honneur de Pierre Goubert,* vol. 1, edited by Alain Croix, Jean Jacquart, and François Lebrun, 175-88. Toulouse: Privat, 1984.

Translated into German in Davis, *Frauen und Gesellschaft* (1986), 93-107, 157-59. Translated into Spanish in Davis, *Society and Culture* (1993), chap. 5.

"Women's History as Women's Education." In *Women's History as Women's Education: Essays by Natalie Zemon Davis and Joan Wallach Scott from a Symposium in Honor of Jill and John Conway,* Smith College, April 17, 1985, 7-22. Northampton, MA: Smith College Archives and the Sophia Smith Collection, 1985.

Reprinted in *Smith Voices: Selected Works by Smith College Women,* 35-47 (Northampton, MA: Smith College, 1990).

"Boundaries and the Sense of Self in Early Modern France." In *Reconstructing Individualism: Autonomy, Individuality, and the Self in Western Thought,* edited by Thomas C. Heller, Morton Sosna, and David E. Wellberry, 53-63, 333-35. Stanford, CA: Stanford University Press, 1986.

Translated into German in Davis, *Frauen und Gesellschaft* (1986), 7-18, 133-35.

"Scoperta e rinnovamento nella storia delle donne." In *Profil di donne: Mio Immagine Realtà fra Medioevo et Età Contemporanea,* edited by B. Vetere and Paolo Renzi, 303-22. Università degli Studie di Lecce, Dipartimento di Scienza Storiche e Sociali, Saggi e Ricerche 19. Galatina: Congedo Editor, 1986.

"Fame and Secrecy: Leon Modena's Life as an Early Modern Autobiography." In *The Autobiography of a Seventeenth-Century Venetian Rabbi: Leon Modena's "Life of Judah,"* translated and edited by Mark Cohen, 50-70. Princeton, NJ: Princeton University Press, 1988.

Reprinted in *Essays in Jewish Historiography,* edited by Ada Rapoport-Albert, 103-18. History and Theory 27 (Middletown, CT: Wesleyan University Press, 1988). Translated into Italian by Caterina Grendi Baglietto, *Quaderni Storici* 64 (April 1987): 39-60. Translated into German by Wolfgang Kaiser, *Freibeuter* 54 (1992): 9-32.

"Life-Saving Stories." In *A New History of French Literature,* edited by Denis Hollier and R. Howard Bloch, 139-44. Cambridge, MA: Harvard University Press, 1989.

Translated into French in *De la littérature française,* edited by Denis Hollier and R. Howard Bloch, 136-42 (Paris: Bordas Editeur, 1993).

"Donne e politica." In *Dal Rinascimento all'età Moderna,* edited by Davis and Farge, 201-19. Vol. 3 of *Storia delle Donne in Occidente,* edited by Georges Duby and Michelle Perrot. Rome: Laterza, 1991.

Translated into French by Pascale de Mézamat, 175-90 (Paris: Plon, 1991). Translated into Dutch by Margreet Blok, 157-70 (Amsterdam: Agon, 1992). Translated into Spanish by Marco Aurelio Galmarini, 211-27 (Madrid: Taurus, 1992). Original in English as "Women and Politics," in Davis and Farge, *Renaissance and Enlightenment Paradoxes,* vol. 3 of *A History of Women in the West* (1993), 167-83.

Translated into Portuguese by João Barrote, 229–49 (Porto: Edições Afrontamento; São Paulo: Ebradil, 1994). Translated into Japanese, 261–87 (Tokyo: Fujiwara, 1995). Translated into Korean by Hyung-Jun Cho (Seoul: Sealmulgyul, 1999).

Preface to *Liste Otto: The Official List of French Books Banned under the German Occupation, 1940,* iii–ix. Cambridge: Harvard College Library, 1992.

"Iroquois Women, European Women." In *Women, "Race," and Writing in the Early Modern Period,* edited by Margo Hendricks and Patricia Parker, 243–58, 349–61. London: Routledge, 1993.

Reprinted in *European and Non-European Societies, 1450–1660,* edited by Robert Forster, vol. 2, chap. 22 (Ashgate: Variorum, 1997). Reprinted in *American Encounters: Natives and Newcomers from European Contact to Indian Removal, 1500–1850,* edited by Peter C. Mancall and James H. Merrell, 96–118 (New York: Routledge, 2000). Reprinted in *Feminist Postcolonial Theory: A Reader,* edited by Reina Lewis and Sara Mills, 135–60 (Edinburgh: Edinburgh University Press, 2003).

"Gifts and Bribes in Sixteenth Century France." Iredell Lecture, 14 February 1995, Lancaster University. Translated into Japanese, *Shiso* 10 (1997): 63–77.

"Riches and Dangers: Glikl bas Judah Leib on Court Jews." In *From Court Jews to the Rothschilds, 1600–1800,* edited by Vivian Mann and Richard Cohen, 45–57. Munich: Prestel; New York: Jewish Museum, 1996.

"Remaking Impostors: From Martin Guerre to Sommersby." Hayes Robinson Lecture, 7 March 1995, Royal Holloway, University of London, 1997. Available online at http://www.rhul.ac.uk/history/Research/research_HayesRobinson.html.

Translated into Japanese, *Shiso* 10, no. 880 (1997): 44–62. Translated into German in Davis, *Lebensgänge* (1998). Translated into Russian in *Homo Historicus: Essays of Yuri Bessmertny on the 80th Anniversary of His Birth,* 2:171–88 (Moscow: Nauka, 2003).

"From Heinous to Prodigious: Simon Goulart and the Reframing of Imposture." In *L'Histoire grande ouverte: Hommages à Emmanuel Le Roy Ladurie,* edited by A. Burguière et al., 274–83. Paris: Fayard, 1997.

"Foreword." In *Changing Identities in Early Modern France,* edited by Michael Wolfe. Durham, NC: Duke University Press, 1997.

A Life of Learning. Charles Homer Haskins Lecture for 1997. American Council of Learned Societies Occasional Paper, no. 39. Available online at www.acis.org.

Translated into German in *Lebensgänge* (Berlin, 1998). Translated into Chinese in *The Birth of Historians: Special Topics on Western Historiography,* edited by Chien-shou Chen, 1–48 (Taipei: Taiwan Elite, 2008). Translated into Hebrew by Gadi Algazi, *Zmanim: A Historical Quarterly* 71 (Summer 2000): 4–19. Excerpt reprinted in *The Little, Brown Reader,* 8th ed., edited by Marcia Stubbs and Sylvan Barnet, 158–63 (New York: Longman, 1999).

"Foreword." In *The Book of the City of Ladies,* by Christine de Pizan, translated by Earl Jeffrey Richards, xv–xxii. Revised edition, New York: Persea Books, 1998.

"Beyond Babel." In *Confronting the Turkish Dogs: A Conversation on Rabelais and His Critics,* by Davis and Timothy Hampton, 15–28. Occasional Papers 10. Berkeley: University of California–Berkeley, Townsend Center for the Humanities, 1996.

Translated into German by Jutta Held and Ute Széll (Osnabrück: Rasch, 1998).

"Beyond Evolution: Comparative History and Its Goals." In *Swiat historii: Prace z metodologii historii i historii historiografii dedykowane Jerzemu Topolskiemu,* edited by Wojciecha Wrozsaka, 149–57. Pozna: Instytut Historii, 1998.

"Neue Perspektiven für die Geschlechterforschung in der Frühen Neuzeit," translated by Josefine Danneberg. In *Geschlechter Perspektiven: Forschungen zur Frühen Neuzeit,* edited by Heide Wunder and Gisela Engel, 16–41. Königstein: Ulrike Helmer Verlag, 1998.

"Displacing and Displeasing: Writing about Women in the Early Modern Period." In *Attending to Early Modern Women,* edited by Susan D. Amussen and Adele Seeff, 25–37. Newark: University of Delaware Press, 1998.

"Who Owns History?" In *Historical Perspectives on Memory,* edited by Anne Ollila, 19–34. Helsinki: Studia Historica, 1999. This essay is a revised and considerably enlarged version of a paper that appeared in *Perspectives* 34, no. 8 (November 2006): 1, 4–6.

"Global History, Many Stories." In *Eine Welt—Eine Geschichte? 43: Deutscher Historikertag in Aachen, 26. bis 29. September 2000,* 373–80. Munich: Berichtsband, 2001.

Translated into German in *Lettre International* 51 (Winter 2000): 86–88.

"Polarities, Hybridities: What Strategies for Decentring?" In *Decentring the Renaissance: Canada and Europe in Multidisciplinary Perspective, 1500–1700,* edited by Germaine Warkentin and Carolyn Podruchny, 19–32. Toronto: University of Toronto Press, 2001.

"Glikl bas Judah Leib—ein jüdisches, ein europäisches Leben." In *Die Hamburger Kauffrau Glikl: Jüdische Existenz in der Frühen Neuzeit,* edited by Monika Richarz, 27–48. Hamburg: Christians Verlag, 2001.

"Foreword." In *Rebellion, Community and Custom in Early Modern Germany,* by Norbert Schindler, ix–xiv. Cambridge: Cambridge University Press, 2002.

"Voices." In *Diaspora: Homelands in Exile,* 2 vols., by Frédéric Brenner, 2:38, 56, 62, 74, 99. New York: Harper Collins, 2003.

"Conclusion." In *Poverty and Charity in Middle Eastern Contexts,* edited by Michael Bonner, Mine Ener, and Amy Singer, 315–24. Albany: SUNY Press, 2003.

"Preface." In *Martin Luther: Üks inimsaatus,* by Lucien Febvre, 7–8. Tallinn: Varrak Publishers, 2003.

"Clifford Geertz on Time and Change." In *Clifford Geertz by His Colleagues,* edited by Richard A. Shweder and Byron Good, 38–44. Chicago: University of Chicago Press, 2005.

"Conclusion." In *Autour de Polanyi: Vocabulaires, théories et modalités des échanges,* edited by Philippe Clancier, F. Joannès, Pierre Rouillard, and Aline Tenu, 283–90. Paris: De Boccard, 2005.

"Henri Hauser: Historien, Citoyen, Pionnier." In *Henri Hauser (1866–1946): Humaniste, Historien, Républicain,* edited by Séverine-Antigone Marin and Georges-Henri Soutou, 13–23. Paris: PUPS, 2006.

"What Is Universal about History?" In *Transnationale Geschichte: Themen, Tendenzen und Theorien,* edited by Gunilla Budde, Sebastian Conrad, and Oliver Janz, 15–20. Göttingen: Vandenhoeck & Ruprecht, 2006.

Translated into Italian, *Quaderni Storici* 41, no. 3 (December 2006): 1-7. Translated into German, *Historische Anthropologie* 15 (2007): 126-31.

"'Leo Africanus.'" In *The New Encyclopedia of Africa,* edited by John Middleton and Joseph C. Miller, 3:281-82. Detroit: Thomason Gale, 2007.

"Stedman's *Suriname* Book in Sweden." In *Vänskap over Gränser: En Festskrift till Eva Österberg,* edited by Kenneth Johansson and Marie Lindstedt Cronberg, 77-98. Lund: Förtfattarna, 2007.

"Feminism and a Scholarly Friendship," with Jill Ker Conway. In *Minds of Our Own: Inventing Feminist Scholarship in Canada and Quebec, 1966-76,* edited by Wendy Roberts, 78-88. Waterloo, Ont.: Wilfrid Laurier University Press, 2008.

"About an Inventory: A Conversation Between Natalie Zemon Davis and Peter N. Miller," with Peter N. Miller. In *Dutch New York Between East and West: The World of Margrieta van Varick,* edited by Deborah L. Krohn and Peter N. Miller, 117-29. New York: Bard Graduate Center, New York Historical Society; New Haven: Yale University Press, 2009. Also available as a BGC film, directed by Han Vu, at http://www.bgc.bard.edu.

"Le conte de l'amphibie et les ruses d'al-Hasan al-Wazzān." In *Léon l'Africain,* edited by François Pouillon, 311-23. Paris: Karthala and IISMM, 2009.

"La *Cosmographia de Afriqua* de Jean-Léon l'Africain." In *Histoire du monde au XVe siècle,* edited by Patrick Boucheron, 627-32. Paris: Librairie Arthème Fayard, 2009.

"Epilogue." In *Atlantic Diasporas. Jews, Conversos, and Crypto-Jews in the Age of Mercantilism, 1500-1800,* edited by Richad Kagan and Philip Morgan, 213-17. Baltimore: Johns Hopkins University Press, 2009.

"Conclusion." In *Inventing Collateral Damage: Civilian Casualties, War, and Empire,* edited by Stephen J. Rockel and Rick Halpern, 329-38. Toronto: Between the Lines, 2009.

Articles

"On the Protestantism of Benoît Rigaud." *Bibliothèque d'humanisme et renaissance* 17 (1955): 246-51.

"Holbein's *Pictures of Death* and the Reformation at Lyons." *Studies in the Renaissance* 3 (1956): 97-130.

"Christophe Plantin's Childhood at Saint Just." *De Gulden Passer* 35 (1957): 107-20.

"Mathematicians in the Sixteenth-Century French Academies: Some Further Evidence." *Renaissance News* 11 (1958): 3-10.

"Sixteenth-Century French Arithmetics on the Business Life." *Journal of the History of Ideas* 21 (1960): 18-48.

"The Good Name of Martin Ponthus." *Bibliothèque d'humanisme et renaissance* 22 (1960): 287-93.

"Peletier and Beza Part Company." *Studies in the Renaissance* 11 (1964): 188-222.

"Strikes and Salvation at Lyons." *Archiv für Reformationsgeschichte* 56 (1965): 48-64. Reprinted in *Society and Culture in Early Modern France,* chap. 1.

"A Trade Union in Sixteenth-Century France." *Economic History Review* 19 (1966): 48–69. Reprinted as "Van oproeren en Stakingen," in *Sociale en politeke movilisering in Europa, 1500–1850,* edited by H. A. Diederiks (The Hague: M. Nijhoff, 1981), 25–52. Reprinted in *The History of the Book in the West: 1455–1700,* vol. 2, edited by Ian Gadd (Aldershot, UK: Ashgate, 2010).

"The Protestantism of Jacques Besson." *Technology and Culture* 7 (1966): 513.

"A Finding List of Renaissance Legal Literature to 1700," with R. J. Schoeck and J. K. McConica. *Renaissance and Reformation* 4 (1967/68): 2–28, 33–85, 98–126.

"Gregory Nazianzen in the Service of Humanist Social Reform." *Renaissance Quarterly* 20 (1967): 455–64.

"Poor Relief, Humanism and Heresy: The Case of Lyon." *Studies in Medieval and Renaissance History* 5 (1968): 217–75. Translated into French in *Étude sur l'histoire de la pauvreté (Moyen Age–XVIe siècle),* 2 vols., edited by Michel Mollat, 761–822 (Paris: Publications de la Sorbonne, 1974). Reprinted in Davis, *Society and Culture in Early Modern France* (1975), chap. 2.

"Sixteenth-Century Continental Editions of Authors in the Forbes Collection." *Renaissance and Reformation* 5, no. 1 (November 1968): 8–13.

"René Choppin on More's *Utopia.*" *Moreana* 19/20 (1968): 91–96.

"A Checklist of French Political and Religious Pamphlets, 1560–1635, in the University of Toronto Library," with J. A. McLelland. *Renaissance and Reformation* 5, no. 3 (May 1969): 18–41.

"The Reasons of Misrule: Youth-Groups and Charivaris in Sixteenth-Century France." *Past and Present* 50 (February 1971): 41–75. Reprinted in Davis, *Society and Culture in Early Modern France* (1975), chap. 4.

"Erasmus at Moscow." *Renaissance and Reformation* 7 (1971): 84–86.

"New Monarchs and Prudent Priests." *Canadian Journal of History* 6 (1971): 69–74.

"A Note on the Publishers of a Lyon Bible of 1566." *Bibliothèque d'humanisme et renaissance* 34 (1972): 501–3.

"The Rites of Violence: Religious Riot in Sixteenth-Century France." *Past and Present* 59 (May 1973): 51–91. Reprinted in *The Massacre of St. Bartholomew: Reappraisals and Documents,* edited by Alfred Soman, 203–42 (The Hague: M. Nijhoff, 1974). Reprinted in Davis, *Society and Culture in Early Modern France* (1975), chap. 6.

"A Rejoinder" [to Janine Estèbe, "Debate. The Rites of Violence: Religious Riot in Sixteenth-Century France"]. *Past and Present* 67 (May 1975): 131–35.

"'Women's History' in Transition: The European Case." *Feminist Studies* 3 (Spring/Summer 1976): 83–93. Reprinted in *Women's Lives: Perspectives on Progress and Change,* edited by Virginia Lee Lussier and Joyce Jennings Walstedt, 5–25 (Newark: University of Delaware Press, 1977); and in *Feminism and History,* edited by Joan Wallach Scott, 79–104 (Oxford: Oxford University Press, 1996). Excerpt reprinted in *The European Women's History Reader,* edited by Fiona Montgomery and Christine Collette, 11–13 (London: Routledge, 2002). Translated into Italian in *Donna Woman Femme* 3 (April-June 1977): 7–33; and in *Altre storie: La critica femminista alla storia,* edited by Paola Di Cori, 67–103 (Bologna: CLUEB, 1996). Translated into Dutch by Els Kloek and Nenneke Quast, in *Tweede Jaarboek voor Vrouwengeschiedenis,* 236–63 (Nijmegen: Socialistese Uitgeveri Nijmegen, 1981). Translated into German in Davis, *Frauen und Gesellschaft* (1986), 117–32, 161–71.

"Ghosts, Kin and Progeny: Some Features of Family Life in Early Modern France." *Daedalus* 106, no. 2 (Spring 1977): 87–114. Reprinted in *The Family,* edited by Alice Ross et al., 87–117 (New York: Norton, 1978). Translated into German in Davis, *Frauen und Gesellschaft* (1986), 19–51, 1135–44. Translated into Russian in *Thesis* 6 (1994): 201–41.

"Men, Women and Violence: Some Reflections on Equality." *Smith Alumni Quarterly* (April 1977): 12-15. Reprinted in *The Role of Women in Conflict and Peace,* edited by Dorothy G. McGuigan, 19–29 (Ann Arbor: University of Michigan Center for Continuing Education of Women, 1977).

"Le Milieu social de Corneille de La Haye (Lyon, 1533–1575)." *Revue de l'art* 47 (1980): 21–28.

"The Sacred and the Body Social in Sixteenth-Century Lyon." *Past and Present* 90 (February 1981): 40–70. Reprinted in *Humanities in Review,* vol. 1, edited by Ronald Dworkin, Karl Miller, and Richard Sennett, 40–79 (Cambridge: Cambridge University Press, 1982). Excerpted in *The Other Side of Western Civilization: Readings in Everyday Life,* vol. 2, *The Sixteenth Century to the Present,* 3rd edition, edited by Peter Stearns, 29–35 (New York: Harcourt Brace Jovanovich, 1984). Translated into German in Davis, *Frauen und Gesellschaft* (1986), 64–92, 145–57.

"Anthropology and History in the 1980s: The Possibilities of the Past." *Journal of Interdisciplinary History* 12, no. 2 (Autumn 1981): 267–75. Reprinted in *The New History: The 1980s and Beyond,* edited by Theodore K. Rabb and Robert I. Rotberg, 267–75 (Princeton, NJ: Princeton University Press, 1982). Translated into German in *Vom Umschreiben der Geschichte: Neue historische Perspektiven,* edited by Ulrich Raulff, 45–53 (Berlin: Wagenbach, 1986). Translated into Portuguese by Antonio Maurício Dias da Costa, *Revista Estudos Amazônicos* 5, no. 1 (2010).

"Misprint and Minerva: Printers' Journeymen in Sixteenth-Century Lyon." *Printing History* 3, no. 1 (1981): 72–83.

"Beyond the Market: Books as Gifts in Sixteenth-Century France." *Transactions of the Royal Historical Society,* 5th ser., 33 (1983): 69–88.

"About Dedications," in "Radical History Review Special Supplement: The David Abraham Case." *Radical History Review* 32 (1985): 94–96.

"A Renaissance Text to the Historian's Eye: The Gifts of Montaigne." *Journal of Medieval and Renaissance Studies* 15, no. 1 (Spring 1985): 47–56. Translated into German in Davis, *Frauen und Gesellschaft* (1986), 108–16, 159–61. Revised as "Art and Society in the Gifts of Montaigne." *Representations* 12 (Fall 1985): 24–32.

"What Is Women's History?" *History Today* 35 (June 1985): 40–42.

"'Any Resemblance to Persons Living or Dead': Film and the Challenge of Authenticity." Fifth Patricia Wise Lecture, American Film Institute. *Yale Review* 76 (Summer 1987): 457–82. Reprinted in *Historical Journal of Film, Radio and Television* 8 (1988): 269–83; and in *The History on Film Reader,* edited by Marnie Hughes-Warrington, 17–29 (London: Routledge, 2009). Translated into German by Robert Cackett in

Bilder schrieben Geschichte: Der Historiker im Kino, edited by Rainer Rother, 37-64 (Berlin: Klaus Wagenbach, 1991).

"A Symposium: Feminist Book Reviewing," with Julia Penelope, Marge Wolf, Cynthia Neverdon-Morton, and Linda Gardiner. *Feminist Studies* 14, no. 3 (1988): 601-22.

"History's Two Bodies." Presidential Address, American Historical Association. *American Historical Review* 93, no. 1 (February 1988): 1-30. Translated into German by Ebba D. Drolshagen in *Der Historker als Menschenfresser: Uber den Beruf des Geschichtesschreibers,* by Fernand Braudel et al., 46-84 (Berlin: Klaus Wagenbach, 1990, 1998). Translated into Chinese in *The Challenge of Modern Historiography: The Presidential Addresses of AHA Presidents, 1961-1988,* edited by Wang Jianhua, 505-29 (Shanghai: Shanghai Academy of Social Sciences, 1990).

"'On the Lame.'" In "AHR Forum: The Return of Martin Guerre." *American Historical Review* 93, no. 3 (June 1988): 507-603.

"Du conte et de l'histoire." *Le débat* 54 (March-April 1989): 138-43.

"Women's History: Multiple Stories." *In de Ban van het Verhall (Jaarboek voor Vrouwengeschiedenis)* 11 (1990): 98-106.

"The Shapes of Social History." *Storia della Storiografia* 17 (1990): 28-34. Translated into Spanish by Ferrandis Garrayo, *Historia Social* 10 (Spring-Summer 1991): 177-82. Translated into German in *Mikro-Historie: Neue Pfade in die Sozialgeschichte,* edited by Hans Medick (Frankfurt am Main: Fischer Taschenbuch Verlag, 1994). Translated into Finnish in *Matkoja moderniin. Lähikuvia suomalaisten elämästä,* edited by Marjatta Rahikainen, 9-17 (Helsinki: Suomen Historiallen Seura, 1996).

"Rabelais Among the Censors (1940s, 1540s)." *Representations* 32 (Fall 1990): 1-32. Translated into German by Wolfgang Kaiser, *Freibeuter* 58 (November 1993): 33-76.

"Stories and the Hunger to Know." *Literaria Pragensia: Studies in Literature and Culture* 1 (1991): 12-13. Expanded and republished in *Yale Journal of Criticism* 5, no 4 (Spring 1992): 159-63.

"Censorship, Silence and Resistance: The *Annales* during the German Occupation of France." *Literaria Pragensia: Studies in Literature and Criticism* 1 (1991): 13-23. Translated into Russian in *Sur un point crucial: Débat autour des "Annales," ou: Comment écrire l'histoire aujourd'hui et demain,* edited by Yui Bessmerty, 166-83 (Moscow: Nauka, 1993). Translated into Italian, *Revista di Storia della Storiografia Moderna* 13, nos. 1-2 (1993): 161-81. Reprinted in *Historical Reflections/Réflexions historiques* 24 (1998): 351-74; and in *After History,* edited by Martin Procházka, 9-31 (Prague: Litteraria Pragensia, 2006).

"Yom Kippur in Moscow, 5750." *Radical History Review* 49 (1991): 155-60.

"The Rights and Responsibilities of Historians in Regard to Historical Films and Video," with Daniel J. Walkowitz for the AHA Ad Hoc Committee on History and Film. *Perspectives* 30, no. 6 (September 1992): 15, 17.

"Women and the World of the *Annales.*" *History Workshop* 33 (Spring 1992): 121-37. Reprinted in *The Annales School,* edited by Stuart Clark, 1:203-23 (London: Routledge, 1999).

"Toward Mixtures and Margins." In "AHR Forum: The Folklore of Industrial Society: Popular Culture and Its Audiences." *American Historial Review* 97 (1992): 1409-16.

"Commemorating 1492: A Roundtable," with Sacvan Bercovitch, Aron Rodrigue, Victor Perera, and Sean Wilentz. *Tikkun* 7, no. 5 (September-October 1992): 53-62.

"Gifts, Markets and Communities in Sixteenth-Century France" [in Russian], translated by Irina Bessmertny. *Odysseus* (1992): 193-203.

"Az imposztor" [in Hungarian], translated by Emese Lafferton and Marcell Sebök. *Café Bábel* no. 3 (1994): 119-28.

"Leere Hände bitten vergebens. Komische Kritik an der Welt: Rabelais und die Geschichten, Sprichwörter und Bilder des sechzehnten Jahrhunderts." *Frankfurter Allgemeine Zeitung* 106, 7 May 1994, Literatur Section.

"Métissage culturel et méditation historique." *Le Monde,* 18-19 Juin 1995, 11. Reprinted in English in *Budapest Review of Books* 7, no. 1 (Spring 1997): 6-9.

"Religion and Capitalism Once Again? Jewish Merchant Culture in the Seventeenth Century." *Representations* 59 (Summer 1997): 57-84. Reprinted in *The Fate of "Culture": Geertz and Beyond,* edited by Sherry B. Ortner, 56-85 (Berkeley: University of California Press, 1999); and in *Trading Cultures,* edited by Jeremy Adelman and Stephen Aron, 59-86 (Brepols Publishers, 2001). Reprinted in German in *Lebensgänge,* 7-40 (Berlin, 1998).

"Literature, Language, and Hierarchy in Early Modern Europe." *Ritsumeikan Studies in Language and Culture* 9, nos. 5-6 (March 1998): 293-302.

"Dialogue: On the Strategy of Culture Mixture," with Masao Yamaguchi [in Japanese]. *Eureka* 11, vol. 29-14 (1997): 36-51. English version in *Ritsumeikan Studies in Language and Culture* 9, nos. 5-6 (March 1998): 381-410.

"Rethinking Cultural Mixture" [in Japanese]. *Revue de la pensée d'aujourd'hui* 26-5, no. 4 (1998): 20-37.

"Millennium and Historical Hope" [essay based on talk presented at the fifth Millennium Evening at the White House, 25 January 1999]. *Tikkun* 14, no. 6 (November/December 1999): 57-59, 61.

"The Rest of the Story," with Jill Ker Conway. In "The Shadow Story of the Millennium: Women." Special issue, *New York Times Magazine,* 16 May 1999, 80-85. Reprinted in Frank Madden, *Exploring Literature: Writing and Thinking about Fiction, Poetry, Drama, and the Essay,* by Frank Madden (New York: Longman, 2001).

"Cannibalism and Knowledge," *Historien* 2 (2000): 13-30.

"Heroes, Heroines, Protagonists." In "Heldinnen?" Special issue, *L'Homme* 12, no. 2 (2001): 322-28.

"Traditions of Gift-Giving in Early Modern France." *BBC History* 2, no. 12 (December 2001): 46-47.

"The Author's Response," in "Natalie Zemon Davis's *Slaves on Screen*: A Review Forum," edited by Vanessa Schwartz. *Perspectives* 39, no. 6 (September 2001): 25-27. Available online at http://www.historians.org/perspectives/issues/2001/0109/.

"The History of Women and Gender (1970-2003): Achievements and the Challenges Ahead." *Pedralbes: Revista d'història Moderna* 22 (2002): 15-28.

"Trumbo and Kubrick Argue History." *Raritan: A Quarterly Review* 22 (August 2002):

173-90. Translated into French, *Actes de la recherche en sciences sociales* 161-62 (2006): 80-96.

"Movie or Monograph? A Historian/Filmmaker's Perspective." *The Public Historian* 25, no. 3 (Summer 2003): 45-48.

"The Historian and Literary Uses." *Profession* (2003): 21-27.

"Being Grateful to Edward Said." *Comparative Studies of South Asia, Africa and the Middle East* 23, nos. 1-2 (2003): 3-4.

"Non-European Stories, European Listeners." In "Berichten, Erzählen, Beherrschen." Special issue, *Zeitsprünge Forschungen zur Frühen Neuzeit* 7 (2003): 200-219.

"Commentary." In "Mobility in French History." Special issue, *French Historical Studies* 29 (2006): 509-11.

"Remembering Aron Gurevich" [in Russian]. *New Literary Review* 81 (2006). Available online at http://magazines.russ.ru/nlo/2006/81/.

"Els viatges d'un bergant: Un musulmà del segle XVI entre dos mons," translated by Aitana Guia I Conca. In "Les mirades del viatger." Special issue, *Afers* 57 (2007): 295-320.

"Remembering Clifford Geertz." *History Workshop Journal* 65, no. 1 (2008): 188-94.

"Le silence des archives, le renom de l'histoire." In "Martin Guerre, retour sur une histoire célèbre." Special issue, *Annales du Midi* 120, no. 264 (Oct.-Dec. 2008): 467-83. Translated into Portuguese in Davis, *El Regresso de Martin Guerre* (2009), 139-59.

"Creole Languages and Their Uses: The Example of Colonial Suriname." *Historical Research* 82 (May 2009): 268-84.

Reviews

Review of *Geneva and the Coming of the Wars of Religion in France, 1555-1563,* by Robert M. Kingdon. *History of Ideas Newsletter* 2, no. 4 (October 1956): 90-92.

Review of *Le Miracle de Laon en Lannoys,* edited by A. H. Chaubard. *History of Ideas Newsletter* 3, no. 2 (April 1957): 18-19.

Review of *Le Livre du recteur de l'Académie de Genève (1559-1878),* edited by S. Stelling Michaud. *Renaissance News* 14 (1961): 43-45.

Review of *The Massacre of Saint Bartholomew,* by Henri Noguères, translated by Claire Eliane Engel. *American Historical Review* 68 (1962/63): 517-18.

Review of *Lyons, 1473-1503: The Beginnings of Cosmopolitanism,* by James B. Wadsworth. *Renaissance News* 16, no. 2 (1963): 118-21.

Review of *Science and the Renaissance,* 2 vols., by W. P. D. Wightman. *Bibliothèque d'humanisme et renaissance* 25 (1963): 433-36.

Review of *Renaissance Studies,* by Wallace K. Ferguson. *Canadian Historical Review* 45, no. 4 (1964): 344-45.

Review of *The Renaissance Reconsidered: A Symposium,* by Leona Gabel et al. *American Historical Review* 70 (1964/65): 851-52.

Review of René de Lucinge's *Lettres sur les débuts de la Ligue (1585)*, edited by Alain Dufour and Eustorg de Beaulieu; and *Les Divers rapports*, edited by M. A. Pegg. *Renaissance News* 18 (1965): 150-52.

Review of *Change in Medieval Society: Europe North of the Alps, 1050–1500*, edited by Sylvia A. Thrupp. *Canadian Journal of Economics and Political Science* 31, no. 4 (1965): 608-9.

Review of *Studies in Genevan Government (1536–1605)*, by E. William Monter. *Archiv für Reformationsgeschichte* 57, nos. 1-2 (1966): 276-78.

Review of *The Political Ideas of Pierre Viret*, by Robert Dean Linder. *Renaissance News* 19, no. 4 (1966): 371-73.

Review of *The Library Catalogue of Anthony Higgen, Dean of Ripon (1608–1624)*, edited by Jean E. Mortimer. *Bibliothèque d'humanisme et renaissance* 30 (1968): 413-14.

Review of *Strasbourg and the Reform: A Study in the Process of Change*, by Miriam Usher Chrisman. *Journal of Modern History* 40, no. 4 (December 1968): 588-91.

Review of *Geneva and the Consolidation of the French Protestant Movement, 1564–1572*, by Robert Kingdon. *Renaissance Quarterly* 22, no. 1 (1969): 54-56.

"Deforming the Reformation." Review of *Religion and Regime*, by Guy E. Swanson. *New York Review of Books* 12, no. 7 (April 10, 1969): 35-38.

"Missed Connections: Religion and Regime." Review of *Religion and Regime*, by Guy E. Swanson. *Journal of Interdisciplinary History* 1 (1971): 384-94.

Review of *Grand commerce et vie urbaine au XVIe siècle: Lyon et ses marchands (environs de 1520–environs de 1580)*, 2 vols., by Richard Gascon. *American Historical Review* 79, no. 1 (February 1974): 158-61.

"Les conteurs de Montaillou." Review of *Montaillou, village occitan de 1294 à 1324*, by Emmanuel Le Roy Ladurie. *Annales, économies, sociétés, civilisations* 34 (1979): 61-73.

Review of *The Renaissance Notion of Women: A Study in the Fortunes of Scholasticism and Medical Science in European Intellectual Life*, by Ian Maclean. *Renaissance Quarterly* 34, no. 2 (1981): 211-13.

"Revolution and Revelation." Review of *The Three Orders: Feudal Society Imagined*, by Georges Duby, translated by Arthur Goldhammer; and *The Age of Cathedrals: Art and Society, 980–1420*, by Georges Duby, translated by Eleanor Levieux and Barbara Thompson. *New York Review of Books* 31, no. 1 (2 February 1984): 32-34.

"The Harvest of Sorcery." Review of *The Night Battles: Witchcraft and Agrarian Cults in the Sixteenth and Seventeenth Centuries*, by Carlo Ginzburg, translated by Anne Tedeschi and John Tedeschi; and *La sorcière de Jasmin*, by Emmanuel Le Roy Ladurie. *Times Literary Supplement* 221, no. 4 (24 February 1984): 179-80.

Review of *The Development of the Family and Marriage in Europe*, by Jack Goody. *American Ethnologist* 12, no. 1 (1985): 149-51.

Review of *Rouen during the Wars of Religion*, by Philip Benedict; and *The Making of a State: Württemberg, 1593–1793*, by James Allen Vann. *Renaissance Quarterly* 38, no. 2 (1985): 327-32.

"Happy Endings." Review of *The Birth of Purgatory*, by Jacques Le Goff, translated by Arthur Goldhammer. *New York Review of Books* 32, no. 12 (18 July 1985): 31-33.

"A New Montaigne." Review of *Montaigne in Motion,* by Jean Starobinski, translated by Arthur Goldhammer. *New York Review of Books* 34, no. 18 (19 November 1987): 50–54.

"A Modern Hero." Review of *Marc Bloch: A Life in History,* by Carole Fink. *New York Review of Books* 27, no. 7 (26 April 1990): 27–30. Translated into Japanese in *Misuzu* 354 (September 1990): 2–13.

Review of *Liquid Assets, Dangers Gifts: Presents and Politics at the End of the Middle Ages,* by Valentine Groebner. *Sixteenth Century Journal* 34 (2003): 1250–52.

Review of *Middle Eastern Languages and the Print Revolution: A Cross Cultural Encounter. A Catalogue and Companion to the Exhibition,* by Eva Hanebutt-Benz, Dagmar Glass, and Geoffrey Roper. *MIT Electronic Journal of Middle Eastern Studies* 5 (Fall 2005): 84–87.

Review of *The Quest for Global Justice in the Twenty-first Century,* by Arthur Mitzman. *Common Knowledge* (2006): 306.

Review of *Sir John Harrington and the Book as Gift,* by Jason Scott-Wren. *Common Knowledge* 13, no. 1 (2007): 142–43.

Review of *Wooden Eyes: Nine Reflections on Distance,* by Carlo Ginzburg. *Common Knowledge* 13, no. 2 (2007): 458–59.

"Kingdoms of Paper." Review of *Who Are You? Identification, Deception and Surveillance in Early Modern Europe,* by Valentin Groebner. *London Review of Books* 29, no. 20 (18 October 2007): 17–18.

"The Quest of Michel de Certeau." Review of *The Capture of Speech and Other Political Writings,* translated from the French and with an afterword by Tom Conley, edited and with an introduction by Luce Giard; *The Certeau Reader,* edited by Graham Ward; *Heterologies: Discourse on the Other,* translated from the French by Brian Massumi, foreword by Wlad Godzich; *Culture in the Plural,* translated from the French and with an afterword by Tom Conley, edited and with an introduction by Luce Giard; *The Mystic Fable,* vol. 1, *The Sixteenth and Seventeenth Centuries,* translated from the French by Michael B. Smith; *The Practice of Everyday Life,* translated from the French by Steven F. Rendall; *Michel de Certeau: Interpretation and Its Other,* by Jeremy Ahearne; *The Writing of History,* translated from the French by Tom Conley; *The Possession at Loudun,* translated from the French by Michael B. Smith, with a foreword by Stephen Greenblatt. *New York Review of Books* 55, no. 8 (15 May 2008). Translated into German in *WestEnd: Neue Zeitschrift für Sozialforschung* 5, no. 2 (2008): 162–73.

Review of *An Ottoman Tragedy: History and Historiography at Play,* by Gabriel Piterberg. *Common Knowledge* 14, no. 1 (Winter 2008): 151–53.

Review of *The Politics of the Veil,* by Joan Wallach Scott. *Common Knowledge* 15 (Winter 2009): 96.

Review of *The Interpretation of Cultures: Selected Essays,* by Clifford Geertz. *Sixteenth Century Journal* 11 (Spring 2009): 58–61.

Film, Television, and Opera

Historical consultant for *Le Retour de Martin Guerre* (movie), directed by Daniel Vigne and produced by Société française de production cinématographique. Premiered in Paris, May 1982; in New York, June 1983. Awarded Belgian Prix Femina (1982); three Césars (1983); Academy Award nominee for Best Costume (1984).

Consultant for *Renaissance* (televison series), created by Theodore K. Rabb and produced by the Medici Foundation. Broadcast by PBS in January-March 1983.

Historical consultant for *The House of Martin Guerre* (opera), libretto and music by Leslie Arden, directed by Duncan McIntosh. Toronto, Theatre Plus, June 1993; new production directed by David Petrarca, Chicago, Goodman Theatre, July-August 1996; Toronto, St. Lawrence Centre for the Arts, 22 September-25 October 1997.

Interviews

Judy Coffin and Robert Harding. "Politics, Progeny and French History: An Interview with Natalie Zemon Davis." *Radical History Review* 24 (Fall 1980): 115-39. Reprinted as "Natalie Zemon Davis," in *Visions of History: Interviews with E. P. Thompson ... by Marho,* edited by Henry Abelove et al., 99-122 (New York: Pantheon, 1983). Reprinted in Italian in *Memoria: Rivista di storia delle donne* 9, no. 3 (1983): 79-93; and *Quaderni aretini: Laboratorio di Ricerca* 1 (1985): 161-88. Reprinted in German in *Freibeuter* 24 (1985): 65-75. Reprinted in Japanese in *Rekishikatachi: Visions of History,* edited by Kazuhiko Kondo, 83-109 (Nagoya: University of Nagoya Press, 1990; 2nd ed., 1991).

Ed Benson. "Martin Guerre, the Historian and the Filmmakers: An Interview with Natalie Zemon Davis." *Film and History* 13 (September 1983): 49-65.

Marine Valensise, ed. "Una Storia da Film (e poi da Libro): Intervista a Natalie Zemon Davis." *Problemi dell' Informazione* 10, no. 2 (April-June 1985): 245-64.

William McCleery. "Natalie Zemon Davis." In *Conversations on the Character of Princeton,* 33-38, Princeton, NJ: Princeton University Office of Communications, 1986.

Saskia Jansens and Anja Petrakopoulos. "Een 'old pro' over haar vak: Interview met Natalie Zemon Davis." *Skript Historish Tijdschrift* 12 (1990): 79-87.

Asuncion Doménch and Ana Bustelo. "Natalie Zemon Davis." *Historia 16* 15, no. 176 (1990): 123-26.

Roger Adelson. "Interview with Natalie Zemon Davis." *Historian* 53, no. 3 (Spring 1991): 405-22. Reprinted in Roger Adelson, *Speaking of History: Conversations with Historians,* 41-60 (East Lansing: Michigan State University Press, 1997).

Danielle Haase Dubosc and Éliane Viennot. "Entretien avec Natalie Zemon Davis." In *Femmes et pouvoirs sous l'ancien régime,* edited by Danielle Haase Dubosc and Éliane Viennot, 306-9. Paris: Editions Rivages, 1991.

Monika Bernold and Andrea Elmeier. "Geschichte, Hoffnung und Selbstironie: Natalie Zemon Davis im Gespräch." *L'Homme: Zeitschrift für Feminische Geschichtswissenschaft* 3, no. 2 (1992): 98-105.

Antoinette Reerink. "Natalie Zemon Davis over: Vrouwen, Indianen en Politieke Correctheid." *Spiegel Historiael* 28, no. 1 (January 1993): 30-34.

Barbara Basting. "Natalie Zemon Davis. Das Möglische zeigen." *Du* 11 (November 1993): 33-37.

Gisela van Oostveen. "'The pleasure principle': De inspiratie van Natalie Zemon Davis." *Dinamiek* 10, no. 1 (1993): 5-11.

Jorge Halperín. "Cuenta Historias Fascinantes Nathalie Davis." *Clarín* (Buenos Aires) 49, no. 17 (16 January 1994): 20-21.

Rebekka Habermas. "Natalie Zemon Davis. 'In Europa liegen meine Wurzeln, und doch bin ich hier immer noch fremd.'" In *Europa entdecken: Prospekt auf eine neue Buchreihe,* 38-50. Frankfurt am Main: Fischer Taschenbuch Verlag, 1995.

Kazuhiko Kondo, Hiroyuki Nonomiya, and Norihiko Fukui. "Natalie Zemon Davis." *Iichiko* 47 (Spring 1998): 113-27.

"'Something Always Bubbles Up': An interview with Natalie Zemon Davis '59 PhD." *Michigan Today* 32, no. 3 (Fall 2000): 16-17.

Maria Lúcia G. Pallares-Burke. "Natalie Zemon Davis." In *As muitas faces da história: Nove entrevistas,* 81-119. São Paulo: Editora UNESP, 2000. Translated into English in *The New History: Confessions and Conversations,* 50-79 (Cambridge, MA: Polity Press; Malden, MA: Blackwell, 2002). Translated into Spanish in *La Nueva Historia: Nueve Entrevistas,* 67-98 (Valencia: Publicacions de la Universitat de València and Granada: Editorial Universidad de Granada, 2005). Also translated into Chinese and Korean.

"'Forschung ist westlich dominiert': Mit Natalie Zemon Davis sprach Simone Meier." *Tages-Anzeiger* (6 May 2002): 57.

Joan Lluís Palos. "'Me interesa la vida de las mujeres normales': Entrevista a Natalie Z. Davis." *La Vanguardia* (28 January 2004): 14-15.

"Natalie Zemon Davis: An e-mail interview with Martin Lyons and Monica Azzolini." *History Australia* 2, no. 3 (2005): 91.1-91.10.

"Babelis Nėra Paskutinis žodis: Istorikę Natalie Zemon Davis kalbina Violeta Davoliūtė." *Kulturos Barai* 482, no. 1 (2005): 52-56.

Carlos Subosky, "Entrevista a Natalie Zemon Davis en Radio Nacional de Argentina," 26 January 2007. Available at www.concienciaytrabajo.blogspot.com.

Derin Terzioğlu. "Natalie Zemon Davis: 'Tarihçiler iyi öyküleri sever...,'" *Virgul* 108 (June 2007): 8-15.

Andrea Feldman. In *Povijesno gledamo: Razgovori s povjesničarima* [Historians' Gaze: Conversations with Historians], 21-35. Zagreb: Antibarbarus, 2007.

Aitana Guia. "Els tombants de la historia: Entrevista a Natalie Z. Davis." *El Contemporani* 35-36 (2007): 43-64.

Emmanuelle Loyer. "A voix nue: Natalie Zemon Davis s'entretient avec Emmanuelle Loyer," 30 April to 1 May 2007. France-Culture (archives INA).

Unpublished papers

"Operation Mind: A Brief Documentary Account of the House Committee on Un-American Activities," with Elizabeth Douvan. Ann Arbor: University of Michigan

Council of the Arts, Sciences and Professions, 1952. Circulated anonymously in dittoed and then in photo-offset.

"A study of 42 women who have children and who are in Graduate Programs at the University of Toronto. Preliminary Report," with Josephine Grimshaw, Elizabeth Mandelle, Alison Smith Prentice, and Germaine Warkentin. Toronto: University of Toronto, 1966.

"Society and the Sexes in Early Modern Europe, 15th-18th Centuries: A Bibliography," with the assistance of Elizabeth Cohen, Sherrill Cohen, Ian Dengler, Barbara B. Diefendorf, Gillian Grebler, Alison Klairmont Lingo, and Kirk Robinson. University of Toronto, 1971; University of California, Berkeley, 1972-73.

Works by Denis Crouzet

Books

Les Guerriers de Dieu: La violence au temps des troubles de religion (vers 1525–vers 1610). 2 vols. Thèse de Doctorat d'Etat; preface by Pierre Chaunu, foreword by Denis Richet. Seyssel: Editions du Champ Vallon, 1990. Reprinted in one volume, 2005.

Symphorien Champier, Les gestes ensemble la vie du preulx Chevalier Bayard, édition du texte de 1525. Introduction by Denis Crouzet. Paris: Imprimerie nationale, 1992.

La nuit de la Saint-Barthélemy: Un rêve perdu de la Renaissance. Paris: Fayard, 1994, 1998.

La genèse de la Réforme française 1520–1562. Regards sur l'histoire 109. Paris: SEDES-Nathan, Paris, 1996. Reprint, Paris: Belin, 2008.

La sagesse et le Malheur: Michel de L'Hospital chancelier de France. Seyssel: Champ Vallon, 1998.

Jean Calvin: Vies parallèles. Paris: Fayard, 2000. Translated into Spanish as *Calvino* (Barcelona: Ariel Press, 2001).

Charles de Bourbon connétable de France. Paris: Fayard, 2003.

Le haut cœur de Catherine de Médicis: Une raison politique aux temps du massacre de la Saint-Barthélemy. Paris: Albin Michel, 2005.

Christophe Colomb: Héraut de l'Apocalypse. Paris: Payot, 2006.

Dieu en ses royaumes: Une histoire des guerres de religion. Seyssel: Champ Vallon, 2008.

Coauthored and Edited Works

L'histoire tout feu tout flamme, with Natalie Zemon Davis. Paris: Albin Michel, 2004.

Translated into Spanish by Anaclet Pons and Justo Serna (Valencia: Publicaciones Universitat de València, 2006). Translated into Italian by Angiolina Arru and Sofia Boesch Gajano (Rome: Viella, 2007).

Frontières religieuses: Rejets et passages, dissimulation et contrebande spirituelle, with Francisco Bethencourt, eds. Paris: Presses de l'université de Paris-Sorbonne, forthcoming.

Contributions to Books

"Sur le concept de barbarie au XVIe siècle." In *La conscience européenne au XVe et au XVIe siècle: Actes du colloque international organisé à l'E. N. S. de jeunes filles n. 22,* edited by Françoise Autrand and Nicole Cazauran, 106-26. Paris: L'Ecole, 1982.

"La Ligue (1588-1589): Un enracinement panique?" In *La guerra del sale (1680–1699): Rivolte e frontiere del Piemonte barocco, Actes du colloque international de Mondovi,* edited by G. Lombardi, 255-73. Turin: Franco Angeli, 1986.

"Henri IV, King of Reason?" In *From Valois to Bourbon. Dynasty, State and Society in Early Modern France,* edited by Keith Cameron, 73-106. Exeter, UK: Exeter University Press, 1988.

"Le langage politique de la Ligue." In *Henri IV et la reconstruction du royaume, catalogue de l'exposition du Musée national du château de Pau et des Archives Nationales,* 75-80. Paris: Archives Nationales, 1989.

"Les fondements idéologiques de la royauté d'Henri IV." In *Henri IV le roi et la reconstruction du royaume: Actes du colloque Henri IV, Pau-Nérac 14–17 septembre 1989,* edited by Pierre Tucoo-Chala, 165-94. Pau: L'Association Henri IV, 1990.

"Imaginaire du corps et violence aux temps des troubles de religion." In *Le corps à la Renaissance—Actes du XXXe colloque de Tours 1987,* edited by Jean Céard, Marie-Madeleine Fontaine, and Jean-Claude Margolin, 115-27. Paris: Amateurs des livres, 1990.

"Le règne d'Henri III et la violence." In *Henri III et son temps: Colloque international du Centre de la Renaissance de Tours, oct. 1989,* edited by Robert Sauzet, 211-25. Paris: J. Vrin, 1992.

"Un chevalier entre 'les mâchoires de la mort': Note à propos de Bayard et de la guerre au début du XVIe siècle." In *La vie, la mort, la foi, Mélanges offerts à Pierre Chaunu,* edited by Pierre Chaunu, Jean-Pierre Bardet, and Madeleine Foisil, 285-94. Paris: Presses Universitaires de France, 1993.

"Ecriture de l'Histoire et idéologie urbaine: Le cas de Lyon au Grand siècle." In *Etat, marine et société: Hommage à Jean Meyer,* edited by Martine Acerra, 135-60. Paris: Presses de l'Université de Paris-Sorbonne, 1995.

"Un texte fondateur? Note sur l'*Histoire et recueil de la triomphante et glorieuse victoire....*" In *Foi, fidélité, amitié en Europe à la période moderne: Mélanges offerts à Robert Sauzet,* 2 vols., edited by Brigitte Maillard and Robert Sauzet, 2:311-31. Tours: Publication de l'Université de Tours, 1995.

"Die Gewalt zur Zeit des Religionkriege im Frankreich des 16. Jahrhundert." In *Physische Gewalt: Studien zur Geschichte der Neuzeit herausgegeben,* edited by Thomas Lindenberger and Alf Lüdtke, 78-105. Frankfort: Suhrkamp, 1995.

"L'intériorisation de la violence: L'exemple du XVIe siècle français de la Saint-Barthélemy aux prémices de la Ligue." In *Les enjeux de la paix,* edited by Pierre Chaunu, 157-71. Paris: Presses Universitaires de France, 1995.

"Edit de Nantes." In *Dictionnaire de L'Ancien Régime: Royaume de France XVIe–XVIIIe siècle,* edited by Lucien Bély, 469-72. Paris: Presses Universitaires de France, 1996.

"Le connétable de Bourbon entre 'pratique,' 'machination,' 'conjuration' et 'trahison.'" In *Complots et conjurations dans l'Europe moderne: Actes du Colloque international organisé par l'Ecole française de Rome. 30 septembre–2 octobre 1993,* edited by Yves-Marie Bercé and Elena Fasano Guarini, 253-69. Rome: Ecole française de Rome, 1996.

"Capital identitaire et engagement religieux: Autour du cas des "princes lorrains."" In

Sociétés et idéologies des Temps modernes: Hommages à Arlette Jouanna, 2 vols., edited by Joël Fouilheron et al., 2:573-89. Montpellier: Publications de l'Université Paul-Valéry, 1996.

"A Woman and the Devil: Possession and Exorcism in Sixteenth-Century France." In *Changing Identities in Early Modern France,* edited by Michael Wolfe, 191-215. Durham: Duke University Press, 1997.

"La rencontre de Charles de Bourbon, Connétable de France, et de Princesse dame Renommée (1527)." In *L'Histoire grande ouverte: Hommages à Emmanuel Le Roy Ladurie,* edited by André Burguière, Joseph Goy, and Marie-Jeanne Tits-Dieuaide, 127-32. Paris: Fayard, 1997.

"Sur la signification eschatologique des 'canards' (France, fin XVe-milieu XVIe siècle)." In *Rumeurs et nouvelles au temps de la Renaissance,* edited by Marie-Thérèse Jones-Davies, 25-45. Paris: Klincksieck, 1997.

"A propos de quelques regards de voyageurs français sur le Brésil (vers 1610-vers 1720): Entre espérance, malédiction, et dégénérescence." In *Naissance du Brésil moderne, 1500-1808 (XXe Colloque de l'IRCOM),* edited by Katia de Queiros Mattoso, Idelette Muzart-Fonseca dos Santos, and Denis Rolland, 67-117. Paris: Presses de l'Université de Paris-Sorbonne, 1998.

"Chrétienté et Europe: Aperçus sur une sourde interrogation du XVIe siècle." In *L'ordre européen du XVIe au XXe siècle: Actes du colloque de l'IRCOM 15-16 mars 1996,* edited by Georges Soutou and Jean Bérenger, 11-50. Paris: Presses de l'Université de Paris-Sorbonne, 1998.

"La foi, la politique, la parole: Une problématique de l'Edit de janvier 1562." In *Axes et méthodes de l'histoire politique,* edited by Serge Berstein and Pierre Milza, 13-40. Paris: Presses Universitaires de France, 1998.

"Calvin," "Catherine de Médicis," "Charles IX," "Henri Ier de Guise," "Henri III," "Henri IV," "Ligue," "Edit de Nantes," "Réforme," "Guerres de Religion," "Saint-Barthélemy," and "Sully." In *Dictionnaire de l'Histoire de France,* edited by Jean-François Sirinelli. Paris: Armand Colin, 1999, 2006.

"La nuit de la Saint Barthélemy: Confirmations et compléments." In *Le second ordre: L'idéal nobiliaire; Hommage à Ellery Schalk,* edited by Chantal Grell and Arnaud Ramière de Fortanier, 55-81. Paris: Presses de l'Université de Paris-Sorbonne, 1999.

"Calvinism and the Uses of the Political and the Religious (France, ca. 1560-ca. 1572)." In *Reformation and Civil War in France and the Netherlands 1555-1585,* edited by Philip Benedict, Guido Marnef, Henk van Nierop, and Marc Venard, 99-113. Amsterdam: Royal Netherlands Academy of Arts and Sciences, 1999.

"Michel de L'Hospital et l'idée de la paix." In *Krieg und Frieden im Ubergang vom Mittelalter zur Neuzeit: Theorie, Praxis, Bilder,* edited by Heinz Durchardt and Patrice Veit, 103-18. Mainz: Verlag Philipp von Zabern, 2000.

"Préface." In *Grenoble au temps de la Ligue: Etude politique, sociale et religieuse d'une cité en crise (vers 1562-vers 1598),* by Stéphane Gal, 11-15. Grenoble: Presses Universitaires de Grenoble, 2000.

"Patrie, antihispanisme et quête de la paix dans la pensée de Michel de L'Hospital." In *Le Traité de Vervins: Guerre et paix en Europe (fin XVIe-début XVIIe siècle; Quatrième centenaire de la paix de Vervins, Mai 1998,* edited by Jean-François Labourdette, Jean-Pierre Poussou and Marie-Catherine Vignal, 97–115. Paris: Fédération des Sociétés d'Histoire et d'Archéologie de l'Aisne, 2000.

"Le connétable de Bourbon ou une métaphysique de l'action." In *Formen internationaler Beziehungen in der Frühen Neuzeit: Frankreich und das Alte Reich im europäischen Staatssystem; Festschrift für Klaus Malettke zum 65. Geburtstag,* edited by Sven Externbrink and Jörg Ulbert, 199–207. Berlin: Duncker und Humblot, 2001.

"Louis Dorleans ou le massacre de la Saint-Barthélemy comme un 'coup d'estat': à propos d'un manuscrit inédit." In *Conflits politiques, controverses religieuses: Essais d'histoire européenne aux 16e–18e siècles; Mélanges offerts à Myriam Yardeni,* edited by Ouzi Eliada and Jacques Le Brun, 77–99. Paris: Éditions de l'École des hautes études en sciences sociales, 2002.

"Un Calvin introspectif?" In *Institut d'Histoire de la Réformation: Bulletin annuel XXII (2000–2001),* 41–56. Geneva: Droz, 2002.

"Grâce et liberté dans les *Carmina* de Michel de l'Hospital." In *De Michel de L'Hospital à l'Edit de Nantes: Politique et religion face aux Eglises,* edited by Thierry Wanegffelen, 223–42. Clermont-Ferrand: Presse Universitaire-Blaise Pascal, 2002.

"Préface." In *"Practiques" et "Practiqueurs": La vie politique à la fin du règne de Henri III (1584–1589),* by Xavier Le Person, 11–20. Geneva: Droz, 2002.

"Le pouvoir monarchique et la violence: à propos du massacre de la Saint-Barthélemy." In *Actes du colloque "La nuit de la Saint-Barthélemy: Problématiques et débats"; Moscou, Institut d'Histoire universelle, Académie des Sciences de Russie, mai 1997* [in Russian], edited by Pavel Uvarov, 82–99. Moscow: RGGU éditions, 2002.

"Mourir en Milanais au début du règne de François Ier." In *Louis XII en Milanais: XLIe Colloque d'études humanistes 30 juin–3 juillet 1998,* edited by Philippe Contamine and Jean Guillaume, 173–88. Paris: Centre d'Etudes Supérieures de la Renaissance, 2003.

"L'Etat français et la violence au XVIe siècle." In *Etat et société en France sous l'Ancien Régime: The Proceedings of the International Conference on the Formation of Global History and the Role of Hegemonic States* [in Japanese], edited by V. Minonya and Y. Aga, 63–100. Tokyo: Yamakawa éditions, 2003.

"Préface." In Yann Lignereux, *Lyon et le roi: De la "bonne ville" à l'absolutisme municipal, 1594–1654,* 9–19. Seyssel: Champ Vallon, 2003.

"Préface" and "Chronologie." In Jules Verne, *Christophe Colomb,* 5–23, 93–95. Paris: Librio, 2003.

"Postface." In Lucien Febvre, *Le problème de l'incroyance au XVIe siècle: La religion de Rabelais,* new edition, 479–517. Paris: Albin Michel, 2003.

"Lucien Febvre." In *Les historiens,* edited by Véronique Sales, 58–84. Paris: Armand Colin, 2003.

"Identity and Violence: French Protestants and the Early Wars of Religion." In *Toleration and Religious Identity: The Edict of Nantes and Its Implications in France, Britain and Ireland,* edited by Ruth Whelan and Carol Baxter, 73–91. Dublin: Four Courts Press, 2003.

"Une mort qui fut une vengeance: Le connétable de Bourbon. Rome, mai 1527." In *Vengeance: Le face-à-face victime/agresseur,* edited by Raymond Verdier, 170–79. Paris: Edition Autrement, 2004.

"Craindre Dieu autrement dans les sermons et pamphlets de Calvin." In *Les deux réformes chrétiennes: Propagation et diffusion, Colloque international, Les réformes religieuses des XVI–XVIIe siècles, Haïfa, 2000,* edited by Ilana Zinguer and Myriam Yardeni, 3-22. Leiden: Brill, 2004.

"Königliche und religiöse Gewalt im Massaker der Bartholomaüsnacht oder der 'Wille' Karls IX." In *Gewalt in der frühen Neuzeit: Beiträge zur 5. Tagung der Arbeitsgemeinschaft frühe Neuzeit im VHD,* edited by Claudia Ulbricg, Claudia Jarzbowski, and Michaela Hohkamp, 33–58. Berlin: Duncker & Humblot, 2005.

"Une princesse qui voulait faire rêver de paix et sérénité." In *Pouvoirs, contestations et comportements dans l'Europe moderne: Mélanges en l'honneur du professeur à Yves-Marie Bercé,* edited by Bernard Barbiche, Jean-Pierre Poussou, and Alain Tallon, 123–64. Paris: Presses de l'Université de Paris-Sorbonne, 2005.

"Préface." In Sylvie Daubresse, *Le parlement de Paris ou la voix de la raison (1559–1589).* Geneva: Droz, 2005.

"1572: Les protestants sont massacrés la nuit de la Saint-Barthélemy sous le règne de Charles IX." In *1515: Les grandes dates de l'histoire de France revisitées par les historiens d'aujourd'hui,* edited by Alain Corbin. Paris: Seuil, 2005, 2008.

"A propos de quelques usages de la monarchie française du XVIe siècle dans le discours historique du XVIIe siècle." In *Monarchies, noblesses et diplomaties européennes: Mélanges en l'honneur de Jean-François Labourdette,* edited by Jean-Pierre Poussou, Roger Baury, and Marie-Catherine Vignal-Souleyrou, 355–83. Paris: Presse de l'Université de Paris-Sorbonne, 2005.

"1588: Le roi Henri III fait assassiner son rival Henri de Guise au château de Blois." In *1515: Les grandes dates de l'histoire de France revisitées par les historiens d'aujourd'hui,* edited by Alain Corbin. Paris: Seuil, 2005, 2008.

"Préface." In Sylvie Daubresse, *Le parlement de Paris ou la voix de la raison (1559–1589),* vii-xv. Geneva: Droz, 2005.

"Préface." In Frédéric Jacquin, *Affaires de poison: Un crime et son imaginaire au XVIIIe siècle.* Paris: Belin, 2005.

"Ira Dei Super Nos." In *Early Modern Europe: Issues and Interpretations,* edited by James B. Collins and Karen L. Taylor, 90–100. Oxford: Blackwell Publishing, 2006.

"Dieu et les petits enfants pendant les troubles de religion." In *Istoricheskaya antropologiya: New Directions in Historical Research,* vol. 3, edited by Gadi Algazi, Mikhail Krom, and David Sabean, 163–89. Göttingen: Max-Planck-Institut für Geschichte/ European University at St. Petersburg, 2006.

"Intolérance et tolérance en France au XVIe siècle." In *Stratégies de la Contre-Réforme en France et en Pologne,* edited by Chantal Grell and Macej Servanski, 23–44. Poznan: Instytut Histgorii UAM, 2006.

"Une loi qui fut une confession de foi évangélique: Autour de l'Edit de janvier 1562." In *Religious Differences in France: Past and Present,* edited by Kathleen Perry Long,

1-18. Sixteenth Century Essays and Studies 74. Kirksville, MO: Truman State University Press, 2006.

"Les stratégies d'occupation de l'espace urbain au temps des premières guerres de Religion." In *Die besetzte res publica: Zum Verhältnis von ziviler Obrigkeit und militärischer Herrschaft in besetzten Gebieten vom Spätmittelalter bis zum 18. Jahrhundert,* edited by Markus Meumann and Jörg Rogge, 167-93. Berlin: LIT Verlag, 2006.

"Sainthood and Heroism: Images and Imagery in Sixteenth-Century Europe." In *Finding Europe. Discourses on Margins, Communities, Images,* edited by Antony Molho and Diego Curto, 335-57. New York: Berghahn Book, 2007.

"La question du millénarisme dans *L'Ethique protestante et l'esprit du capitalisme.*" In *Histoire des familles de la démographie et des comportements en hommage à Jean-Pierre Bardet,* edited by Jean-Pierre Poussou and Isabelle Robin, 777-805. Paris: Presse de l'Université de Paris-Sorbonne, 2007.

"Le mythe savoyard, Bayard et le regret d'un temps perdu." In *Bayard et la Maison de Savoie: Actes des rencontres Bayard 2002. Chambéry, 18 et 19 octobre 2002, Université de Chambéry-Association des amis de Bayard,* 81-101. Pontcharra, 2003. Revised version in *Bayard: Histoires croisées du chevalier,* edited by Stéphane Gal, 131-45. Grenoble: Presses Universitaires de Grenoble, 2007.

"Sur la symbolique du refus de la 'farce' papiste: La France des années 1530-1560." In *La Réforme en France et en Italie: Contacts, comparaisons et contrastes,* edited by Ph. Benedict, S. Seidel, and A. Tallon, 403-30. Rome: Ecole Française de Rome, 2007.

"Mystique royale et sentiment national? Les visions du frère Fiacre de Sainte-Marguerite." In *Le sentiment national dans l'Europe méridionale (France, Espagne, Italie) aux XVIe et XVIIe siècles,* edited by Alain Tallon and Benoît Pellistrandi, 295-322. Madrid: Casa de Velasquez, 2007.

"Langages de l'absoluité royale (1560-1576)." In *Absolutismus, ein unersetzliches Forschungskonzept? Eine deutsch-französische Bilanz: L'Absolutisme, un concept irremplaçable? Une mise au point franco-allemande,* edited by Lothar Schilling, 107-39. Munich: Institut Historique Allemand, 2008.

"Les guerres de Religion, violences pour Dieu." In *La guerre dans tous ses états: Concordance des temps,* edited by Jean-Noël Jeanneney, 57-83. Paris: Nouveau Monde Editions, 2008.

"Préface." In Florence Buttay, *"Fortuna": Usages politiques d'une allégorie morale à la Renaissance,* 7-16. Paris: Presse de l'Université de Paris-Sorbonne, 2008.

"Sur le désenchantement des corps saints au temps des troubles de religion." In *Reliques modernes: Cultes et usages chrétiens des corps saints des Réformes aux révolutions,* 2 vols., edited by Philippe Boutry, Pierre Antoine Fabre, and Dominique Julia, 2:436-82. Paris: Centre National de Recherche Scientifique, 2009.

"Deux hommes dans un bateau, Lucien Febvre et Fernand Braudel: Leçons inaugurales au Collège de France." In *Le Moyen Âge et la Renaissance au Collège de France,* edited by Pierre Toubert and Michel Zink, 299-318. Paris: Fayard, 2009.

Articles

"Recherches sur la crise de l'aristocratie en France au XVIe siècle: Les dettes de la Maison de Nevers." *Histoire Economie et Société* 1 (1982): 7-50.

"Recherches sur les processions blanches, 1583-1584." *Histoire, Economie et Société* 4 (1982): 511-63.

"La représentation du temps à l'époque de la Ligue." *Revue historique* 270, no. 2 (1983): 297-388.

"La violence au temps des troubles de religion vers 1525-vers 1610." *Histoire, Economie et Société* 4 (1989): 507-25.

"Royalty, Nobility and Religion: Research on the Wars of Italy." In *Eighteenth Annual Meeting: Papers,* 1-14. Proceedings of the Annual Meeting of the Western Society for French History 18. N.p., 1991.

"Désir de mort et puissance absolue de Charles VIII à Henri IV." *Revue de synthèse* 3-4 (July-December 1991): 423-41.

"Crise du Sacré et politique: Sur le désir de Dieu au XVIe siècle." *Tumultes* 1, no. 1 (1992): 49-71.

"Au temps des premières guerres de Religion: Violence catholique et désir de Dieu." *Notre Histoire, L'Eglise et la guerre* 88 (April 1992): 36-40.

"Le massacre et son désir au temps des premières guerres de Religion," in "Medium, médiatisation et fanatisme." *Revue internationale de psychanalyse* 2 (1992): 31-54.

"Aux origines de la Saint-Barthélemy: De la concorde à la violence ou de l'Amour au crime." *L'information historique* 57 (1995): 1-9.

"La caravane des perles: Note critique à propos de l'histoire de la "dame aux chameaux."" *L'information historique* 57 (1995): 58.

"Charles IX ou le roi sanglant malgré lui?" *Bulletin de la société de l'Histoire du protestantisme français* (July-September 1995): 323-39.

"L'étrange Génie du Mythe de croisade." *Le Débat* 99 (March-April 1998): 85-92.

"Introduction: L'Etat comme fonctionnement socio-symbolique (1547-1635)." *Histoire, Economie et Société* 3 (1998): 339-40.

"Un édit qui fut une confession de foi: Une lointaine 'mémoire' de l'édit de Nantes." In "L'Edit de Nantes: Sa genèse, son application en Languedoc: Actes du colloque organisé le 15 mai 1998 par la ville de Montpellier," edited by Arlette Jouanna and Michel Péronnet. Special issue, *Bulletin historique de la ville de Montpellier* 23 (1999): 6-28.

"Circa 1533: Anxieties, Desires, and Dreams." *Journal of Early Modern History* 5, no. 1 (2001): 22-61.

"A propos de la plasticité de la violence réformée au temps des premières guerres de Religion." *Bulletin de la Société de l'Histoire du Protestantisme Français* 148 (October-December 2002): 907-51.

"Le devoir d'obéissance à Dieu: Imaginaires du pouvoir royal," in "Métaphysique et politique de l'obéissance dans la France du XVIe siècle," special issue, *Nouvelle revue du XVIe siècle* 22, no. 1 (2004): 19-47.

"La représentation de l'altérité au temps des premières guerres de Religion: Trois figures de l'exclusivisme," in "Tolerancias, intolerancias," special issue, *Revista de Historia das Ideias* 25 (2004): 209-45.

"Le zèle ligueur: Entre conversion et possession." *Historien: A Review of the Past and Other Stories* 6 (2006): 106-33.

"Veillées d'armes," in "Les protestants: Leur histoire, leurs valeurs, leur influence." *Historia thématique* 109 (September-October 2007): 30-33.

"Catherine de Médicis actrice d'une mutation dans l'imaginaire politique (1578-1579)." In *La coexistence confessionnelle à l'épreuve: Etudes sur les relations entre protestants et catholiques dans la France moderne,* edited by Yves Krumenacker and Didier Boisson, 17-50. Chrétiens et sociétés: Documents et mémoires 9. Lyon: RESEA. Religions, sociétés et acculturation, 2009.

"Veillée d'armes," in "Les protestants: Leur histoire, leurs valeurs, leur influence," *Historia thématique* 109 (September-October 2007): 30-33.

"Postscript." In *Political Culture in Early Modern France: Essays in Honour of R. J. Knecht,* edited by Penny Roberts and Robert J. Knecht, 226-30. *French History* 21, no. 2. Oxford: Oxford University Press, 2007.

"Impossibles biographies, histoire possible? Entre Pierre de Bayard, Michel de l'Hospital, Charles de Bourbon, Jean Calvin, Catherine de Médicis et Christophe Colomb." *Institut d'Histoire de la Réformation: Bulletin annuel* 28 (2006-2007): 49-73.

"'A strong desire to be a mother to all your subjects': A Rhetorical Experiment by Catherine de Medici." *Journal of Medieval and Early Modern History* 38, no. 1 (Winter 2008): 103-18.

Interviews

"Enquête sur un massacre: La Saint-Barthélemy." *L'Histoire,* March 1994, 94-101.

"Une immense angoisse traverse la Renaissance..." *L'Histoire,* December 2002, 44-49.

"Pourquoi fut-elle si détestée." *L'Histoire*, November 2006, 50-57.

About the Authors

Natalie Zemon Davis is a social and cultural historian of early modern times. Her published works have been translated into various languages including French, Italian, German, and Japanese. She was historical consultant for the film *Le Retour de Martin Guerre* and the opera *The House of Martin Guerre*. Davis has taught at major universities including the University of Toronto, the University of California at Berkeley, and Princeton University. She was awarded the Holberg International Memorial Prize 2010 for her imaginative approach to history coupled with intensive archival research. Davis is a former president of the American Historical Association, fellow of the American Academy of Arts and Sciences, corresponding fellow of the British Academy, and Chevalier de l'Ordre des Palmes Académique. She has received honorary degrees from Harvard University, the University of Toronto, Memorial University of Newfoundland, Cambridge University, Université de Lyon, and Oxford University. Emerita from Princeton University, Davis is now adjunct professor of history and professor of medieval studies at the University of Toronto. She is currently researching slavery and sociability in 18th-century Suriname.

Denis Crouzet is professor of modern history at the Université de Paris 4-Sorbonne, director of the Roland Mousnier Center, and director of the Research Institute on the Civilizations of the Modern West. He is the author or editor of twelve books, including *Les Guerriers de Dieu* and *Dieu en ses royaumes*.

Michael Wolfe is professor of history and graduate dean of arts and sciences at St. John's University in Queens, New York. He is the author or editor of six books, including *The Conversion of Henri IV* and most recently *Walled Towns and the Shaping of France*.

Index

Addams, Jane, 155n22
Afghanistan, 153, 161, 180
Africa, contemporary conflicts in, 161, 176n13
aging, 37-38
Agrippa von Nettesheim, Heinrich Cornelius, 11, 27n7
Agulhon, Maurice, 39, 42, 59n19
al-ʿArabi, Ibn, 21, 28n20
al-Farid, Umar Ibn, 21, 28n19, 36
al-Ghazālī, Abū Hāmid, 20, 28n15
al-Hamadhānī, Badī' al-Zamān, 20-21, 28n16, 36
al-Hariri, Muhammad al-Qasim ibn Ali ibn Muhammad ibn Uthman, 20, 28n17
Alberto Pio, Prince of Carpi, 35, 58n4
Algazi, Gadi, 164, 177n24
Alpers, Svetlana, 158, 176n1
al-Wazzān, al-Hasan (Leo Africanus), 8-10, 13-20, 21-23, 34-37, 77, 165-66, 173-74, 181-83
Anabaptists, 167, 177n29, 178n35
the *Annales*, 26, 44, 88-89, 125, 152
Annales school, 59nn 15, 17, 28, 61n65
Annie Get Your Gun, 134, 155n18
Anouilh, Jean, 3, 27n3
anthropology, 45-51, 88, 113, 152, 158, 175
anti-Semitism, 80, 91n19, 92n34, 96, 130, 154n5
anti-war movement, 44, 63-64, 153
Arbaleste, Charlotte, 112, 127-28n9
Ariès, Philippe, 42, 59n30, 152
Aristotle, 28n9, 127n3, 173, 178n47
Armstrong, Elizabeth, 43, 60n35
Ashkenazic Jews, 108n8, 100

Baez, Joan, 153, 157nn46, 47
Bakhtin, Mikhail, 39, 43, 59n20
Bancroft, Aaron, 135, 155n21
Barenblatt v. United States, 148, 156nn35, 36, 37
Bataille, Georges, 133, 154n15
Beard, Charles, 127n2
Beard, Mary Ritter, 109, 127n2
Beauvoir, Simone de, 125, 129n29, 138
Bellay, Jean du, 36, 58n8
Benedict, Philip, 45, 60n47
Bercé, Yves-Marie, 40, 59n22
Berkeley, University of California at, ix, 64-65, 114, 152-53, 156n45, 158, 159
Berkshire Conference of Women Historians, 128n16
Berkshire Conference on the History of Women, 114, 128n16
Berque, Jacques, 50, 61n61
Berlin, Irving, 97, 108n4, 155n18
Berr, Henri, 41, 59n27
biographies, writing, 74-75, 106-7
Blanc, Judith, 164, 177n23
Bloch, Marc, 41, 42, 51, 59nn28, 29, 61, 87-89, 90, 173
Boccaccio, Giovanni, 74, 91n9
Boethius, Ancius Manlius Severinus, 172, 178n45
Bosnia, 24, 28n27
Bossy, John, 55, 62n67
Bouwsma, William, 158, 176n2
Bretonne, Nicolas Edmé Restif de la, 25, 29n31
British Mandate, 162, 177n18, 177n21
Brucker, Gene A., 158, 176n4
Buber, Martin, 162, 177nn19, 20
Budé, Guillaume, 2, 27n2, 110, 139
Burke, Peter, 43, 60n44
Bush, George W., 161, 166, 168, 169, 171, 178n44

Calvin, Jean, 19, 25, 28n14, 69, 73, 86
Calvinism, 19, 55, 60n47, 66, 91n3, 167-68
Cardano, Girolamo, 56, 62n70
Castiglione, Baldassar, 109, 127n5
Catholic Church. *See* Catholicism
Catholic Holy League, 68, 69, 91n3
Catholicism, 52-55, 64, 68-71, 115, 175. *See also* St. Bartholomew's Day Massacre; *Women on the Margins: Three Seventeenth-Century Lives*
Caudwell, Christopher, 132-33, 154n13

Certeau, Michel de, 50–51, 61n63
Chakrabarty, Dipesh, x, 76, 78, 79–80, 81, 91n10
Chandler, Lucretia, 155n21
charivaris, 8, 17, 39, 76
Charles III, Duke of Bourbon, 82, 92n24
Charles V, Emperor, 82, 92nn24, 28
Chéreau, Patrice, 24, 28nn21, 26
Christianity, 9, 163, 170, 180, 181–82
Cixous, Hélène, 125, 129n31
Clampitt, Amy, 174, 178n49
Coburn, Nathaniel, 156n34
Cohen, Mark, 56
Colie, Rosalie, 26, 29n32, 40, 42–43, 150
Collège de France, 27, 49, 89, 127, 129n40
communism, 59n13, 140–41, 154n16
The Communist Manifesto, 132, 154n8
Conway, Jill Ker, 43, 60n39, 111, 113–14, 152
Coornaert, Émile, 39, 59n17
Coquéry-Vidrovitch, Catherine, 126–27, 129n39
Coras, Jean de, 5, 19, 22, 69, 75
Corneau, Alain, 25, 28–29n28
Coughlin, Charles, 130, 154n4
Coxeter, Donald, 151, 156n42

d'Orléans, King Louis-Philippe, 24, 28n23
Danbury Correctional Institution, 148–49, 151, 156nn39, 40
Dante, 82, 92n27, 118
Darnton, Robert, 160, 176n10
Daston, Lorraine, 122, 129n26
Davis, Chandler, 13, 103–4, 110, 161
  Hallowell ancestors of, 135, 155n20
  HUAC and, 141, 143–48
  marriage to Natalie Zemon, 134–40
  prison experience of, 148–49, 150, 151, 156n40
  at University of Toronto, 151, 152, 159, 160
"decisionism," 169–70
Delmas-Marty, Mireille, 127, 129n42
Demme, Robert Jonathan, 17–18, 28n13
de Pizan, Christine, ix–x, 2, 27n1, 109–10, 110–11, 112, 114, 139
Detroit race riots, 131, 154n7
Diefendorf, Barbara, 40, 45, 59n21
Dognon, Suzanne, 92n34
Douglas, Mary, 47, 61n53
Douglas, William O., 148, 156n37
Douvan, Elizabeth, 140, 155n29
Droz, Eugénie, 37, 58n9
Duby, Georges, 124, 126, 127, 129n28
Dumas, Alexandre, 24, 28n25
du Plessis-Mornay, Philippe, 112, 127–28n9, 128n10

Engels, Friedrich, 132, 154n8
Enlightenment, 3, 91n13, 102
Enron scandal, 148, 156n40
Erasmus, Desiderius, 73, 87–88, 90, 91n7
eschatology, 56–57, 62n71, 65–66, 67, 68, 70, 166–71
evangelicalism, American, 168, 169
Existentialism, 27n4
Ezrahi, Sidra, 164, 177n26

family history, 93–108
Farge, Arlette, 126, 129n37
Fass, Paula, 158, 176n6
Febvre, Lucien, 53, 59n28, 61n65, 87–90, 92nn32, 34
Feilchenfeld, Alfred, 119–20, 128n23
Feminine Mystique, 125, 129n33
feminism, 111, 120, 134
feminist criticism in France, 125
Fiction in the Archives: Pardon Tales and their Tellers in Sixteenth-Century France, 31–33, 119, 123
Foucault, Michel, 85, 86, 92n29, 127, 152
Fournier, Jacques, 26, 29n35, 31
François I, King, 27n2, 74, 82, 91n8, 92n24, 128n20
Free Speech movement, Berkeley's, 153, 156n45
French Revolution, 1–2, 3, 25, 29n30, 102, 109, 128n14
Friedan, Betty, 125, 129n33

Gabel, Leona C., 109, 127n1
Galison, Peter, 122, 129n27
Garrisson, Janine, 54, 61n66
Gascon, Richard, 38–39, 58n11
Geertz, Clifford, 46–47, 49, 50, 61nn51, 52, 70, 160
gender inversion, 46
gender as genre, 113–14, 124–25
gender in writing women's history, 11, 113–17, 122–27
Geneva Accord, 164, 177n27
Geremek, Bronisław, 43, 60n40
Germaine de Staël, Anne Louise, 128n14
Gershwin, George, 97, 108n5
Gershwin, Ira, 97, 108n5

The Gift in Sixteenth-Century France, 7, 123, 133
Gilles de Viterbo, 35, 58n2
Gilmore, Myron, 139, 155n25
Ginzburg, Carlo, 43, 60n40
Godelier, Maurice, 49, 61nn57, 60
Goldman family, 94-96, 98, 99
Goubert, Pierre, 59n15, 39, 42
Grafton, Anthony, 160, 176n11
Greenblatt, Stephen, 26, 29n33, 70, 158

Hallowell family, 135, 155n20
Harris, David, 153, 157n46
Hart, Lorenz, 96, 108n3
Hatcher, Harlan, 144, 145-46, 150, 155n31
Hauser, Henri, 39, 41-42, 53, 59n14, 139, 152
Hayden, Robert, 82, 92n23
Haywood, DuBose, 97, 108n6
Hegel, Georg Wilhelm Friedrich, 79, 91n14
Heidegger, Martin, 79, 91n15
Héritier, Françoise, 127, 129n41
Herzl, Theodor, 132, 154n9
Herzog family, 99, 101, 107, 163
historical analysis, 6-7, 23, 172-74
historical films, 23-25
historiography
  French, 39, 52-53, 78
  Western, 78-80
  women's, 11, 107, 109-20, 122-27
history
  and forms of transmission, 39-40
  interdisciplinary approach to, 51-52
  intuitive approach to, 48-49
"history of hope," 117-18
Hollywood Ten, 140, 147, 148, 156n39
Holocaust, 24, 63, 64, 82, 92n23, 93, 103-4, 118, 128n19, 145, 162, 170
Holt, Mack P., 45, 60n46
Houbre, Gabrielle, 126, 129n36
House Un-American Activities Committee (HUAC), 156n34, 156n35, 156n38
  Chandler Davis and, 143-45, 147-49
  creation of, 155n28
  Hollywood Ten and, 140, 147, 148, 156n39
  Operation Mind and, 140-41, 143
Hufton, Olwen, 118, 128n18
Hull House, 135, 155n22
humanism, 58n4, 91n7, 139
Hume, David, 79, 91n13
Hunt, Lynn, 158, 176n5

influences, 41-44, 45-48
inversion, rituals of, 46
Iraq, U.S. policy toward, 153, 161, 166, 171, 180
the Irgun, 163, 177n21
Irigary, Luce, 125, 129n30
Islam, 50, 161, 163, 166-67, 168, 170-71, 180-83. *See also* al-Wazzān, al-Hasan (Leo Africanus)
Israel and Palestine issue, 81, 162-64, 170, 177n20, 177n27, 178n32

Jaeger, Werner, 41, 59n24
Jancke, Gabriele, 119, 128n22
Jansenism, 25, 29n29, 68
Jesuits, 33-34, 51, 58n1, 71
"Joe Hill," 134, 154-55n17
Jordan, W. K., 139, 155n26
Joyce, James, 102, 108n10
Judaism, 167, 169-70, 178n41. See also *Women on the Margins: Three Seventeenth-Century Lives*

Karlstadt, Andreas, 167, 178n33
Khaldun, Ibn, 81, 91n20
Khionrea, Thérèse, 174, 178-79n50
Kittredge, George Lyman, 96, 108n2
Klapisch-Zuber, Christiane, 43, 60n38, 126
Knights of Pythias, Order of, 98, 108n7
Kohn, Hans, 162, 177n19
Kristeva, Julia, 125, 129n32
Kubrick, Stanley, 17-18, 28n11
Kuhn, Thomas, 85, 92n30

Labadists, 166, 177-78n30
La Boétie, Étienne de, 72, 91n6
Ladurie, Emmanuel Le Roy, 26-27, 29n35, 39, 42, 43
Lamming, George, 81-82, 92n22
Lamport family, 98-102, 104, 107-8, 136, 162
Landon, Alf, 130, 153n1
La Reine Margot, 24, 28n21, 28n25
Le Goff, Jacques, 49, 61nn58, 60
Lenin, Vladimir Ilyich, 132, 154n10
Leo Africanus. *See* al-Wazzān, al-Hasan (Leo Africanus)
Leo X, Pope, 35, 58n6
Lerner, Max, 130, 154n3

letters of pardon, 31-34, 96-97, 105
Lévi-Strauss, Claude, 47-48, 60n40, 61n54
Levi, Giovanni, 43, 60n40
Levi, Primo, 118, 128n19
Lewalski, Barbara, 151, 156n43
Lewalski, Kenneth, 151, 156n44
Lewis, Bernard, 16, 28n10
"Los Cuatro Generales," 134, 154n17
Louise, Duchess of Montpensier, 82, 92n25
Lucas, Margaret, 112, 128n12
Lukács, Georg, 132-33, 154n14
Luther, Martin, 53, 58n6, 70, 88, 178n34
Lutherans, 66, 133
Lyon, France
  archives of, 3-5, 8, 38
  religious conflicts of, 53, 63,
  sixteenth-century printers of, xi, 9, 43, 45, 110, 141-43
  women's history in, 112, 118

Macaulay, Catherine Sawbridge, 112-13, 128n13
Mandela, Nelson, 161, 176n14
Manifest Destiny, 168, 178n36
Manuel I, king of Portugal, 35, 58n5
maqāmāt, genre of the, 20-21, 28n16, 36
Marguerite de Navarre, 74, 89, 119, 128n20
Markert, Clement, 156n32
marriage, 110, 135-39
Marx, Karl, 39, 59n13, 76, 79, 110, 132, 154n8
Marxism, 41, 43, 47, 53, 104, 132-33
Mauss, Marcel, 12-13, 49, 61n56, 154n15
McCarthyism, 154n4, 155n28
Mennonites, 166, 177n29, 178n34
the *menu peuple,* 33-34
Merian, Maria Sibylla, 8, 12, 30, 32, 57, 75, 117-18, 166
Merton, Robert, 173, 178n46
millenarianism, 62n71, 168
Mirandola, Pico della, 65, 91n1
Modena, Leon, 56, 62n68, 106
Molière, 78, 91n11
Montaigne, Michel de, xi, 10, 27n6, 56, 72-74
Montaillou: The Promised Land of Error, 26-27, 29n34
Monzie, Anatole de, 88, 92nn31, 32
Moody, John N., 150, 156n41
Morrison, Toni, 81, 91-92n21
Mundy, John H., 38, 58n10
Müntzer, Thomas, 167, 178n34

neoconservatism, 169-70, 178n39
Newcomb, Theodore M., 109, 127n5
New Historians, 163, 177n22
Nickerson, Mark, 145, 156n33
Nietzsche, Friedrich, 169, 178n38

Obama, Barack, 180-81
Operation Mind, 140-41, 143, 155n30
"otherness,", 9-10, 49-50

Palestine. *See* Israel and Palestine issue
Pappenheim, Bertha, 119, 120, 128n24, 129n25
"Peatbog Soldiers Song," 134, 155n17
Penrose, Hannah, 138, 155n20
Perrot, Michelle, 43, 60n37, 124, 126, 129n35
Piaf, Edith, 51, 61n64
Plekanov, Georgi, 154n9
PM, 130, 153n2, 154n3
Polanyi, Karl, 162, 176-77n15
political experiences, 140-41, 143-45, 147-51
political influences, 130-35
politics, contemporary, 161-62, 180-81
Pomponazzi, Pietro, 109, 127n3
Porgy and Bess, 97, 108n6
Postel, Guillaume, 34-35, 58n2
Power, Eileen, xi, 42, 59-60n31
Prentice, Alison, 111, 127n8
Princeton University, 43, 47, 56, 114, 115, 159-60, 176
Progressive Party, 134-35, 155n19
Protestantism, 53, 54-55, 68-69, 75, 112, 135, 151, 163
Protestant Reformation, 25-26, 28n14, 39, 53, 178n33, 34
Protocols of the Elders of Zion, 80, 81, 91n19

Quakers, 135, 137, 138, 155n20, 166, 178n31
"queer theory," 123-24
the Qur'an, 170, 178n42

Rabelais, François, 25-26, 27n5, 34, 35-38, 73-74, 87-88, 89, 90, 182
Raphael, 35, 58n7
Reader's Digest, 102, 108n11
The Return of Martin Guerre, xii, 5, 10, 18-19, 48, 70, 74, 114, 174
Rice, Condoleezza, 171, 178n44
Rites and Customs of the Jews, 106, 108n12
"The Rites of Violence," 47, 54-55, 63-65, 145

Roche, Daniel, 127, 129n44
Rodgers, Richard, 96, 108n3
Roelker, Nancy L., 43, 60n33, 150
Rosaldo, Renato, 50, 61n62
Rosen, Ruth, 160, 176n8
Rushd, Abū'l-Walīd ibn (Averroës), 15, 28n9

Saarinen, Eero, 102, 108n9
Sartre, Jean-Paul, 3, 27n4
Schmitt, Carl, 169-70, 178n40
Schmitt, Jean-Claude, 49, 61nn59, 60, 81
Schorske, Carl, 160, 176n12
Scola, Ettore, 25, 29n30
Scott, Joan W., x, 114-15, 125, 128n17
self-fashioning, 10-12, 18, 63, 71, 72, 75, 83, 146
Sen, Amartya, 162, 177n16
sexuality
  gender and, 123-24
  religion and, 71-72, 169
Sforza, Caterina, 109, 127n1
Shapin, Steven, 80, 91n18
Shelby Cullom Davis Center for Historical Studies, 160, 176n9
slavery, 2, 17-18, 82, 123, 178n31, 181, 183
Slaves on Screen: Film and Historical Vision, 17-18, 23
Smith College, 41, 42, 103, 109-10, 131-34, 140, 154n16, 162-63
"Solidarity Forever," 134, 154-55n17
Solidarność, 43, 60n42
Spielberg, Steven, 17-18, 28n12
Spinoza, Baruch, 162, 177n17
St. Bartholomew's Day Massacre, 24, 28n24, 54, 63, 145, 146
Starn, Randolph, 158, 176n3
Stone, I. F., 130, 154n4
Stone, Lawrence, 159, 160, 176n7
subaltern theory, 76, 91n10
Suleyman I, 170, 178n43

Ta'ayush, 164, 166, 177n25
Teresa of Avila, 69, 91n5
Thomas, J. Parnell, 148, 156nn38, 39
Thomas, Keith, 43, 60n43
Thomas, Norman, 131, 154n6
Thompson, Edward P., 43-44, 60n45, 125, 129n34
Throop, Palmer, 109-10, 127n4, 139
Thrupp, Sylvia, xi, 42, 60n32
Thucydides, 79, 91n17, 173, 178n48
Tilly, Louise, x, 111, 114-15, 125, 127n6
Toronto, University of, 43, 111-12, 113-14, 138-39, 151, 152, 164
Tous les matins du monde, 25, 28-29n28
Trickster Travels: A Sixteenth-Century Muslim Between Worlds, 180, 181-82. *See also* al-Wazzān, al-Hasan (Leo Africanus)
Trinkaus, Charles, 41, 59n25
Troeltsch, Ernst, 166, 177n28
Trotskyists, 133, 154n16
Turner, Victor, 46, 61n50
Turniansky, Chava, 119, 128n21

Ursulines, 33-34, 51, 57, 58n1, 71

Valensi, Lucette, 14, 27n8
Valois, Marguerite de (Queen Margot), 24, 28n21, 125, 126
van Gennep, 45-46, 61n48
Varga, Lucie, 89, 92n34
Vichy regime, 39, 59n18, 92n31
Vico, Giambattista, 41, 59n23, 132
Viennot, Éliane, 24, 28n22, 125, 126
Vietnam War, 44, 63-64, 153, 156n45, 157n47
violence, 40, 47, 54, 63-68, 79, 145
Virgil, 82, 92n26

Walesa, Lech, 60n42
Wallace, Henry, 134-35, 155n19
Warkentin, Germaine, 111, 127n7
Wars of Religion, French, 28n24, 72, 91n3, 166, 167
Weber, Max, 39, 58n12, 70-71, 110, 132, 166, 169, 173
Weil, Françoise, 43, 60n36
Weil, Simone, xi, 138
Wilson, Woodrow, 168, 178n37
Winchevsky Centre, 139, 155n24
Wollstonecraft, Mary, 120, 128-29n25
women's historiography, 11, 107, 109-20, 122-27
women's suffrage, 127n2, 128n13, 137
Women on the Margins: Three Seventeenth-Century Lives, 7, 30, 48, 55-58, 74, 75, 84, 123, 182

Xenophon, 79, 91n16

Yugoslav Wars, 161, 176n13

Zemon family, 95-98, 99, 101-4, 138-39, 162

Zemon-Davis family, 40, 103–4, 110, 137–39, 149, 150
Zhiri, Oumelbanine, 14, 27–28n8
Zilsel, Edgar, 41, 59n26
Zionism, 65, 100, 103, 107, 132, 154n9, 162–63, 177n19